SHOWTIME

SHOWTIME

SHOWTIME

ONE TEAM, ONE YEAR,
ONE STEP FROM THE NHL

ED ARNOLD

Collins

Published by Collins, an imprint of HarperCollins Publishers Ltd

First edition

HarperCollins books may be purchased for educational, business,
or sales promotional use through our Special Markets Department.

HarperCollins Publishers Ltd
2 Bloor Street East, 20th Floor
Toronto, Ontario, Canada
M4W 1A8

www.harpercollins.ca

Library and Archives Canada Cataloguing in Publication
information is available upon request.

ISBN 978-1-44341-594-1

Printed in the United States of America

RRD 9 8 7 6 5 4 3 2 1

For Matt and Luke Bradica: May you always pursue your dreams.
The fun, after all, is in the pursuit.

CONTENTS

PROLOGUE

Hockey Day in Canada: February 9, 2013

The Peterborough Petes had been on a mission. It wasn't so much to win, but to make sure the team did not lose on this special night.

Goalie Andrew "Dagger" D'Agostini had written on the whiteboard before the game, "Every victory is won before you play under the lights." It was an echo of boxing great Muhammad Ali's line, "The fight is won or lost far away from the witnesses—behind the lines, in the gym and out there on the road, long before I dance under those lights." In other words, practice makes perfect.

The day-long entertainment package was soon wrapped in a ribbon of perfection: the Petes did not disappoint the city, its people or the CBC. The Petes won.

"There were great individual efforts out there tonight," said coach Jody Hull. "You all did your job, put in the effort that was needed. The entire defence played well. You can all look at the player beside you and know that he emptied his tank tonight. Remember this feeling, remember how tired the extra effort makes you feel, but remember that feeling is what we need. I think [Nick] Ritch played a great game, showing that scoring points is not all that matters. It was just a great team effort." His pride in what they had accomplished was bursting from his breaking voice as he spoke. The Petes had played Hull hockey—textbook hockey.

Inside their dressing room, after Hull's short talk, the players looked at each other knowing they had given it everything. Their tanks were empty. It was 9:50 P.M. Hull joked that curfew was 10. Stick boy Iain Norrie, who had again predicted a 5–0 win, quietly walked about the dressing room, then added more magic when he spoke up, saying more than his usual "Showstopper!" "Well done, guys, good game, play as a team. I mean it!" he yelled. The players, coaches and training staff cheered, clapped, laughed. But for fans and the team, the night was Showtime.

The players had heard the crowd chanting, no longer the familiar smattering of scattered applause and weak attempts at "Go Petes Go," but the sound of almost 4,000 voices, all wanting the players to hear them. They agreed that if they had this crowd to boost and urge them on every night, it would be a different team, a better team, a team assured that it had that seventh player. It was this night—not the firings, not the trades, not the past, but this night—that marked the turning point in the season. This night was when 23 players became a team.

When the night was over, the CBC crew packed up and left behind another city brimming with pride at what it had revealed to the nation: that Peterborough was the best city in Canada. Obviously, there would be arguments about that from people in almost every other part of the country, but for now, Peterborough, one of the best-kept secrets in Canada, was part of the public record from coast to coast. A national spotlight had been shone on the community, and it shone back. Every athlete knew, however, that sunshine could be quickly covered by a cloud. Would the team be able to continue basking in the glow of this weekend for the rest of the regular season?

CHAPTER 1

Hockey Mafia Background

The Peterborough Petes are known in hockey circles as the Hockey Mafia or the Hockey Factory. The team has put more players into the NHL than any other. It has connections with every NHL franchise. It has made more appearances in the modern-day Memorial Cup than any other team.

But for a time, that supremacy was in serious doubt. In fact, by 2012, the Petes' record had begun to seem dismal. But their prospects looked better for the 2012–13 season. Little did I, or anyone else, know it would be a historic season in so many ways.

My journey began in March of 2012, after the team failed to make the playoffs for its second consecutive year, a first in its history. I would spend 13 months with the Petes, observing their operations. I enjoyed access never before offered to a writer, watching how the team was put together and what went into its various stages. I attended team functions, all team practices and all games but two, went on scouting missions, attended the private draft and closed-door board meetings and obtained confidential documents while interviewing players, parents, coaches, fans and management along the way.

The dream chasing, the team building, the business of hockey and the work on the next season began that March in Mississauga at the OHL midget hockey tournament. It was here that dreams began and, in so many instances, ended.

It was an unexpected journey, a ride so controversial and riveting, with so many coaching, management and player changes, including a threat of the team being purchased by former Petes stars Greg Millen and Keith Acton, who had both gone on to good NHL careers.

Along the way, many of the fans were found to be fickle, with short memories. They were convinced that in the "good old days," 4,000 fans would come to watch the team in regular-season games. It had never happened since the Montreal Canadiens brought the team to the city in 1956—the norm was fewer than 2,800. Before the season was over, at different points the fans would be disappointed, despairing and angry before finally becoming believers again. In the final weeks, they would sing hosannas to the team they had started out disparaging. They would dream of making the playoffs; some even thought of winning a championship.

The ride the fans jumped onto was only on the ice; unlike me, they were not on board for the part of the team's journey that transpired behind the scenes—discovering the billets, the education program, parents, scouts and team lifestyles—where the real stories took life.

The players, all between the ages of 16 and 20, shared many of their personal stories and opinions. (These conversations were never shared with anyone else during the year, and all who were interviewed knew their words wouldn't be made public or shared until the book came out. It was the only way I could gain trust, even though there were so many times I wanted to tell others what was happening with their team.)

I began to come to terms with the complex reality of this hockey factory, the legendary Peterborough Petes, and all of its struggles. It was a team not owned by a private investor, but instead left by the Montreal Canadiens in the 1960s to a community board of directors whose members did not share in any revenue.

The Ontario Hockey League began as a farm system for the NHL; today, it is the minor hockey graduates' taste of a mini-NHL, where they experience the travel, competition and play found in the pros, but not the big bucks. They are paid from $50 a week to a maximum of $150 if they're overage. All players, not just the team's favourites, are now covered for the costs of any books, tuition and other fees for high school, college, university or trade schools while playing. They are required to have an academic advisor, a tutor if needed, monthly academic progress reports and the latest technical support. Summer courses for undergraduate degrees are also covered. Seven players on each team are allowed a full ride toward their undergraduate degree. Once a player signs a professional contract, the junior team is not obligated to cover that cost. In addition, any player who chooses not to go to university, college or trade school within 18 months of leaving the CHL loses the education package.

Packages range from $3,000 for a year to $20,000 annually for four-year deals. The Petes' education costs were $29,000 back in 2003; 10 years later, they were at the $100,000 level. Those packages were just one of the financial issues that posed a challenge. The

Petes' day-to-day expenses rose inexorably from one year to the next. Their stick budget alone in the previous season was $54,000; skates cost $17,000; $30,000 was spent on clothing, and $94,000 on the players' stipends. The team also paid for room, board, insurance, gas mileage, equipment and a travel allowance of up to $100 monthly. There were playoff bonuses ranging from $100 for the first round to $450 for the last round. There could be other perks, but the league had to approve them.

In the 1980s, Peterborough became the first team to offer $3,000 educational scholarships to all players, not just to first- and some second-rounders. Future NHL superstar Chris Pronger came along in 1993, changing everything. Dick Todd was both coach and GM at the time. According to longtime board member Pat Casey, Todd drafted Pronger late, "even though he said he was going the U.S. route. We flew him and his parents here [from Dryden, Ontario], gave them a tour and dinner. We didn't know if he was that good. He was a tall, skinny kid that Dick said he had seen a few times, but he looked more like a basketball player. Pronger had an agent who said if the team wanted Pronger, it would have to be for a five-year education package to Western University [the University of Western Ontario in London] at $10,000 per year, guaranteed. The Petes had never done anything like that before. . . . We invited him to camp, and at the first practice we thought he was the Wayne Gretzky of defence and didn't have to look back. However, it changed everything. It started the agents, and they now come asking for everything.

"We can't afford it," said Casey. "The league has gone haywire and it's not fair. It's putting us out of business. We lose money every year and have to dip into a reserve fund unless we make the playoffs. The money goes fast."

The league is now a multimillion-dollar business involving 20 teams, some playing in $45 million rinks. The Petes, once leaders not only in hockey success but also on the business side, had fallen behind. Its own community had no idea how far. The community, like the team, hung on proudly to the past, but even that had become mythical, out of proportion to what it had really been like.

These 13 months would be crazy, unpredictable, exhilarating and eye-opening. The journey would be interrupted by nightmares along the way as 23 young men—just kids, really—chased their dreams.

CHAPTER 2

High Expectations

The fans were pumped for the 2012–13 Peterborough Petes season. Sure, they had seen their team fail to make the playoffs in the last two years, but on opening day this fall the team would have the top draft pick of last season, Nick Ritchie, back as well as fourth-year goalie Andrew D'Agostini and superb rookie prospect Michael Giugovaz. Combine this with five veteran defencemen—including Tampa Bay Lightning first-round pick Slater Koekkoek; the Petes' top sniper, Matt Puempel, an Ottawa Senators draft pick; and another top midget pick they would get to draft this year—and things appeared to be good.

Team manager Dave Reid, who had won two Stanley Cups as an NHL player, and coach Mike Pelino, who had coached at every level, were also returning. There was plenty to be hopeful for. The team had suffered some bad injuries in the previous season, but when fans looked at what they thought would be the lineup for next season, they were sure of success.

Peterborough's team was a David among Goliaths, a small-market upstart that had often swung its slingshot and slain giants. It had been one of the best junior hockey teams in the world, seldom been one of the worst, and was not a team owned by people thirsting for—or even making—a profit, but by volunteers whose only interest was in developing young hockey players. The players performed in a quiet arena, the Memorial Centre on Roger Neilson Way. It has one of the quietest fan bases in the league; at times, it was like they were attending a funeral, forgetting they were there not only to be entertained but also to support and become part of their hometown team.

Fan support for the Petes wasn't the weakest in the league, but it was getting closer to the bottom. The team had gone to the conference finals in 2005 and captured the league championship a year later. Only six seasons had passed since then, a short time in the life of a hockey team. By any reasonable measure, the team's management had done a creditable job. And yet, the Petes' declining fan base was getting restless. You could hear their complaints in the stands and read them in the local newspaper and on Internet message boards. They wanted new blood, new ideas and changes in the way things were run. Petes fans were a tough crowd; they wanted a winner every year.

It wasn't as if the club's board of directors had been sitting on their hands. They had been making moves clearly intended to improve the team.

Two years earlier, they had fired Jeff Twohey, who had been general manager for 17 years and a dedicated, well-liked and hard-working Petes employee for close to three decades. When he left, a number of Petes scouts, upset by the firing, walked out in a show of support. There had been some major holes to fill.

The board took its time hiring a new GM. Then president Ken Jackman said, "We know we have to get this right." They finally hired television hockey analyst and former Petes captain Reid to take Twohey's place. Reid's hockey credentials were impeccable. He had a public profile, what appeared to be great communication skills, and an impressive hockey background. The board liked his talk and believed he could walk the walk. Besides, the 46-year-old was one of their own: a Petes alumnus and former team captain. The fans and media cheered the choice . . . it was a public relations coup. Reid signed a four-year deal, promising and expecting big things. After all, as a former hard-working defensive specialist, he had reached the summit: he had drunk from hockey's silver chalice and gained a rink full of hockey knowledge along the way.

But those were his achievements as a player. He was not familiar with his job, his team or his role in the league. He had never coached or managed anything comparable, a fact that soon became apparent. Reid's first month on the job back in 2010–11 was short of a startling success. After his first seven games, the Petes were in last place. Since then, he had not had a winning season and had not made the playoffs even once.

It didn't matter to the team, Reid or the fans that their two most prolific players, defenceman Koekkoek and forward Puempel, had been injured for much of 2011–12, as were up-and-coming defencemen Clark Seymour and Connor Boland. It also didn't matter that the team had been obliged to trade its scoring star, Austin Watson, for indiscretions that included using his cell phone during games and sometimes-excessive indulgence in alcohol off the ice—minor issues to some observers, major to others. Watson, while playing for his

U.S. junior team in the world championships at Christmas, discovered that the Petes were trying to trade him and had agreed to a deal with Sarnia that would have brought rookie star Nick Ritchie's older brother, Brett, to Peterborough. Watson had the right to turn down any move, and he declined this one because another former Petes top draft pick, Ryan Spooner, was now playing in Sarnia and they didn't get along. Neither wanted that trade. He refused to return to the Petes, and Reid was forced to trade him to London for a raw up-and-comer—eighth-round midget draft pick Chase Hatcher (whose father was former NHL great Derian)—and some draft picks. Watson, meanwhile, went on to lead London to the Memorial Cup tournament. Petes fans were incredulous. The board had approved and encouraged the deal.

Reid hadn't made excuses for his losing seasons. Neither fans nor the team cared about or survived on excuses. Excuses in sports were like wrapped presents—nobody cared about the outside, and when stripped to bare essentials, they had better be worth the anticipation. Reid took the blame and responsibility. He said he hadn't given the coaching staff the assets they needed to succeed. He took the blame for everything from complaints about bad trades to not giving fans a better off-ice experience on game nights.

Fans were saying the team "sucked." They were especially upset because what had appeared to be a promising 2011–12 season, with the team in first place after two months, turned out to be another failure. At its conclusion, they were the third-worst team in the league. Reid and his staff took failure personally. Their only reward would be picking third in the 2012 draft, and Reid was looking forward to it as his chance at redemption. He knew his most important decisions depended on the ability of his scouts to spot upcoming talent. Both his future and the team's ultimately were the product of the winter scouting that took his dedicated, mostly part-time and ill-paid staff to hundreds of rinks across the province, where they survived on bad coffee, warm bottled water, cold hot dogs and greasy french fries, costing the Petes about $60,000 annually. If the fans' complaints were to be answered, Reid's judgment—and that of his scouts— would have to be correct.

Peterborough Examiner beat writer Mike Davies was optimistic about the forthcoming year. Since being hired by the *Examiner* in 1992, he had been the eyes and ears of Petes fans. Nobody in the media knew as much inside dope about the team as he did.

Davies had an eye disease, retinitis pigmentosa (RP), that caused sight problems that had become worse over time. He was legally blind. He still had some peripheral vision, but he likened it to "a jigsaw puzzle. Randomly remove pieces and eventually you begin to lose portions of the picture."

Davies was not only a respected journalist but also an insider who had earned the respect of past and present Petes coaches and also had the ear of some club directors, who actually consulted him and listened to what he had to say. He was as aware as anyone of the fans' unhappiness and had written that the Petes "should be a much-improved team. If the Petes don't end their two-year streak of missing the playoffs then there is something seriously rotten in Denmark." He had no idea that this year he would see and hear things he had never seen or heard before while with the team.

What would be exposed were issues inside the boardroom, from scouting to drafting and player selection. Management seemed to be inside a time capsule, acknowledging the team's great past, waiting for its better future, but stuck in its poor present. Nobody seemed to be moving the wheels along. The team appeared trapped. They did not have the players to win a championship four years ago, nor three or even two years ago, and while Davies and the team were optimistic, the club didn't seem to have the players this season, either. They had traded their best players for little and drafted some players in the later rounds who had been good minor hockey players but who weren't good juniors.

For some outsiders, the team's present and future looked bleak. Unlike the team, they were not so sure that a turnaround was in the cards. And as the team was to find out, some people, such as Millen and Acton, were willing to take the team over, which triggered the Petes' biggest community controversy in a season full of them, long before the games even began.

It all began in March 2012. It was a warm day outside the Hershey Centre on Rose Cherry Place, the street named for Canadian hockey celebrity Don Cherry's deceased wife, Rose. Two days earlier, driving snow and biting wind had provided exactly the right backdrop for hockey thoughts, but now the grey chill had been replaced by a summer-blue sky, sunshine and a temperature in the 20s. Golf courses were already opening in southern Ontario west of Toronto.

The front parking lot of the home of the Ontario Hockey League's Mississauga St. Michael's Majors (the name would be changed to Steelheads a few months later) appeared full with close to a thousand cars, a surprising number for a midget hockey tournament.

This was the season-ending Ontario Hockey League Showcase Cup, a big deal. It was full of players who would make up the bulk of the OHL's rosters in the near future. Many of the onlookers were here to watch and assess particular players. Their decisions were consequential: the OHL is the biggest supplier of hockey players to the National Hockey League. In 2012 alone, 30 per cent of NHL players were OHL graduates. Fourteen of those players were from the Peterborough Petes.

The majority of the 303 players eligible for the next month's OHL midget priority draft were playing in this tournament. Almost all were long shots to make junior teams. Some would choose not to play in the Ontario league, taking collegiate scholarships in the United States instead. Some would stay away from OHL camps in order to protect their future options. Maybe one potentially great player—and that's a big maybe—would go unnoticed and not be drafted but still find his way to the NHL.

Those who wanted to play in the OHL and were lucky enough to be selected in the midget draft would try to fill one of the few spots that come open each year in a league that allowed each of its teams a maximum of four 16-year-olds each season. If every OHL team kept four 16-year-olds, which most would not, then 80 of the prospects on the ice today would play in the OHL in September. But being drafted meant only that the team thought the chosen player might just possibly make it someday. Only the top selections made by each OHL team could realistically expect to play for that team in the fall. The other selections would be developed (if at all) more slowly and at a lower level.

The duration of the apprenticeship depended on the player's talent, and its outcome was variable. Experience, timing and luck were required. The odds were against every kid here. The statistics showed that only a handful, maybe an average of one from every OHL team, would ever see any NHL action.

Of course, the odds of making it in any career that paid a minimum of $550,000 annually were also slim. The odds of getting accepted into Harvard were 7 per cent; the odds of becoming a neurosurgeon even lower, with only about 200 in Canada; a rock star much lower (you can probably count them on two hands in Canada); an author who doesn't need another income to live on, even lower. Of all these pursuits, only the OHL also supplied its novitiates with room, board and education costs while they acquired experience and honed their skills.

On the Friday night of the weekend of the tournament, the Petes' staff gathered in a Mississauga hotel room for a mock draft, trying to anticipate all the possible situations that could develop on draft day. They argued about the players they should select and speculated on the choices that other teams would make. There was a minor argument over their proposed first pick—Eric Cornel versus Jared McCann—which continued up until draft day. Reid was stubborn, however, and most of them knew whom the team would be picking.

Two players at or near the top of Reid's and his scouts' minds were not at this showcase tournament because their teams had been deemed not good enough to be invited. One purpose for this week-long scouting trek was to watch the other top players to see if any were better than the one they planned on picking. Another was to look at choices that might be available later in the draft. The midget tournament was a sort of cattle auction where people compared sizes, skills, attitudes and bloodlines. First-round selections were obvious and known to most scouts, just as the best racehorses were familiar to all trainers. It was the players they coveted as later-round picks that they tried to keep confidential. These other players could also become important to the teams that took them, but their prospects were much more difficult to project.

Reid, a well-known face among those present, stood to watch some games, sat with his scouts for others, observing the action on the ice intently while the scouts were busy with their notebooks,

BlackBerrys, laptops, iPads and diaries. The scouting team was led by Mike Oke, the player personnel director and son of Petes board member John Oke. Mike had a solid background in Ontario hockey. He was a former Tier II coach, assistant coach and assistant manager and had been director of player personnel and assistant coach with the OHL's Oshawa Generals from 2004 to 2006. After that, he was a scout, and then chief scout for International Scouting Services. Oke's knowledge of players and the game, which had long impressed Reid, would prove helpful as they prepared for the upcoming draft.

Reid and the scouts were looking at skating skills first and foremost. If a guy couldn't skate, he couldn't play. How were the kid's wheels going forward, backward, laterally? How well did he stop and start? Was he first on the puck? Was he good along the boards? Did he make that all-important pass? How was his worth ethic? Would he be able to compete against much older, bigger, stronger, meaner players in the OHL?

Apart from the qualities that could be seen and analyzed in the course of a game, there were others that the scouts would inquire about. *Did a player have any legal problems? Did he have focus? Did he get along with teammates? Did he have any drinking or drug problems? Was he hooked up with a longtime girlfriend? Would he get homesick?* In earlier times, teams wanted to know only if the kid could play; now they wanted to know everything they could discover, including his parents' occupations, home life, size, fitness and sports genes.

Before this week's tournament, the Petes had had parent-player interviews with many of the kids they were interested in. Some failed miserably by showing no interest at all. They might have blown their chance of being drafted. Team officials had seen players who didn't look them in the eye or show any excitement, who just shrugged their shoulders in response to significant questions or simply watched the clock as if bored. Try that at your next job interview. Young hockey players are no different from other teens: they can be shy, indifferent and ignorant of the ways of the world. They can be antsy and disrespectful. But for a team whose choices shape a good or bad season, these traits take on particular importance.

Reid and his staff watched the on-ice action not caring who won, just how certain players were performing. The scouts had their lists of players they had spent more time watching—not only the best players but also ones willing to sign and play in Peterborough. Ideally, they wanted someone who could step right into next season's lineup, as 2011's top pick, Nick Ritchie, had done. The Petes and other OHL teams played not only to win but to develop young boys into better hockey players and young adults as well.

CHAPTER 3

Draft Day

Draft day came the next month, on Saturday, April 7, 2012. It should have been a day for hoping that the Petes just might find the piece that had been missing from the jigsaw puzzle that makes a winning team. People who cared about the Petes should have been focused on that Saturday. Instead, the headline running across the front page of the *Peterborough Examiner* was about the possibility of a more fundamental change: an offer to buy the team, put forward by a group of investors called NorthLight Entertainment, led by Greg Millen and Keith Acton. This was absolutely the wrong time for this kind of upheaval.

NorthLight had made its secret offer to the board of directors the previous September. They proposed to build a $50 million complex consisting of a hotel and 6,500-seat arena to replace the existing 4,069-seat rink and turn the team's on-ice failure around. The Petes board kept it quiet, but at the end of the 2011–12 season, board president Jim Devlin, upset by fan verbal abuse, expressed his skepticism in an interview with the *Examiner* about finding anyone willing to spend $50 million to build a private rink in his hometown. The NorthLight group couldn't believe it—he was pretending there wasn't already an offer in place—and responded by making the proposal public. The news hit the community on draft day. It started an uproar unlike any seen in decades, with people questioning the board's secrecy and fans expressing widespread unhappiness about the team's on-ice failures, which they blamed squarely on what they viewed as the board's meddling and ineptitude. What they didn't know was that the Millen group's offer wasn't the only one they had received, including an offer from a group proposing a casino/rink project.

Some fans and others grumbled that the board had become an old boys' club, out of touch with the community, and that its proceedings lacked transparency. They didn't know that the relationship between the board and the rink's owner, the municipal government, had become dysfunctional to the point of hostility. The city was taking close to $1 million a year from the Petes and treating the team like a bad tenant, unwilling to share parking and many advertising revenue opportunities. Ugly closed-door negotiations between the city and club only made the tension worse. For the first time in history, the two groups had resorted to arbitration.

Devlin, the Petes' slim, white-haired president, was a successful businessman who had grown up playing hockey and baseball in the town and had joined the Petes' board in 1996. For his part, Devlin had privately entertained an idea to explore the ownership model of the Green Bay Packers of the National Football League. That team sold non-dividend, non-transferable shares to the public. The board of directors he presided over was made up of local people, including family doctor Bob Neville; John Oke, a banker; Ken Jackman, a deputy police chief; Wilf Hughes, a high school principal (all three retired); and Pat Casey, an investment counsellor.

The team had always been about growing boys into men, making sure they got their education. As board member Dr. Neville proudly told players, "We are here for you. We are a nonprofit company. We are all about you, not money. That's what makes us different." But, of course, the team needed to stay profitable to continue existing.

The Petes were running a team valued in the millions of dollars on a shoestring budget. Costs were skyrocketing while income was either unpredictable or stagnant. There was a reserve fund sufficient to see them through a few bad years, and Devlin said that if the team had made the playoffs in 2012, it would have made money. He insisted, though, that "the model has been successful and it will be successful going forward, but not without challenges." The lack of money made it difficult for the team to compete with deeper-pocketed teams in larger markets, but the board maintained that every team in the Ontario Hockey League had to operate under the same rules, able to offer players no more than what the Petes could offer.

Many fans snickered at this naive, gullible attitude. There had been rumours throughout the league that some teams were paying players—or their parents—big dollars, as well as giving them perks such as cash and luxury suites, but none of these allegations had been proven. The league was aware of the talk, though, and in August 2012 it fined the Windsor Spitfires $400,000 and took away several of the team's top draft choices for recruitment violations.

But the financial imbalance between OHL clubs was obvious. Some teams had better equipment and facilities, even their own buses. Kitchener, the only other "community-based" team in the OHL, had revenues more than double those of the Petes. The Petes' board members admitted they would love to have a new arena but warned this could mean higher ticket prices. Publicly, the board wasn't budging in its decision not to sell. Privately, it was banking on the team to come through with a much-improved season. The club badly needed to win and was relying on draft day for help.

It was against this backdrop that the draft took place.

Back in the Memorial Centre, and in prospective players' homes across the country, many nervous people were waiting for the draft to begin. That morning, there were 303 '96ers praying for a phone call. (Hockey people invariably use the year of a player's birth as an identifying mark—birthdate first, name second. Even the players routinely do this.) Most of them hoped to be picked early. Realistically, if they weren't selected in the first two rounds, there was little chance they would make their team in the upcoming season. In a change from what had been a long-standing tradition, however, most waited in the comfort and privacy of their own homes.

Twelve years earlier, the OHL's midget priority draft, which began in 1969, had been conducted in an arena or hotel ballroom, with team tables arranged around the floor, in a setup similar to the NHL draft. Teenagers sat in the stands, anxiously waiting to hear their names called amid all the anxiety and pressure of a public spectacle. The current online draft gave more privacy to the teams, because outsiders couldn't hear their sometimes caustic remarks about the character and ability of this or that 15-year-old.

Petes staff members had been busy the day before the draft, fixing up the alumni room in the Memorial Centre for Saturday. This, too, was a change: for the previous 11 years, the Petes had met in a local hotel room, but Reid thought their own space, with mementos of the team's rich tradition adorning the walls, was better.

There were 12 people around the Petes' main table, including Reid, Oke, the scouts, me and Aaron Garfat, the assistant general manager who, with the help of office administrator Cathie Webster, took care of everything from booking buses to overseeing ticket sales to negotiating sponsorships. We had all arrived at 7:30 A.M. for the 9:12 draft start. Seated at separate tables were the directors, who mostly dropped by later, and the coaches: Mike Pelino, Jody Hull and Wayne Clark.

The quiet, somewhat introverted Pelino resembled a high school teacher from the '70s: he was good-looking, always well-dressed and groomed and, at 51, one of the oldest coaches ever hired by the Petes (only one other 50-year-old had taken on the job). OHL coaches generally are young up-and-comers with their eye on the NHL. Pelino was well qualified to coach, better than many: he had taken courses, acquired the highest certification—he had even written a dissertation on the subject. He had been either an assistant coach or head coach at almost every possible level, including stints assisting coach Mike Keenan in Florida and Tom Renney in New York.

Sitting next to Pelino was former Petes star and longtime NHLer Jody Hull, a quiet, blue-collar type who lived in the area and loved to help local hockey teams. Hull, 42, had been an assistant coach for the Petes for a few years until Twohey suddenly, and surprisingly, fired him just before the 2008–09 season began, leaving him without a chance to join another OHL team. He had been with the local Tier II junior team as an assistant until Reid was hired.

Rounding out the coaching staff was another former Petes star, goalie Ron Tugnutt (not at the draft), who had enjoyed a long NHL career, and Wayne Clark, a 34-year-old Peterborough native, local high school teacher, minor hockey coach and student of the game with whom Reid had become familiar while in Peterborough youth hockey. Clark had coached at various AAA levels, including four years as a minor midget coach and two years as assistant coach with St. Mike's high school, a team that had won an Ontario championship.

Draft day represented the culmination—and in some respects, a celebration—of the work done by the scouts throughout the winter. Scouts were Preparation H's dreams come true, Goodyear's and Tim Hortons' best customers and an expense account's nightmare. They sat endlessly on hard benches, drove countless miles to towns and cities across the province and were among the most frugal travellers on Earth. They had met with Oke, the Petes' personnel director, three months earlier to slim 1,600 players to fewer than 200, first debating which players were the best at their positions, and then narrowing the discussion to the best players overall. The scouts, along with Oke, then focused their attention on the smaller group, interviewing players plus their parents, coaches and agents.

The scouts' reports included each player's statistics and rated him on competitiveness, offensive and defensive play, physical play, OHL potential, skating, shooting, hockey sense, scoring, puck skills, intangibles, game rating, draft projection, player type and a best guess about whether he would report to the Petes. With these reports in hand, and after extensive discussion, the Petes had narrowed their choices to a pool of 133, arranged in order from best to worst and further divided by position. They had eliminated 170 players from the OHL list of 303 according to different criteria. Besides talent, for example, some players were crossed off the list because they were Americans in the U.S. development program who said they would not report to an OHL team.

The Petes' ratings differed from those indicated on the list compiled by OHL Central Scouting that was shared with all OHL teams. They needed forwards after their three top goal scorers had graduated. They had seven returning defencemen and two goalies eligible to return. The goalies' (and team's) goals-against average had not been good, almost last in the league, but the Petes felt their defence would be their strength.

There were high expectations for the 16-year-old goalie selected in the 2011 draft, Michael "Giggy" Giugovaz, who starred in Tier II for Georgetown in the previous season and helped get that team to the provincial finals. It was likely that Peterborough's oldest goalie, Mike Morrison, wouldn't be returning or would be playing a less significant role. Although Morrison didn't know this, he should have expected something was up when the Petes turned down his request for new goalie pads to break in over the summer.

The draft began when league commissioner David Branch prompted the team with the first pick, the basement-dwelling Erie Otters, to make its selection. Everyone knew the Otters would select Connor McDavid of the Toronto Marlboros minor midgets, a 1997-born bantam-age player granted "exceptional player" status for the draft. All the other players would have a 1996 birth date or earlier. Kingston, with the next pick, was expected to select defenceman Roland McKeown from Listowel, who'd also played midget for the Toronto Marlies. (Many of the Marlie players didn't grow up in Toronto; four of the 10 players drafted off the team in 2012 were raised in other places, such as Newmarket, Hamilton, Thornhill and Brampton. Parents get them set up in Toronto residences or have them attend a private school so they will be eligible for the team.) These picks were widely anticipated before draft day.

The Petes hadn't revealed whom they would pick but said they needed a big playmaking centre. Their choice was Eric Cornel, a tall, gangly, good-looking, blond-haired, shy teen, who had never had a stitch on his face, which he still had to shave only occasionally.

Cornel's midget team hadn't made it to the playoffs, and while that result was disappointing, it was a blessing for him and for the Petes. His team wasn't at Mississauga's showcase tournament. Instead, the Kemptville Tier II Junior A team had called him up for the rest of its season, and he had played well with, and against, players up to five years older. Reid, watching Cornel's playmaking ability, knew the Petes had winger Ritchie, the team's rookie of the year, to play with him.

Reid couldn't find enough superlatives for the young centre: high-level skills, good ice vision, an ability to find the open man—Cornel wasn't quite capable of leaping over tall buildings at a single bound, but maybe he possessed the potential to be a star player. It helped that Eric's minor midget coach said that in his 15 years of coaching he had never seen anyone with this teen's work ethic or leadership qualities. Peterborough scouts had been watching Cornel for the last two years. Reid had travelled to Ottawa to watch him play minor midget, where he scored 50 points in 26 games.

"Eric is an offensive-minded centre that carries his minor midget team in every game if they have any chance of winning," stated the team's scouting report. The Petes' scouts wrote about his hard, accurate shot and his skating ability but added "he will not go out of his way to finish a check, but then again that's not what most teams are looking for out of a player of his calibre. . . . I do not think Eric will be a great goal scorer, but he will score; I see him as a playmaker. He is a positive team player who shows some leadership skills. He works hard in all areas of the ice. He makes everyone on the ice better. He is willing to engage physically, and this is likely to increase as he adds muscle to what still appears to be a fairly thin frame."

Reid was convinced the Petes had their man—er, boy. (His grandfather George Hollingdrake had also played junior in the Montreal Metro League against Petes board member Pat Casey, but the team didn't find that out until later.) The kid had even been born in Peterborough before moving at an early age. More importantly, Reid knew they needed forwards if they were going to have a successful year, and this forward would be able to step in at 16, the age he'd be at fall training camp, to help right away. He also knew how difficult it was to find good, big centremen.

We had met Eric Cornel and his parents on Good Friday, the night before the draft, in the restaurant at the Memorial Centre for a private dinner attended by members of the executive, management, staff and scouts, along with many of their wives. Most were seeing the boy for the first time. It was only when you saw him not wearing skates and equipment that you realized how young he was. Cornel was tall, at six feet, two inches, but slim at 165 pounds. It was not his size or innocent personality that radiated "boyhood," however, so much as the silver braces on his upper teeth.

Eric's parents, a couple in their 30s, had considered the U.S. scholarship route for their son. He had an average in the high 80s at school and was considering Boston College, Harvard and Cornell. But Peterborough seemed a comfortable choice. The Cornels still were new to the attention and draft excitement and their son being the focus of all these adults. They knew, though, that they would no longer have to buy sticks, skates or equipment for their hockey-passionate child as he began his apprenticeship. Nor would they have to pay registration and monthly fees to his team, or pay for tournament hotel rooms and meals. They would not even have to worry about his post-secondary education costs if a pro hockey career didn't work out. He was guaranteed four years of university, just like all the other first-round picks in the OHL who didn't sign pro contracts. It was a big change for parents who had been picking up the tab for everything from registration fees to hockey camp since their prodigy was seven. Just the cost of university was roughly equivalent to the down payment on a new home.

Now, instead of financial concerns, the parents would have different worries. Their oldest boy (he had two siblings) would be leaving home. He had been away before, at the World Youth Olympics in Austria, playing for Team Canada and scoring nine points in the last five games to help the team win a bronze medal, but his family had been there watching, knowing they would return home in 10 days. And even though Cornel, like his father before him, had been born in Peterborough, this would be different, a big step.

It was made easier, however, because Eric's grandparents and other relatives lived in and around the area. Eric had moved with his parents to Ottawa when he was only two, but he knew Peterborough well. The family had hoped he might stay in the home of one of these relatives, at least for the first year, but decided that, like the other players, he should move in with landparents, as billets were called in OHL towns. They would be strangers in the beginning but would become his winter hockey parents over the course of the season. They met those landparents within a month after the draft, which eliminated many concerns. It seemed this kid was born to play in Peterborough, but as he shyly told me before dinner, "Now I have to make the team."

And when Reid called Cornel's name Saturday morning, his journey began, as it did for the other 14 players the team selected in the day-long draft.

**

All OHL scouts would be following the top picks throughout the 2012–13 season to determine who had made the right choices. The Petes' Cornel would be judged against those picked after him— players the Petes had thought wouldn't be as productive. Jared McCann, Joshua Ho-Sang, Robert Fabbri, Michael Dal Colle, Jacob Middleton, Sam Bennett and Niki Petti rounded out the top 10 and would surprise the Petes' scouts.

Junior hockey deals are sometimes made in conversations before the draft. One name that came up quite often as a possible second-round choice was Spencer Watson. Reid told his draft team that Spencer's father had said Spencer would only go to the team that took his twin brother by at least the fourth round. His brother wasn't as high on scouts' lists, but the father was insistent. Reid called Spencer's father and asked if they took the other son in the fifth round, would he come to Peterborough. The answer was yes, but it turned out to be academic. Kingston selected Spencer one pick before the Petes' turn, and later, in the fifth round, picked the brother. Spencer would turn out to be a jewel.

The Petes had five minutes to make their second choice now that Spencer was gone.

The Soo's Michael Amadio and Quinte's Josh Maguire were on their list. They knew they could probably get one or the other. There was a discussion while computer charts and internal scouting reports were pulled up. Leading the discussion was the Petes' scouting coordinator, Chris McNamara. The 32-year-old looked after the Greater Toronto Area. He had been on the Kingston Frontenacs' scouting staff for two seasons, was a regional scout with the Oshawa Generals for a season, and was OHL head scout for International Scouting Services before joining the Petes. He had attended St. Francis Xavier University, where he obtained a degree in human kinetics.

Born and raised in Nova Scotia and now living in Markham, McNamara held a full-time job, as all the Petes' scouts did; he was hockey program director at the Canadian Ice Academy in Mississauga. He looked like a teen among adults in this room, but he seemed to have almost everyone's ear. He said Maguire could be a future Petes captain. Maguire's father, a former policeman, owned a sporting goods and trophy shop in Peterborough. His mother, with whom he lived in nearby Cobourg, had been a star hockey player. The scouts said the 15-year-old would go into the corners and come out with the puck, the hungrier of two dogs after a bone. Like Cornel, Maguire had not played in the OHL midget tournament, and scouts weren't as enthusiastic about him as Reid for a second-round choice. Reid surprised many hockey observers by selecting him in the second round, 24th overall.

A very poorly kept secret in junior hockey is that some players are only willing to go to specific teams, so they get word out that they will be taking a U.S. scholarship offer instead of heading to the OHL. Sometimes they do, but other times the kid goes to the OHL. Names of some of these kids came up in this year's draft. One player the scouts suspected might be doing this was Jake Evans. Petes scouts thought he was bluffing about taking a full deal to Notre Dame, but Reid insisted he wasn't.

Reid told them the Petes wouldn't be picking him, and he was emphatic about it. Evans's name came up again later, but Reid reiterated, "We're not taking him. Evans wants that full deal at Notre Dame."

Team president Devlin was in the room when this happened, and while Evans's name didn't mean anything to him, Devlin found it strange that Reid wasn't listening to the people they paid to do the scouting. He made a mental note of the incident.

Kitchener finally took Evans as the 147th pick. McNamara immediately got a sarcastic email from a scouting friend stating, "Welcome to the Kitchener 'Notre Dame' Rangers," but Evans later signed with Notre Dame, just as Reid had foretold.

Sitting around the draft table was a mental grind. It was boring, to the point it could put a summer bear back into hibernation. There was no drama in the procedure, except sometimes in the teams' draft rooms, and even that was low-key, like a playoff hockey pool without the beer and pizza.

Throughout the day, the alumni room reverberated with pithy, sometimes admiring, scathing or skeptical comments: "He's got heavy boots." "His boots don't move." "He's got good feet, great feet." "He's a good one." "Is that height the Marlies' measurement?" "He's too small." "He can skate." "He's got a $10 million body and a 10-cent brain."

Size mattered to many teams, but these were 15- and 16-year-old kids who, for the most part, hadn't even grown enough to lose the squeak in their voices. They didn't have to make the team this coming season; they could wait for another year. While most boys reach their adult height by the time they're 15, many don't reach maturity until they are 17 or older. Their ultimate size could only be guessed at. Scouts looked at their parents to get some idea, but even that was not a reliable guide.

Some of the directors drifted in and out during the day, without saying a word, but most left before the fifth-round break at 1:30.

Devlin wouldn't leave until 4 P.M., with two hours and five rounds still to go.

The draft took nearly nine hours. In that time, the Petes selected 15 players, of whom only two would make the team in 2012–13. Others might have to wait for another year; still others would never make it. The Petes had drafted two goalies, three defencemen and 10 forwards, including a last-round pick of Ron Tugnutt's son, the only Peterborough minor hockey player chosen by the Petes (not picking local boys was yet another minor controversy in the community). Reid figured he now had plenty of assets, because his past moves had netted him higher draft picks not only this year but also in the future—a good situation to be in. The upcoming season was going to be his and his team's time to taste the playoffs. He was determined to do things his way, to be a "honey badger" or badass this season, no more Mr. Nice Guy. It was a tough fit for Reid: outwardly, he maintained a tough image, but he had a friendly heart.

Despite the controversy about the sale stealing the team's thunder, draft day had been long but rewarding. When everyone left the alumni room that night, it was with a good feeling about the upcoming season. All were pumped about the team's future. They couldn't wait for the puck to drop in the first game. Reid was happy too, though he had another worry to distract him. There was a player problem brewing, one with serious ramifications. Even Reid couldn't guess how much trouble it would cause.

CHAPTER 4

Summer Storm

Matt Puempel was the Petes' captain, their best forward, an Ottawa Senators draft pick, Canadian Hockey League rookie of the year in 2010–11 and the team's shining light. He had been selected by the former GM in the first round, as the sixth pick over-all, in 2009. He was the Petes' golden boy. He had set up, through the team, a small foundation to raise money for the Children's Wish Fund. The foundation had raised $9,000, but Puempel, surprisingly, didn't show up to present the cheque to the charity; it was his idea, after all. It seemed to some that Puempel was going through the motions to establish himself as an admirable figure in the community but that he was insincere or lacked real commitment. Or was there an agent or parent behind the problem? Or were the Petes the problem?

Reid wasn't about to divulge anything; he knew that finger-pointing was a mug's game that would hurt only the team's reputation. The staff tried to keep problems private, as they had in the past. Austin Watson, the top scorer who had been controversially traded midway through the 2011–12 season, might have been perceived as a problem off the ice, but on the ice he had always given his best. He had never given the team the private Puempel pout.

Puempel's mother was involved in her 19-year-old son's hockey life and not reticent about expressing an opinion on everything from his ice time to expenses, but the team put up with this for the sake of a talented player. Besides, it isn't that unusual in today's junior hockey. The Petes had very few parental interference problems, and Puempel's mother wasn't even an issue until a trade demand popped up. Puempel hadn't been injury-free in his time with the Petes: he had required hip surgery one year and had missed the last two months of 2011–12 with a concussion. Remarkably, the day after the season ended, he was able to play for the Senators' American Hockey League farm team in Binghamton. The media never asked, but some fans certainly wondered what medical miracle had made him healthy enough to play in a bigger, tougher league against much older, stronger players, when he couldn't even play in the Petes' last home game. Privately, the Petes had left it up to Puempel when the playoffs were out of their reach. He chose not to play, even though that last home game was practically sold out. To some, Puempel's absence showed a lack of leadership and dedication to the Petes.

A few weeks after the 2012 season ended, on the night before rookie camp opened, the Petes held their annual banquet. The well-liked captain was a no-show. It was left to the team's other stars, Nick Ritchie and Slater Koekkoek, to welcome Cornel and the other rookies to the Petes organization. The public was told that Puempel was on "a prearranged vacation in Mexico with family," but it was actually an unscheduled trip after Binghamton's season ended. The buzz in the community was that their favourite son wasn't showing much family love. While the critics questioned the kid's commitment and leadership, they didn't know he wanted out of Peterborough. It was another headache for management—and Reid in particular—as the team prepared for its annual rookie camp weekend.

Rookie camp gave the GM and coaches an early chance to see their draft picks in action. It was something of an innovation for the team: in the past, players had just shown up for training camp in the fall. Reid saw it as a useful exercise, however, that let management watch their prospects, not just with current and future seasons in mind. At the same time, the camp also was an opportunity for head coach Mike Pelino to make an impression and establish a rapport with the youngsters. It was a chance to set the tone for the coming year.

The first day of the two-day rookie camp had been devoted to fitness testing, on-ice drills and a full-game scrimmage. Many of the people who were there, including Petes scouts and coaches, were surprised by the ability of some players but worried by the lack of intensity in others. They hoped the second day would be different. There was a game scheduled for 11 A.M., after the boys had had a good, although probably restless, sleep. Some players showed signs of stiffness, the result of the previous day's exertions, but all said they were ready to roll. Some had been questioned not only by Petes staff but also by parents who wondered where their sons' drive and determination had gone. A few kids were complimented on their play and competitive spirit.

If there was one word the Petes used to describe the players they wanted, it was *competitor*. The word was written on the fitness centre wall alongside the names of past competitors that included Doug Jarvis, Bob Gainey, Steve Yzerman, Chris Pronger and Eric and Jordan Staal. It was an illustrious, and perhaps intimidating, list.

The word was repeated throughout the players' summer training manual, which had been sent out to them before camp opened. Reid, Pelino and the scouts frequently used it in their group meetings. If you weren't competing in rookie camp, they told the boys, you wouldn't make it to the main camp at summer's end. This wasn't quite true: rookie camp was not meant to be a tryout so much as an initiation. But the coaches wanted to see the players make a real effort. Reid told them, "Our goal of a championship begins today."

He reminded everyone that a Pete was a "player who competes every single shift, displays a high level of skill and ability, practises and plays each shift at a high tempo, understands his role within the team and is both mentally and physically strong. Some of these traits you already possess, and some you are developing. By holding yourself accountable and not accepting anything but your best, you are giving yourself an opportunity to be a Peterborough Pete."

Pelino addressed the rookies next. He told the 40 teenagers that when, or how high, they had been drafted as midgets didn't matter. The staff wanted the best players, and all had a shot. He told one of his favourite stories to illustrate the point: New York Rangers captain Ryan Callahan wasn't drafted by Guelph until the 15th round—but he went on to play in the NHL. A more-or-less random survey of Petes drafts from 2000 to 2006 underlined Pelino's argument: six players drafted in the eighth round or later eventually made it into the Petes lineup. Pelino was right; they all had a shot at making it. Of course, the obverse was true: they had a bigger shot at not making it.

Some of the players might have still been thinking of assistant coach Wayne Clark's earlier story about the genie and the pond full of crocodiles. The genie told a crowd gathered around a pond that he was looking for a really courageous individual. He promised everything from riches to a better life to anyone who jumped in with the crocodiles and swam across the pond. One man went in, finally, and swam desperately across the pond, escaping with only torn clothes and minor lacerations. The genie was impressed. He asked what the man wanted as his reward, and the man replied, "I want to know who pushed me in."

The Petes coaches were there to push hard, even when players didn't think they needed it, toward the main camp, where dreams began or ended.

Pelino was hoping there would be pleasant surprises and that some of the players would force him to make tough decisions. He knew it would be difficult to cut veterans, but he'd cut them if it made the team better. Pelino told the rookies, "It is a tremendous honour to wear the maroon and white, and all of you should be very proud of getting to this point."

Reid also was hoping for surprises, brighter lights to give his team more depth and ammunition.

The sunny, mid-20s weather made rookie camp seem longer for the scouts, who were stuck in the gloom of the Memorial Centre from 8 A.M. to 8 P.M. each day. "It wouldn't be as long if it was raining outside," scout Ron Ringler observed. Whatever the weather, their attention was focused on kids. There were big kids, thick kids, short kids, tall kids. There were boisterous kids (not many of these) and strangely quiet kids. Some had short hair, others' locks fell to their shoulders. Some were nervous and paced anxiously, like relatives outside a maternity ward, when they couldn't be on the ice. Most of the players were strangers to the town and to one another, as wary as any family moving into a new neighbourhood. They ached to get in uniform, to tie their skates and pick up their sticks. They needed to act to overcome their fluttering stomachs and anxious thoughts. Being on the ice brought freedom from life's cares. It wiped away everything but the game from their minds. Perhaps nothing drove people to be involved in hockey, or any sport, more than this hour or two of freedom.

The Petes, in fact, had few openings, but the players either didn't know this, didn't care to think about it or had confidence that they were good enough, not only to make the Petes but to beat out a veteran as well. There was not a player among them who hadn't survived—and triumphed—in numerous tryout camps over the years. Some had been making all-star teams since they were seven. This time, they faced all-stars from all over Ontario, and many were facing, for the first time, the ugly prospect of being cut. If they wanted to continue in professional hockey, they would forever be competing against the best players for a position on teams.

Cornel didn't know what to expect at his first OHL rookie camp, but by the time he had arrived, he and just about everyone else knew he wasn't ready. The first clue was the wire facemask he wore—not like the half-mask shields all the others had on, which symbolized the graduation out of minor hockey. The next clue was his lack of energy.

Watching his son on the first day, Rob Cornel understood that Eric wasn't as prepared as many of the others. He had been at Ontario's under-17 team tryouts three weeks earlier, but he hadn't hit the ice again since then. Instead, he had played for his high school's soccer team in the season-ending championship tournament. The family's naïveté was showing; not even the team knew Cornel hadn't been skating. Still, because they had witnessed his amazing skating ability, they weren't especially worried about his apparent rustiness on his feet. Despite one NHL scout's private confident comment ("He's a keeper"), they were a bit concerned about his willingness to compete. (That word again.) How would he make out against bigger, stronger and much older players? He hadn't exactly excelled in the physical tests conducted on the first day, either: he scored low in weightlifting, vertical jumping and stretching exercises. It was easy to forget that this lanky blond kid, soon to have pimples, had just turned 16.

Meanwhile, the team's second-round pick, Josh Maguire, helped himself with a strong showing on the ice and in the fitness room. He dug for the puck, competed in the corners, took out his man and showed great determination getting to the net. The Petes were committed to Cornel and signed him to a contract, despite their transient misgivings. They signed Maguire too, so both players would probably start the season with the big team. This meant there were even fewer openings for other newcomers.

Many of the players had personal trainers that their families paid for (some teams paid these trainers directly to avoid players handling the money, as the Petes would the following year) and would get on the ice during the summer. This was a change from an earlier era: from the 1950s through the 1970s, most players went home to play golf, baseball or lacrosse, or to work at summer jobs. They expected to get back into shape when they returned to training camp. In a way, Cornel's soccer-playing interlude was a throwback to olden times. It was an indulgence he was unlikely to repeat.

After the final scrimmage, players would meet one on one with

Reid or the coaches for a pep talk, to get to know one another and determine what the players' plans were for August training camp.

Before leaving, the rookies and parents met with the Petes' staff and their education consultant to discuss the provisions that would be made for school. The Petes also gave each player a fitness training manual with the idea that all of them, including last season's returning players, would come back in even better shape.

The Petes would keep in touch with both rookies and veterans during the summer, making sure they were following fitness programs. Some would even get personal visits. Every member of the Petes' staff was conscious that his job and hockey future were on the line. The coaches were willing to work even harder than last season. The players had better be willing to do the same.

Summer for many of the players meant more rinks, time spent on stationary bikes, weightlifting and stretching. But eight Petes picks, including Cornel and Maguire, were also at evaluation camps for Ontario and Canada under-17 teams. Canada had so many exceptional young players that instead of one Team Canada, it sent regional all-star squads to the tournament. Nick Ritchie, Stephen Nosad and Trevor Murphy had made the squad in 2012, the most of any OHL team. Reid would be on a well-deserved vacation, boating with his wife on Lake Ontario, during the Team Ontario camp in Cornwall in July, but the Petes would be well represented, with coach Clark acting as one of Team Ontario's coaches.

Meanwhile, Ritchie would be named one of 22 players to play for Canada's under-18 team in Slovakia and the Czech Republic from August 13 to 18.

Reid used whatever downtime he had to study possible forward lines and defensive pairings for the coming season. He knew he needed some bigger forwards and scoring power to replace departing players, maybe even Puempel. The Cornel and Maguire signings meant there were only two or three open spaces, since seven defencemen were coming back. Those were not good odds for any of the other rookies. The kids drafted this year who didn't make the team would get experience on other older, bigger teams in Tier II or major midget and could try again with the Petes next year. Realistically, if the Petes had too many rookies in the lineup, they would not make the playoffs at all. The youngest players could not be expected to compete against 19- and 20-year-olds unless their skills were on par with a Crosby or Orr or they had both the size and skill of young Ritchie.

The Petes had four '95s, five '94s, fifteen '93s and three '92s. The good news was they had lost only their three overage players (players in their final season of junior hockey); the bad news was they had nobody to replace them.

Along with Clark, Hull and new goalie coach Andrew Verner (Tugnutt had left the team), Reid attended the NHL draft in Pittsburgh in June that saw Petes star Slater "Koeks" Koekkoek selected in the first round, 10th overall, by the Tampa Bay Lightning. The general manager who chose him was none other than Reid's onetime Petes teammate, Steve Yzerman. It was quite a sight when the former Detroit Red Wings star announced another Petes star as the team's first pick. Al Murray, the Lightning's director of amateur scouting, told his team that Koekkoek was absolutely the best player on the team's list. "He is a terrific skater, going to be a point producer as well as a real solid defensive player."

Murray lived in Wilcox, Saskatchewan, where Koekkoek had

played midget hockey for the Athol Murray College of Notre Dame and was named MVP when the Hounds won the Canadian midget championship in Quebec. Murray had been impressed with the Ottawa-born-and-raised 16-year-old defenceman who had been the youngest player for Canada's under-18 bronze-medal team in 2011.

After Koekkoek was selected, he told the media how cool it was for Yzerman to be the one to announce it and how much he owed the Petes. "It means everything to me," he said at a press conference in Pittsburgh. "Something every kid dreams of when they start. To be here [at the NHL draft and picked] is a huge thing. There is a great heritage around Peterborough; Peterborough is a great spot for anyone to really grow up and play junior hockey. I thank them for all they have done for me and getting me to the next level. I owe them quite a bit." He added that his mom and dad were "the biggest things in my life. I wouldn't be here without them."

Koekkoek's selection made 2012 the fifth consecutive year in which an NHL team had drafted a Pete in the first round. In those five years, Kitchener and Niagara had produced a first-round pick only three times (none of them consecutively); London, Windsor, Guelph, Oshawa, Plymouth, Barrie and Brampton, twice; and Owen Sound, Sarnia, Mississauga and Kingston once.

Of the 211 players drafted, 48 had played in the OHL in 2011–12 (out of 99 who had played in the Canadian Hockey League), the highest number since 1999, when 52 were picked, just more evidence that the OHL was a development factory and a great NHL apprenticeship program. Those first-round drafts meant dollar signs to their junior teams. The NHL paid hefty development fees to the OHL, which passed them on to the players' teams. A top pick could earn the team more than $20,000 via a complicated formula even Reid didn't understand.

Koekkoek's defence partner, Clark Seymour, was also drafted—in the fifth round, 143rd overall, by Pittsburgh. He had been passed over the previous year, but now his perseverance had received its just reward.

The fact that Koekkoek had been taken early in the draft meant Reid had to consider the possibility of his making the move up to the NHL that fall. As it turned out, the NHL was headed toward a lockout: negotiators for the league and the players' association would fail to come to an agreement before the scheduled start of the season, and the standoff would mean no NHL hockey would be played until mid-January of 2013. But in the summer, Reid had to assume that there would be an NHL season—and there was no Koekkoek twin in the Petes' rookie camp. Players like him don't come along very often. (The last defenceman as good as Koeks was Zach Bogosian, who had gone to the Atlanta Thrashers—now the Winnipeg Jets—after being picked third overall in 2008 and never returned.) The slender, muscular, curly-haired, blond, confident kid who at an incredibly early age had always wanted to play with and against older, better players was seen by coaches as the key to a successful team. Koekkoek had been injured in 2011–12 and probably needed more time in the OHL, but the Petes were still looking for another possible star.

And, as luck would have it, out of the haystack came the needle. Greg Norman Betzold hadn't been one of the 303 players on the OHL priority draft list, nor had he been spotted previously by the Petes. The tall (six feet, two inches), gangly youth, weighing in at 178 pounds, came up from the States and shone like a comet in a black sky.

Born a year before Cornel and Maguire, he was invited to the Petes' rookie camp at the suggestion of their American scout, Randy Walker, who knew him from peewee hockey in Philadelphia and had watched his progress while playing for the Shattuck-St. Mary's high school team in Minnesota. This same school had produced such stars as Sidney Crosby, Jack Johnson, Jonathan Toews, Zach Parise and 2012–13 Quebec junior star Nathan MacKinnon (now with Colorado in the NHL), although they had played a level above Betzold. Reid scoured the kid's history. He had scored 42 goals and added 39 assists for 81 points in 60 games while collecting 87 penalty minutes in 2011–12. Great numbers. His dad had gone to college on a golf scholarship and named his son after his favourite golfer, Greg Norman. A family advisor, American law student Alex Linsky, suggested to the kid's parents they give an OHL camp a try to see if he could compete.

He had been one of 15 invited free agents at the Petes' rookie camp and was the best player, playmaker and shooter, as well as one of the top skaters on the ice. It helped that, after he and his family had driven the nine hours from Maryland, they saw the banners commemorating Greg Millen, Cory Stillman and the Staal brothers—all names they recognized—hanging from the Memorial Centre lobby. Betzold, at only two years of age, had watched tapes of New England Whalers games that starred Millen.

Best of all, Betzold competed.

He was only testing an OHL camp while waiting for the United States Hockey League draft on May 22, but Reid had seen enough and knew he couldn't let him escape.

"I was looking around for the police to tell me he had escaped from jail or something. I couldn't believe it," said Reid.

The club offered Betzold a contract right after rookie camp and signed him on May 15, but it took a two-year U.S. university education guarantee. The parents had barely scraped together enough money to get him into the private school the previous season, and now a team wanted to pay for him to play hockey! They were a little overwhelmed. His father fondly remembered watching a game when his son was four (it seemed like only a few years ago). In the stands, he had scrawled some words on a piece of paper, instructing his boy to keep skating, and held it up for him to see. And the kid "came over smiling and waving and, of course, he couldn't even read! So how stupid was I?" Theirs had been a whirlwind ride, taking Greg to hockey rinks in Maryland, Washington, D.C., Philadelphia and Minnesota to get him better competition. Pelino had seen at least one contender, as had the fans, although surprisingly, only 300 of them had shown up to watch their top draft picks that rookie weekend.

Besides the draft, of course, teams could trade for the talent they needed. OHL rules gave them until 5 P.M. on June 27 before trade activity was stopped for a summer hiatus that lasted through July. The Petes hadn't developed their own overagers (20-year-olds, or '92s) and needed trades to get them. Two prospects that caught Reid's eye were Brett Findlay and Francis Menard. The Petes gave up five future draft picks to get them.

The fun-loving, extroverted, sandy-haired Findlay had played for two years in the Soo. After their miserable 2011–12 season, he finished with the minor-pro Texas Brahmas on an amateur contract. If Puempel returned to the Petes, Findlay, with his scoring skills and a six-foot, 178-pound body could be the addition the Petes needed. In his 100 OHL games, he had amassed 40 goals and 60 assists with a dismal team.

Findlay had grown up in Echo Bay, near the Soo, and never played on a top AAA midget hockey team before playing in the OHL.

He came from a family of skaters. His mother, Sandra, was the power skating instructor for the OHL's Soo Greyhounds. His father, Bruce, had played Tier II junior hockey and coached minor hockey. And his older sister, Terra, was a world-class figure skater. Brett's mom had wanted him to take up figure skating, but father Bruce preferred hockey and signed him up at four. At 16 (during his OHL draft year), he broke his leg in two places in an all-terrain vehicle accident. Doctors said he would be lucky to play again. He had two major surgeries in 2007, and for six months he didn't play and didn't know if he ever would again.

He spent painful months, first in a cast and later at the Soo rink, where a therapist helped him recover his strength. As the leg healed, he skated tentatively, a day here or there, then five nights a week on a rink in the Soo or on the frozen river at Echo Bay. When he finally laced up his skates and slipped the shin pad over the leg, which now was held together by pins and rods, it was to play for a local AA midget team. He tried out for the AAA team the following season but was cut. He went to AA and won the 2008–09 scoring championship and MVP award. The following year, he made the AAA squad but chose to go to the Blind River Beavers of the Northern Ontario Jr. Hockey League (NOHL) to play with 21-year-olds. His family still remembers the satisfaction Brett felt when he called the AAA coach, the man who had cut him the previous year, to tell him he wouldn't be joining the team. He had cut the coach.

He was third in league scoring for the Beavers when he was invited to try out for the OHL Greyhounds and surprised them with his scoring ability. When the Petes traded for him, he was excited and told Reid he'd certainly be at camp. No NHL teams had drafted the good-looking kid. "If I had been 16 [and] in my first year, I would have been nervous [about moving to Peterborough], but instead I was excited to get here. At 16, you're not quite mature or ready for the move; it takes a couple of years in junior to mature, and now I'm moving into adulthood. Maybe I can help the younger guys like Ritchie, help him mature and play a part in his success.

"Not every kid has this chance, and you realize how privileged you are and how much an honour it is. No matter if you make it to the NHL or not, you can use your talent for an education and you have different options, maybe to be a coach and pass on what you know to the kids."

OHL teams were allowed only three overage players, but Findlay was an obvious competitor and an effervescent and rapidly maturing young man: maybe a perfect fit for the Petes.

Menard was similarly promising. At six feet and 185 pounds, he was also a forward and Guelph's assistant captain. He had grown up in a French-speaking household in the small town of Embrun, Ontario, between Ottawa and Montreal. He was chasing more than a hockey dream: he wanted to find his biological parents. He was born in Charlottetown, where his 17-year-old parents gave him up for adoption at birth. That was all he knew about them. (Later in the season, unbeknownst to the team, he began meeting with a local group on Wednesday nights that had expertise in finding biological parents.) He loved his adoptive parents—his mom a teacher and his father a farmer who grew up in the French community of St. Pascal, Ontario, near Ottawa—and knew they would always be his family. They had told him about his adoption as a young boy, so he was comfortable with it and considered the Menards his mom and dad. But he longed to meet his biological parents as well as track his genetic medical history. He had a tattoo on his shoulder dedicated to them.

Hockeywise, the French-speaking Francis yearned for better competition and development.

In Grade 9, at the age of 14, after hearing about the Athol Murray College of Notre Dame from his coach, he flew out alone for the school's open house and "liked it, so I left home," he said matter of factly, adding that his parents had paid for the flights and the tuition, which came to $30,000 a year. He stayed at the school for three years, playing hockey, living in a dormitory and learning not only the game but also the English language. The focus was on hockey and church on Sundays. The town of Wilcox, Saskatchewan, had 11,000 people, almost all of them English-speaking, and Francis, at 15 with broken English, played first for the school's bantam squad and then the midget AAA Hounds, for whom the likes of former NHL great Wendel Clark had also played. He averaged a point a game and posted a 75 per cent school average while also becoming fluent in English.

The Guelph Storm selected him in the sixth round of the OHL draft in 2008, but he returned that fall to Notre Dame, getting 47 points in 37 games with the Hounds midgets. Slater Koekkoek enrolled at the school as a bantam in Menard's final year and was called up to the midgets in midseason. Menard was happy to make the Storm in 2009, scoring his first goal in only his second game but racking up only four points in 32 games. "The OHL was different from Notre Dame. There was more liberty, independence. While everyone was always together at Notre Dame and you shared a room with your buddies, the OHL was a different lifestyle." That first year, he was still in high school, so it was school all day and a practice in the afternoon or games at night. Since the age of 14, he had spent his winters away from home, playing hockey.

He kept working harder and his production increased, as did

his ice time. He wasn't selected in the NHL draft in 2010, and he returned to Guelph. The Storm hired a new coach halfway through the season, which seemed to ignite Menard, who got 31 points in 66 regular-season games as well as four goals in six playoff games. In his third season, he was named an assistant captain and finished second in team scoring with 60 points. In his three years with the team, the centre scored 42 goals and 106 points in 199 games. "The NHL dream starts to shrink as you get older," he said. "Hard work will do a lot, but only so much. I'm not too high up in the clouds and know at the end of the day you still have to make a living. I'm chasing the dream, but this dream changes as you get older; you can see the guys who really have potential and will play at a much higher level."

Guelph was looking toward its future and wanted to use its younger players more often. This is part of the constant cycle many OHL teams go through: they don't like to call it rebuilding, preferring to characterize it as "building a team." Menard thought he would be traded and harboured no hard feelings. In fact, upon being traded, the mature young man sent a message thanking the Guelph management, team and city for everything. Notre Dame had taught him well. He was a friendly and appreciative 20-year-old. He was so excited to meet some of his new Petes teammates that he volunteered to arrive two days after the trade so he could take part on the Petes' boat at a cancer fundraising event. His voluntary appearance was a positive development for the Petes' family and community image. The boat race was just one of a number of community functions that Reid involved the team in. The Petes didn't just talk the talk when it came to community; they walked the walk.

The addition of Menard and Findlay gave the team two more experienced centres before training camp opened. Together with Alan Quine, a friend of Menard's who in the summer trained with other Ottawa-area Petes, Koekkoek and Seymour, they came to be called "the Ottawa group" by the rest of the team. They were tight. Too tight, it would turn out.

The June European import draft was also conducted via computer, but far more quickly than the NHL draft, and little attention was paid to it. Reid traded the Petes' ninth-overall import draft choice to London for the Knights' second-round pick in 2013, a fourth-rounder in 2014 and a seventh-rounder in 2015. Reid knew picking import players was a gamble. Professional European teams were willing to pay top-rated prospects to keep their boys playing in Europe, and Canadian major junior teams needed to come up with some cash for these players. Reid selected short (five foot nine), compact (176 pounds) Jonatan Tanus from Kuopio, Finland, a 17-year-old left winger who had earned a silver medal playing for his country's under-18 team.

Reid didn't have a lot of the Petes' cash to offer, so he chose someone he was confident would come to training camp without any financial perks. Tanus wanted a contract, not a tryout, before he would come across the pond. The Petes already had Cornel, Maguire and Betzold signed as newcomers, so the addition of Tanus just made it that much more difficult for other players hoping to make the Petes.

Tanus's parents were both doctors, but their son, when asked about following in their footsteps, chuckled and said, "I don't want to be a doctor; they work too hard." His dad, Michel, was born and raised in Israel and had gone to medical school in Russia, where he met his Finnish wife, Sari, and moved to her homeland four years before Jonatan was born. Michel couldn't speak Finnish then but learned it and several other languages, as did his wife. Their English was limited but passable. Sari's father had been a hockey referee, and her brother, Veli-Pekka Pekkarinen, played hockey in a Finnish pro league. Michel was also a team doctor for an elite hockey team in Finland. Jonatan started playing hockey at five. Unlike in Canada, minor players in Finland had more practices than games. He scored a lot of goals and was moved into a group with players two years older.

When the Petes drafted Tanus, he didn't know a thing about them. He did know that the OHL was a pipeline to the NHL, where he dreamt of one day playing. "I knew the OHL played good hockey and every team was good, with plenty of people watching. We didn't have anything like that." The kid with the broken English, who had never played on the smaller North American ice surface, would take his first plane ride across the ocean alone to get to training camp.

The Petes had 27 players with OHL experience coming to camp for only 22 to 24 positions. It was obvious from Reid's list that there were going to be a lot of disappointed kids, and some of last year's players might even be among them.

The goalie situation was an unknown. Andrew "Dagger" D'Agostini was heading into his fourth year. Mike Morrison had been brought in via a trade the previous season, but he was in his overage year, and Giggy was a promising rookie draft choice who was poised to displace him. It was clear that Morrison's future with the Petes was in jeopardy. When he had asked Reid about his future in May, he was told frankly that he wouldn't be getting much playing time. Morrison demanded a trade, but Reid couldn't get one done.

One of the unique and unpleasant aspects of a GM's job in junior hockey is having to deal not only with disgruntled players and agents in these situations but also with parents. Morrison's parents, unhappy with Reid's inaction, called Devlin. The president maybe should have said he was sticking by his general manager's decision, but he didn't because the Petes liked to deal with their problems and preserve that family image. Morrison was released and eventually was picked up by Kingston. Cross Morrison off the list of players who would be praising the Petes in the future.

Reid thought the team's performance in the rookie camp was weak and let the coaching staff know it. He and Pelino agreed on one point, that goaltending could be a problem. Nineteen-year-old Dagger was back for his fourth year, but he hadn't had a great season in 2011–12, and the 17-year-old rookie, Giggy, with his unusual right-handed catching glove, hadn't played an OHL game. Neither had yet looked brilliant.

Dagger and Giggy were opposites: veteran and rookie, thistle and rose, Bambi and Rambo. In warmups, Dagger stretched, moved and focused while Giggy skated around deking, shooting pucks, goofing off. Dagger had close-cropped black hair and a clean-shaven face; Giggy had long, unruly, sandy hair and a sometimes-whiskered face, depending on the day or his mood. Dagger was early for everything; Giggy was often late. Dagger had favourite NHL teams, knew all the statistics, watched goalie videos and was a student of the game; Giggy had no allegiances.

Dagger was last year's OHL Dan Snyder Humanitarian of the Year award winner. He had been a goalie for Canada's under-18 team in Germany two years before, an event that cost his family $10,000 to attend, but his father, Tony, a former Junior C player, said he would have paid 10 times that to see his son play for Canada. Dagger had matured since his arrival in Peterborough three years ago and said, "It's insane what I've put myself through. My life revolves around hockey, training, focus, discipline, nutrition, watching video, reading books, fitness, sacrificing my time."

While Giggy loved the game, he had yet to capture Dagger's passion. It was Dagger, not Giggy, who said, "You'd have to put me in a body bag to get me out of the game. I don't want any regrets or at 50 say [that] if I had stretched 10 more minutes or did that one extra push-up. . . . I do the work now so I won't regret it later."

Dagger and Giggy had things in common, though: when they got inside their crease, both were competitive and determined not to let anyone score on them, even in practice. Both Petes goalies were Toronto-area kids—Giggy from Brampton, Dagger from Scarborough. They both had uncles who were goalies, and both had borrowed old equipment to start their hockey journey and had fallen in love with goaltending. They had also both suffered through friends' deaths: Giggy, this year when a high school friend died, and Dagger at 15. It was that incident that changed his father's perspective, transforming him from a nervous, excited, sometimes overbearing father to a more understanding one.

The staff was looking forward to July, when most teams reduced operations for much-deserved vacations. Reid, although nominally on vacation, would be wired to his cell phone for any issues that might pop up, as they surely would, before returning to work in August, when trading could resume. But before his holiday could begin, the excrement hit the Petes' fan.

For Reid, Matt Puempel remained a headache. In April, a few

months after vehemently informing the public that he was happy and wanted to stay in Peterborough, he not only asked for a trade but also insisted that he be sent to Kitchener. The reason: he felt it would be better for his career because the coach there was also Team Canada's junior coach. The Petes' coaches took Puempel's demand personally. Obviously, Puempel was not a Pelino fan. Narrowing the list of destinations to Kitchener made it more difficult for Reid to get what the Petes needed.

Puempel's request, although not initially made public, was whispered throughout the sports community. (The Petes had an internal leak that flowed faster than a kitchen faucet.) This was the third star forward, the second captain in three years, who was ticketed for a trade. Demands like this from top players were troubling. And there were some observers—hockey insiders who understood the game—who argued that Reid should have pushed back, should have told the kid to sit and sulk, as Reid had said privately he would, thus sending a message to all players that management had the final say. Giving in would give the wrong impression to prospective players—and their parents—who wondered why these stars wanted out of Peterborough. It also sent current players the wrong message that they too could easily get out. Reid realized he could not let this trade happen unless he and the team won in the deal. They had received only draft choices and a fourth-liner in exchange for the last star player who was traded away. Fans expected a lot more this time. Surely, Reid would put his foot down.

In mid-June, Puempel's agent sent Reid a letter indicating that his client would not be reporting to training camp and formally requesting a trade. Reid had asked for the letter: he wanted Puempel to make his trade demand public so it could not be made to appear that the team was dumping him.

Reid tried to make a three-way deal with Kitchener and Niagara that would benefit the Petes by bringing in Ritchie's older brother, Brett, an excellent player who was Nick's best friend, the kid he had competed against at home, in parks and on outdoor rinks, all of his life. It would have been the perfect team fit and a public relations coup. Kitchener was agreeable and so, it seemed to Reid, was Niagara, but when the trade with Kitchener was done, just minutes before the trade deadline on June 27, neither Ritchie nor Niagara was a part of it. Only Kitchener's Zach Lorentz, a low-scoring 12th-round draft pick in 2009, and three second-round draft picks were coming to Peterborough.

The board of directors was shocked. Devlin understood that Ritchie was part of the deal when he had last talked with Reid. Reid says he told Devlin that wasn't the case. To the board, it was a disappointing, frustrating surprise. To the fans, who weren't told about the Ritchie part of the deal, it looked as though Reid had once again given up more than he got. Even though Reid collected plenty of assets (which he planned to use to make another attractive deal when trading resumed), he got nothing that would please the fans or the board or improve the team for the coming season. When the arrangement was announced, it brought on a barrage of anger and criticism. It would have been even worse had critics known about the Ritchie offer falling through.

Lorentz was a five-foot, eleven-inch left winger who had recorded 19 goals and 33 points in 66 games with the Rangers in 2011–12. Puempel had scored the same number of points in fewer than half the number of games and had totalled 166 points in 144 regular-season games over three seasons. He was OHL and CHL rookie of the year in 2009–10, as well as a silver medal winner in the 2010 world under-17 championships and a first-round draft pick of the

Ottawa Senators. There was no comparison between the two players and no way to massage the trade as a good thing. To all appearances, Reid had blown it—again.

If Puempel had thrust a metaphorical dagger into the Petes' collective back, he gave it an added twist in an interview with the *Examiner's* hockey beat reporter, Mike Davies, on the night the trade was made public. Puempel said he wanted to play for a winner. He said he loved Peterborough, that he might even choose to live there later, and added that he had the "greatest respect" for Reid. But while "Peterborough has made some great additions this year, you don't really go from being a team that misses the playoffs to being a contender. It's a process," said Puempel. "If they do, I'll be the first to call Dave Reid and congratulate him. This being my last year of junior, I wanted to win and be a part of a team that is in a different phase of a rebuild." Puempel said he was also afraid that if the Petes didn't have a good season, he might be trade bait in January, and he didn't want to be in that situation.

Puempel had pushed the Petes under the bus. By saying he wanted to play for a winner, he was telling the team it was a loser. The Petes might have used his words to motivate their players; instead, they let it ride, arguably a big mistake.

Puempel was leaving a coach who had more experience than most of his counterparts in the OHL or CHL, one who had already coached an NHL team, a Canadian university team and Team Canada. Pelino had won and lost at all levels and was respected in many hockey circles as an astute student of the game. But Puempel didn't like his coaching. Some of his former teammates privately agreed.

Reid offered an answer to Puempel and to disillusioned Petes fans, saying maybe it was still part of his becoming the team's GM. "I don't know. We do know that what we're doing here, and the group we have got, we know we're doing the right thing and are developing the players we have on our roster. We believe in what we're doing and that we're going in the right direction. We're not the only one in this situation. I know there are other players in the league who have asked for trades. It's part of the game. We do everything we can to provide a great hockey opportunity for players in Peterborough and a great life experience for young men. I'm not concerned with how our organization is doing things moving forward."

Reid believed the team was now stronger, with more depth and assets than at any time. He also felt the team defence would be one of the best in the OHL. (He was counting on Koekkoek's return.) His message was all about optimism, but the mood in the community was pessimistic. They had lost another top scorer. Reid put as good a face on the deal as possible by saying he was not done "reshaping his team."

Petes president Devlin said he had been livid when Reid told him about the trade. There was trouble brewing between the two men.

The Puempel trade had given bitter fans, and the community, enough ammunition to take potshots at the team for the rest of the summer. There was an extremely tense atmosphere in the organization's boardroom and offices.

So much had happened since the end of the Petes' dismal hockey season: players had come and gone, the city and the Petes battled over rink advertising rights and revenue, there had been a controversial purchase proposal and Puempel had told Peterborough fans he wanted to play for a winner.

There were plenty of vicious people who had no qualms about describing Petes management and coaches in nasty terms. Reid,

Pelino and the board of directors were called everything from bums and assholes to idiots or worse. The atmosphere heading into August was tense. Reid's and Pelino's futures depended on the performance of 23 teenagers in the coming season, and they knew it. Another losing season and they'd be gone.

CHAPTER 5

Training Camp

"The first thing I want to make clear is that we are on a mission to win," coach Mike Pelino told the players gathered in the alumni room at the Memorial Centre. It was the first day of the four-day training camp, and the players had not yet had their physical exams and fitness tests. Soon the coach would have the chance to assess the hand he had been dealt, and the players would discover whether they would become part of the game. But first, Pelino wanted to set the tone.

Pelino was a professional. He had known as soon as he was hired that he was bound to be fired one day. This didn't stop him from hoping Peterborough would be a long-held position. His wife was from the area, his son went to school at nearby Lakefield College and the Petes job was something he had wanted for a while. It was two years ago that the slim, grizzled, black-haired hockey coach heard the

Petes were cleaning house. His friends, former Petes coaches Mike Keenan and Gary Green as well as the Rangers' Tom Renney, all recommended him to Reid, who couldn't believe his luck that someone with Pelino's background was available.

The then 51-year-old had been involved in hockey since he was a child growing up in Welland, Ontario. Life for Pelino was hockey. His father, Louie, who was born in Italy and came to Canada when he was six, played for a junior team near Ottawa that went to the Memorial Cup Eastern Canada semifinal, losing to future Montreal great Jean Beliveau's team in 1951.

When Mike was growing up, sports was "our way of life." He both played and refereed hockey and umpired baseball. Pelino played minor hockey and, at five feet, ten inches, played for the Welland Junior B team at 17, becoming one of the league's best defencemen. He had NCAA scholarship offers but went to the University of Toronto, where he got a degree in education, studying economics and commerce.

He tried out for the varsity team but got cut "by none other than Tom Watt," the hockey guru at U of T. He tried out for the Junior B Oshawa Legionaires, whose coach was another teacher, the not-yet-famous Mike Keenan. Pelino drew inspiration from Watt and Keenan as well as other coaches. He finally made the U of T squad and still holds the record for most career points in Ontario university hockey by a defenceman. He once scored 11 points in a single game.

"My passion was to be a player," he said, "but when it seemed that wasn't going to happen, I became a teacher and hockey coach."

He took a job teaching high school in Woodbridge and became Paul Dennis's assistant coach with the Toronto Marlboros of the OHL in 1985–86. He was also coaching two high school hockey teams and the golf team and helping with the football team. The

Marlies practised every day and played 70 games—he missed only one. Many nights, he slept at the Gardens, where the Marlies played, or in the school or in his car. "It's amazing what you can do when you're single," he said with a chuckle. "It was way too much, and the next year I left the Marlies for a less hectic schedule.

"I loved working with people, trying to inspire and improve and watch them and the team develop. The team is the key. I was good at it and embraced it. It became my life."

He was instructing at Gary Green's Can Am hockey school in Peterborough in 1986 when he met his wife, Kim, working in the school's business office. In 1987 he was hired as sports information coordinator at Brock University and stayed for 10 years. The Pelinos were married in 1989, beginning the nomadic life of a hockey coach together. Over the next few years, he dragged not only himself but also Kim and their two children—a daughter and son—around North America, coaching several under-18 teams before leaving Brock in 1997 for professional hockey. He coached various national teams to international championships, including the Spengler Cup in Switzerland, and helped with Canada's Olympic gold medal team in Salt Lake City.

The quiet, well-spoken career instructor said coaching was like conducting a symphony. "Much like a conductor must ensure all the talented members of his orchestra are in sync in order to create beautiful music, a coach must orchestrate his team," he once wrote. "He must coordinate his group to be on the same page, to execute a game plan and perform at a high level to achieve the synergistic effect of the whole being greater than the sum of its individual parts."

In 2010, while an assistant coach with the San Antonio Rampage of the AHL, he got what he called his "dream job" with the Petes, the legendary team he had heard so much about but that had fallen on hard times. He headed to what people had told him was a hockey hotbed with knowledgeable fans, an excellent organization deep in history and tradition and a new GM who was a former Petes and NHL alumnus. It sounded too good to be true.

You know what they say. . . .

When he had helped coach the Marlies 25 years before, he said, "the players were so team-oriented. Today, the players are better, the competition is better, the skating and skill level is better, but the players have a survival instinct. Many of the players are trying to figure out what is best for them instead of what is best for the team. I'm not sure if that is player-, agent- or parent-driven or intrinsic, but new players are very self-serving when they first get here and it's difficult to deal with as we try to mould a team."

Pelino had his own way of balancing his competitive instincts with a sense of social justice. Each year, unpublicized by the Petes or him, he travelled to Iqaluit, a poverty-stricken northern native community, where he conducted hockey clinics with 100 players from children to teens. He had returned from his 10th session in Iqaluit in August. It was a change and gave him something to feel good about. A coach needs that.

The last season with the Petes, 2011–12, found him working the hardest he ever had as a hockey coach. The team had been in first place at the end of November, but when injuries hit their best players, the team nosedived, not even making the playoffs. He was committed to making sure they made it this season. After two years as coach, he also was beginning to learn that Peterborough didn't quite get behind the team as he had been told it did, and the fans weren't as knowledgeable as the myth had made them seem. He was surprised by this but kept plugging along, just as his nickname, Plugger, suggested. He hadn't become as well known in the community as many past coaches. In fact, his name was so unfamiliar among some people in

Peterborough that they still confused him with former NHLer Mike Foligno.

"I believe as an OHL coach," he once wrote, "I have two primary responsibilities to my players. One is to provide the guidance and leadership to help each individual develop into a champion on and off the ice. The other is to orchestrate this group of individuals into a cohesive, successful unit."

Pelino knew that getting through to some of the players and convincing them to embrace his team philosophy was going to be a challenge. He had seen the same changes to junior hockey many other observers have commented on. "They have grown up learning ways to get to the next level. They ask how do I get to the next level, how do I get noticed, and they think it's by playing on the power play, scoring goals and getting lots of minutes. Instead they should be asking how can *we* be successful and listen to the coach to not only see what he can do to get better but all of us get better. That's very general, of course, not all of them are like that, but I see that change. The other big change is how it is now such a big business."

Pelino was trying to get through to his players in the carefully scripted and rehearsed speech he gave in the alumni room on the first day of camp, telling them determination, hard work, passion and enthusiasm would capture their character.

"We will be successful and we will win.

"We will be the fittest team in the OHL.

"We will be the hardest-working team in the OHL.

"Starting with today's fitness testing, we want to see your best every day.

"We know there are going to be some very tough decisions as to who makes our team. Your job is to make it as hard on us as you can.

"Show us how much you want to be a Peterborough Pete. Being

a Peterborough Pete is special and it is an honour. You represent not only yourself and this group around you, but all of those who ever have been part of the Petes before you—everyone from Bob Gainey and Steve Yzerman to Pat Casey and Dave Reid, from Larry Murphy and Scotty Bowman to Jody Hull and Andrew Verner, from Roger Neilson to Jordan Staal.

"Continue the tradition!"

Mission to win . . . no one will outwork us . . . make every day count . . . compete, compete . . . be a leader . . . believe in yourself . . . play with swagger . . . For the newcomers, the words were motivating, exciting and new to their ears. For some of the veterans, it was just more talk. They had heard it all before.

There were other small signs of discontent among the veterans, though they tended to go unnoticed by the coaching staff—little things like coaches making the guys take off their ball caps outside for the runs. They weren't much, but in light of later developments, they became significant.

The players had arrived for camp, the veterans living in their old billets' homes, rookies doubling up in billets or hotel rooms with their parents. Most of the veterans figured they would be remaining in Peterborough for the season, but still there was uncertainty; others had no idea what was ahead. For some, it was their first time away from home in a strange city and rink and living in homes with strangers. Homesickness is sometimes the most difficult part of the journey. Most players who are homesick agree the toughest part is getting through training camp, followed by the loneliness of the first few weeks in new homes without family.

For 15- and 16-year-olds, living with strangers, getting comfortable in their homes and getting used to their habits, foods and personalities, and having them not know yours, could be a difficult transition. The feeling is similar to that experienced by many youths on their first days in a new school. But here, there would be no returning to your parents' home. There are great players who didn't make it because of this shock to the system. Although they would never admit as much to the team, some cried themselves to sleep with the loneliness, while others just jumped in without missing a beat.

The landparent/billet situation has changed over the years. In the 1950s and '60s, players usually stayed with a widow or older family and lived near the rink in working-class homes. Today, players are spread throughout the city, usually in middle-class homes with families. The Petes were the first OHL team to start this system of landparents, commonly called billets in other centres, in which players are placed with families in their communities. They advertise for families to take in Petes, interview them at their homes and do background checks.

Once approved, the landparents are given a small weekly allowance, but no one takes on the job for financial gain. Sometimes the arrangements don't work out. During his first season with the Petes, 16-year-old Windsor native Trevor Murphy had some bad experiences with his first few landparents, through no fault of his own. At one home, he discovered a landparent's child had some health issues. He reported it to the team and his mother. He was moved out of another home when a daughter who had moved away returned and wanted her room back. He moved three times in his two seasons.

These things happen, but not very often. Occasionally, the fit between the player and the home isn't right. The Petes' experience has generally been positive, however: for the majority of the players, their landparents' family becomes their home away from home. The parents and siblings can become friends for life.

The billet system was overseen by the team's GM and Walter DiClemente. DiClemente was a 30-year police veteran who had been involved with the Petes since 1983. He had also set up a proactive risk-management program that the league later used as a model for other teams. The friendly, helpful former sergeant had arrived in Peterborough in 1980, started attending Petes games and "got the bug." He was a landparent who had looked after 13 players over the years. He didn't do that any longer, now that he had two growing children of his own and his duties as president of the minor Petes hockey program to keep him busy. He said picking the landparent is probably the most important thing the GM can do for future recruiting and player retention. "You have to make sure the bar is set high and always ask, 'Would I leave my son with them?' Basically, you are adopting a teenager. You make sure they get three meals, do their laundry, and make them feel at home." The reward for many is being part of the players' lives, watching them grow—and, in DiClemente's case, getting invited to their weddings, receiving Christmas cards and being friends for life. He was even a member of former NHLer Mike Ricci's wedding party.

Dave and Cindy Crowley were among the Petes' cohort of landparents. They looked after two Petes, Nick Ritchie (although not until later in the season) and Derek Mathers. They also operated a busy local restaurant and had three children. The role was one they had assumed naturally. As they explained it, about three years ago they noticed that players were coming into their restaurant regularly. "I'd ask them about their diets, home life and hear about the meals they were eating," remembered Cindy. "I decided we needed to do something, so I started giving them discounts on their meals, then thought we should be billets and open our house to a player."

Two of their children were still living in their comfortable five-bedroom home when they welcomed their first player. It was the year Reid became GM, and goalie Jason Missiaen, at that time a Montreal Canadiens draft pick, was their first charge. "It was a rough season," said Cindy. "He was put on waivers after training camp and went through a lot of trauma. It was heart-wrenching to have a six-foot-nine kid coming home, crying his eyes out, saying he was put on waivers.

"I'm not a hockey person," said Cindy. "I didn't even know what waivers were—we had to Google it. [Waivers come into effect when a player is cut loose and made available for other teams to claim.] We were trying to reach his parents, his agent. It was an emotional roller coaster. Even though he was no longer with the Petes, he stayed with us for three more weeks before Baie-Comeau [in the Quebec Major Junior Hockey League] picked him up."

The Crowleys didn't take another player that season, but at training camp the next year they tried it again, taking in newcomer Derek Mathers, "the gentle giant," who stayed with the team and became part of the Crowley family. "He's such a wonderful boy, so gentle, he plays with our grandchildren. He's a joy to have around."

Dave Crowley took Mathers aside, three days after he arrived, for "the Talk." "I asked him if he knew who the tough one in this house was, and he gave me the right answer—Cindy, which was so true. She put the fear of the ruler into him and anyone else." They had the same rules for the player as their children. Obey the rules and there would be no problem. "I told him we'd never say no to him as long as he never said no to us."

There were never any issues with Derek, who enthusiastically joined in at family meals, especially Cindy's special Wednesday night

Italian spreads for her children, grandchildren and hockey players. Other players angled for invitations to these meals.

In October, Ritchie would have problems with his billets. The kid didn't observe curfews and loved being out with the older players. He moved in temporarily with Reid, and the team asked the Crowleys to take him in. They were hesitant. They talked to the coaches, and then to Nick, and asked Derek if he would mind. Ritchie had a bit of a reputation for salty language and for not respecting his former billets' rules. "But I can tell you he has never sworn in this house and he's been pretty good," the Crowleys would report months later. "I told him once, when he arrived, and again when he missed a curfew, that he would have to pack up and move if he did it again."

The players had to do their own laundry and volunteered to cook the Crowley meal once a week—usually flatbread pizza. Mathers would make it, while Ritchie set and cleaned the table. They were two of the biggest players on the team and ate "all the time, in fact."

The Crowleys and other billets got $85 a week, but it wasn't long before that money was gone after the necessities like milk, juice and fruit were purchased. Landparents counted on a local bakery for monthly supplies and on food stores that gave Petes discounts. The two boys seldom ate junk food at home, preferring to eat healthy, although outside the home Ritchie tended to eat anything in front of him. Cindy would also make Ritchie's lunch for him to take to high school, which had to tide him over until dinnertime. "If you're in this for the money, you're not going to make anything," said Dave with a smile.

There was more to it than food and shelter, though. Dave even stayed up until the players got home, no matter what time they got in. "I did that for my kids and do it for them. I don't want them coming home to a cold, dark, uncomfortable home." They also told any player on the team that if they were drinking and needed a ride, to call them.

They worried about the two when they weren't home. Cindy, known to the family and players as Nonna, texted or phoned them if they were late. If there was no reply, "my heart jumped.

"Our role is to make sure the parents know these boys are in a safe, happy place, well fed and cared for. We can't replace Mom and Dad, but we can give them that home experience.

"We only wanted them to respect the house and they did."

The Crowleys had no regrets about taking in players. They pointed out that Missiaen, then playing in the American Hockey League, still called weekly.

The players' training camp journey started with testing the day before the Labour Day weekend. Training staff, coaches, general manager and scouts prepared to work 16 hours daily for four straight days until they had whittled the players down to a reasonable number, from 57 to 28. They would make further cuts before the season started, until they had the final 23 or so.

Reid had already told the coaching staff that this was not going to be a development year. They had to win or they wouldn't be around to develop any more Petes. They all had sleepless nights, especially those first four days, because they worried about making cuts, sending most of the boys home, dashing their dreams, telling them they wouldn't be part of the team. There were only 13 or 14 forward, seven or eight defence and two goalie positions available.

Fifty-seven of the 60 invited players had arrived by August 29. Forty-five of them were born in the first half of the year, confirming research that shows that players whose birthdays fall early in the year have a better chance of making it to junior than those born later.

Twenty-four were taller than five foot eleven and heavier than 185 pounds. Twenty-seven had OHL experience. More than half of them were from small towns and cities in Ontario. Their parents were administrators, teachers, farmers, businessmen, pilots, civil engineers—a good mix of hard-working white- and blue-collar workers.

Clark held fitness sessions for those who arrived a week or two before camp. The first camp day, with players at the rink for up to 10 hours, was full of fitness testing, medicals, photographs and sprints. They picked up their equipment: Petes maroon shells to cover their former team pants, gloves, sticks, helmets, T-shirt and shorts.

The first days were much like starting at a new school where personalities are kept hidden until everyone gets a feel for things. There were no hurrahs, no yelling, no quips, no jock talk, just an eerie quiet that acknowledged fear of the unknown and fear of competitors who were all there to capture the same thing: a spot on the squad. Most of the players were new, not knowing how to behave, and feared doing something wrong. This newcomer tentativeness would linger until the team was selected. Then they could relieve their anxiety and nervousness, the tension released like air from an overfilled balloon.

Today's players should have been happy they hadn't arrived back in the 1970s when coach Roger Neilson, a sports workaholic, made players do a five-mile run to start, and end, the day. The plug was pulled on that tough tradition years ago, long before the Reid era. This year, 36-year-old assistant coach Clark, rotund but serious student of hockey fitness, had dryland exercises on the first day, the most daunting being the four 300-metre sprints in the arena parking lot under the hot sun, after a day of testing that had included bench-pressing 150 pounds as many times as you could in two minutes. Koekkoek placed first in the vertical jump test. The players generally were in good shape: only one failed to complete the gruelling sprints. Most of them did the first sprint in under 50 seconds—but only six of those successful sprinters made the team. Five of the six slowest in the last sprint made the team.

The team also measured the boys for height, weight and fat percentage. Only eight of the 57 had less than 9 per cent body fat; Koekkoek was lowest at 8 per cent. (Sidney Crosby reported to his first NHL camp with a percentage of 7.) Of those eight players, only Koekkoek, Cornel and D'Agostini made the team.

One of the players with high fat percentage was the team's rookie of the year in 2011–12, Nick Ritchie. Not 17 until December, he was already six foot two, weighed 218 pounds—13 pounds heavier than the previous year—and had just competed for Canada in Europe at the world under-18 championship. His fat percentage was 12, a team high, but not high for athletes. (Many of us would be happy to have that little body fat.) Surprisingly, not only did Ritchie have a higher body-fat count, but his fitness level didn't measure up to the others, including other members of last year's team. He may learn to train more effectively one day, as his older brother Brett had, training with fitness guru and former NHL star Gary Roberts one summer. Nick kept his eye on his brother's career, always wanting to do better.

The testing, meetings and sprints continued from 1 to 5 P.M. on that first day, with plenty of replenishing liquid breaks but no meals; some energy bars, nothing else. The players were burnt out and hungry when they finished. The landparents, some of whom were taking two players during camp, were waiting in the parking lot, knowing they would be using up a big slice of their weekly $85 budget on tonight's first meal.

Former Petes captain Mike Martone, who was at training camp to encourage the new arrivals and help with various routines and games, knew exactly how the new players felt.

He remembered his first camp, after arriving from the Soo, as pretty tough. "It's everyone for themselves and it takes a while to find out who your new friends are," he said. "Cuts were being made every day. . . . Briane Thompson, a team veteran, had been with the Soo and he introduced me to some other veterans, so I was accepted. I thank him to this day."

He also saw the changes in junior hockey players today from when he came here in the 1990s.

"When I was drafted, it was a privilege and honour to be picked by anyone," he said. "The culture has changed so much. The first priority for me was to get drafted and get an opportunity and play for the team that picked me. Now kids are trying to pick who they play for."

Just like the upcoming season, training camp was not without controversy.

A few weeks earlier, a mysterious organization calling itself the Canadian Hockey League Players' Association—unconnected to the National Hockey League Players' Association—revealed it was forming a union for junior players, claiming it had the widespread support of players. Only Stephen Pierog had been approached, and he wasn't a supporter. Few others had heard of it until the media got wind of it, sending fear through the CHL and team boardrooms.

The Petes board of directors, especially President Devlin, were alarmed by the prospect. He decided to speak to the players and parents at camp. He addressed them, but there were no questions. Hockey was what the players were there for. Besides, Devlin's often long, slow speeches could lull a sleep apnea sufferer to dreamland.

A couple of months later, it was revealed that one of the proposed union's founders had previously been convicted of fraud, and the so-called union collapsed.

National Hockey League players' wives have a different interpretation of the league's abbreviation: No Home Life. By the same token, the OHL could be called the Overtime Hockey League. On the training camp weekend, Wayne Clark was preparing for high school classes and Mike Pelino's daughter was heading to university in Guelph, while Dave Reid's was entering Trent in Peterborough. Goalie coach Verner couldn't go to his young son's provincial baseball championships out of town. The training staff were the busiest people at camp, looking after players' and coaches' requirements. Trainer Brian Miller, known as B-Man, had the washing machines and dryers going continuously every day. B-Man played a vital role on the hockey team, not only looking after the medical care of the players but also seeing to their equipment and maintenance of the dressing room. B-Man, who has his physical education degree from Brock University, had been the trainer for the OHL's Guelph Storm for three years and head trainer and equipment manager of the Saint John Flames of the American Hockey League for six.

Most of the players had arrived, except for three whose dreams had ended with injuries before camp and two others who had decided to forgo camp because they had received U.S. scholarship offers.

Scrimmages over the next few days featured teams named for former Petes who were also Hockey Hall of Famers: Teams (Bob) Gainey, (Steve) Yzerman and (Larry) Murphy. There were about 100 curious people watching each day. Reid, Pelino, Oke and other coaches and scouting staff watched from above as former Petes coached the teams.

Some of the lingering doubts about Cornel were erased. The kid was a hockey player. Staff now remarked on his ability to skate and see developments on the ice. A 16-year-old usually took time to develop and grow, but he looked like a natural; he was not flashy but was intelligent, as one NHL scout said. His father knew Cornel had had a questionable rookie camp, and the player had come back ready to perform. "The experience at rookie camp opened Eric's eyes, but he's back. He wants this. He's adapting well. His mom will be worried as school starts, but it's something Eric wants. I don't know how the [Tanus] family from Finland does it."

Slater Koekkoek, Alan Quine and Greg Betzold had impressive days. Koekkoek's team won the championship in the two-day mini-tournament, during which teams played games when they weren't practising. Veteran fans said it had been the most competitive camp in years, with far more intensity and energy than last year's.

All the '96ers, with the exception of Cornel and Josh Maguire, were sent home. Cornel and Maguire, who had looked good the first day, slowed down, unused to being on the ice seven times in three days. The weekend ended with the annual Maroon and White scrimmage, which included all the best remaining players and attracted about 1,000 fans. Koekkoek starred in that tilt while puck wizard and veteran Quine, with four of his team's five goals, was also impressive.

Betzold had scored three highlight-reel goals at camp, and staff wondered how he had escaped being drafted, especially coming out of the well-scouted Shattuck-St. Mary's private school. But Reid, his colleagues and the scouts knew as well as anyone that the brightest light in training camp could easily lose its brilliance in the regular season. They met between periods and again after the final game. At that point, the decisions left to be made affected a handful of positions. Altogether, 13 players were sent back to their hometown teams; some others would be placed with Petes affiliates. The club had given all its draft picks the training-camp experience, something some teams didn't do. The '96ers left with experience and confidence, knowing that, with more work, they had a chance to someday return.

Of all the cuts Reid had to make that week, one was especially difficult: Dylan Fitze, a city native and a Petes full-timer in 2012–13 who was an overager and three-year OHL veteran. Kids in their final year of eligibility who have put so much of their lives into the game and pursuing their dream are the most difficult cuts on any junior team.

A few eliminated players thanked the Petes on Twitter for giving them the opportunity to play. This was generous and perhaps prudent: it is never a good idea to burn your bridges. Teams have long memories, and thoughtless comments can put an end to any hope of future favour. There are many examples of players who didn't give up and eventually succeeded. Bill Huard, back in the 1980s, kept returning to Petes camp, and on the third try, when he carried 25 more pounds of muscle than at his first tryout, he finally made the team, had two good years and went on to play in the NHL.

Reid said cutting junior players was not much different than in minor hockey: you lose sleep over it and it's the worst part of the job. "It's not easy to dash someone's dreams," he said. "You tell them they don't fit in your plans this year, they need to work on something. You never tell them the dream is over, because for some, it isn't. You don't like doing it, but it has to be done. You tell them they need development, or maybe they are just not what we are looking for. It hurts to tell them." But, as he knew, it hurt much more to be told.

After four gruelling days, 28 players would remain while waiting for the first exhibition game against Mississauga, which had already formed its team. Only four or five cuts were left.

Among the most likely on the bubble were Luke Hietkamp, Chase Hatcher, Cole Murduff and rookies Alex Robinson, Matt McCartney or Cody Thompson.

Hatcher would be a tough cut. Unlike the others, he had an NHL pedigree via his father, Derian, the former captain of the Dallas Stars, and his uncle Kevin, another NHL veteran. Chase was drafted in the eighth round by London in 2010, when he was only five foot ten, but he grew five inches in one year. When he was traded to the Petes in January for superstar Austin Watson, he had two strikes against him: the name on the back of his jersey and the trade; both were met with great fan expectations in Peterborough.

"The name has been helpful and hasn't been," he said. "Some of the players chirp at you, and sometimes it's a lot to live up to. And"— he laughed—"I will probably never be able to."

There had been years when some players eliminated themselves. After working out at camp and seeing for themselves that they weren't ready or good enough, they approached the coach and let him know. This was not one of those years.

Goaltending decisions became easier when a prospect's kneecap was broken in the warmup before the Mississauga game. Giggy and Dagger would be the goalies, as Reid and Pelino had always anticipated.

Reid and Pelino were expecting big things from their defence, figuring that with the blueline corps's experience, size and talent, it was one of the best in the league.

Pelino praised the newcomers for not looking out of place and said of Nick Ritchie, a dominant force at 16, "If he can go from the start of the season to the end like he did today, he's going to make a lot of [NHL] scouts drool about the prospect of drafting him [in 2014]."

They were already drooling. Ritchie's father, Paul, a horse trainer and school administrator who had also played in the OHL—as well as for Pelino at Brock University—and his mother, Tammy, a teacher who was a volleyball star in university, had been impressed by their young sons' skills, so much so that they had spent about $250,000 over the years for Nick and older brother Brett to play hockey. They had given up almost every night and winter weekend for their sons' practices and games, a price paid to a greater or lesser degree by countless hockey parents. The parents remembered Nick's first attempt to skate at two or three, when they put a chair in front of him for him to push and he said angrily, "That's for babies!" Nick proved he was no baby when he and his brother played on the rink their father built for them. This was not a slapdash affair, but a rink with boards, lights and nets. It was not unusual for the boys to shoot 600 pucks almost every night. Nick competed against his older sibling, as only brothers can. It was as if every game was the last game in Orangeville. He was the biggest kid on both his hockey and lacrosse teams, and he starred on both. His parents, just like others in the OHL, including the Quines, had moved their teenage boys from their hometown to the Toronto minor hockey leagues for better competition. Some parents actually set up apartments or rooming houses for their boys. Quine, from Ottawa, had lived in a house with other midget-age players in order to gain residency so they could play there. Nick was the third-youngest Pete behind Cornel and Maguire, but after a year with the Petes in the OHL, he was expected to be one of the team's stars.

There wouldn't be many, if any, more cuts before the regular season, although Pelino hoped to pare the 28 names down to a lineup of 23 before the season began and to keep extra players to fight for the final positions. Reid had talked with four-year veteran Hietkamp about his role, telling him he'd be a fourth-liner and they would be expecting him to be an energy guy who might not play all the games. Hietkamp said he was willing to give it all he had, but no veteran who took on a role as a fourth-liner and became a part-time player in junior hockey could be entirely happy. Hietkamp was no different, but he put up a good front.

Gradually, the pieces were falling into place. After all the intense meetings, the hard decisions and the emotionally charged conversations, the Peterborough Petes were almost ready to put another team on the ice.

The scouts went home prepared for another season on the "hot dog tour."

B-Man and the training staff made sure their equipment and supplies were up to the demands of another long grind.

The players settled into their billets. Some looked forward, or not, to another year at school.

Pelino mentally went over the players in the Petes' lineup as well as his hopes and plans for the games ahead.

"It doesn't look bad," he told me. "It looks good. We're not sure yet if it's great; that will take some time."

But he knew few people within the organization would have time for failure. The camp had gone well, and he had seen many good signs. He knew it had been the most competitive camp of his three years in Peterborough. Now he had to make sure they got on a winning track. They needed wins.

CHAPTER 6

The Captain

There are many variables that go into a winning hockey season. Luck, injuries, good players, management, team togetherness and commitment over the course of a long season are a few. Obviously, coaching plays a role, as does the team's captain. The Petes' captains of bygone years, with a few exceptions, were usually the team's most loyal players. None had been traded or asked to be traded. Team and player had respected the maroon and white and had given the jersey and the *C* sewn on it the allegiance they deserved. In recent years, this tradition had hit a rough patch, but the role of captain remained central to a team's success.

It is the captain who leads the players and keeps them moving forward. The Petes have had some great players as captains and some great captains as players. It was usually the latter who took them the farthest. There were two qualities shared by all of them: a powerful work ethic and natural leadership ability. Not all of them were the best players, or the top NHL draft choices or top scorers, but all of them led by example and were veterans loyal to the team, who outworked and outlistened every other player.

It didn't look from the outside as if the Petes had anyone who could compare to these past captains, so many of whom had gone on to have great professional coaching, managing, scouting and even executive hockey careers. But greatness, after all, is more easily recognized in hindsight than in prospect. What the Petes needed was a player who would grow in the role.

There was a time when the players voted for their captain, but that hadn't happened for years. Now the coaches made the selection, with the approval of the GM. They had not had much luck in the last two seasons, what with Watson's and Puempel's unseemly departures.

Pelino said selecting a captain meant "trying to determine the best candidates who have a good relationship with the players, coaches and who know it is an honour to be chosen." The captain had "to exhibit the qualities and attitude we want in our players and try to do what is best for the group. He has to be a team player and be a guy with ability and unselfishness with determination, commitment."

The coaches figured the Petes' 61st captain, Slater Koekkoek, the 18-year-old with the slim, muscular body, nice smile, curly light-brown hair and confident attitude, fulfilled those requirements. He was the guy who, although injured last year, had shown his leadership by attending this year's banquet to welcome newcomers and applaud award winners. He also was the hardest worker at practice, the team's best player and a top NHL draft pick.

Koekkoek, whose father's parents had come to Canada from Holland and had a farm near Ottawa, was not even two years old when his amused neighbours watched the precocious kid play with a little wooden stick and beach ball in front of his parents' home in Winchester. When he wasn't outside playing, he was inside with his mini-sticks. His mother, a nurse, who had been a figure skater, took him to figure skating classes when he was three. He skated circles around the other kids even when he wasn't supposed to be doing it, especially when the group was gathered to listen to their instructor. But once the lad hit the ice, he had to be moving. He was dressed in a cowboy outfit for one event and took off doing impromptu laps around the Winchester rink, earning the laughter and applause of the crowd. It was obvious, even at that age, that he needed more action. His parents enrolled him in hockey.

Like most Petes and OHL players, Koekkoek usually played hockey against, and with, older boys. He thrived on being the best player, said his parents. "He always wanted to be number one in everything he did, whether it was in public speaking, [in] which he was number one; cross-country running, which he was; Canada Swim, which he was. Anything he did, he had to win or give it his best try." He was in Grade 8 and just 12 years old when he attended a hockey tournament in Toronto and was spellbound watching a team from Saskatchewan. He wanted to know more about these Notre Dame Hounds. "When we got home," said his mother, Karen, "he started talking about it. We thought he'd let it go, but he started researching Notre Dame.

"One thing about him is, he won't let go. If he wants something he is persistent.

"We were not jumping up and down about Notre Dame. We didn't really take much time to think about it. He was playing AAA on good teams, but he wanted to play on better teams, and they wouldn't let him play on the older teams. He told us, 'You're going to be holding me up if I don't go to Notre Dame.'" As the best player on his team, he didn't think he was getting enough ice time and proper direction. His parents, meanwhile, heard whispers at the rink about Slater thinking he was a superstar. The whispers hurt his parents so much, they hadn't talked to some of those other parents since. "I won't give them the time of day," said the normally friendly Brian. The parents of many budding hockey stars, from Gretzky to Yzerman, have had similar experiences, dealing with complaints not only from the opposition but also from teammates' parents.

The family made huge sacrifices for their children. Brian, a rugged rock of a man, worked overtime as a lineman at Ontario Hydro. Karen would rush home from work to get Slater to practices, feeding him Kraft Dinner on the way or at the rink while also getting their daughter to all her sports and academic functions. The family travelled throughout Ontario for summer and winter hockey, baseball and swimming—and now Slater was thinking about private schools.

They first visited the American prep school Shattuck-St. Mary's, and then Notre Dame in Wilcox, Saskatchewan, in the spring. "We went on the tour of Notre Dame [everyone, including the grandparents]. The school was in the middle of nowhere and freezing; there were no trees and it was surrounded by nothing. It looked like it was out on a lake," said his mother. "But Slater tried out with a group there and he loved it. They thought he was good and the idea blossomed for him."

The tuition was a big financial gulp: $30,000, which didn't include travel or parents' expenses to watch him play. There were no Caribbean vacations in the Koekkoek family's future. That August, when Slater was 14, the family returned to set up his room. Crickets filled the hallway—the province was going through a dry spell. "I cried," said his mother. "Here was my little boy in the middle of nowhere. . . . What are we doing? What are we getting into? He was

14 and leaving home." His roommates were strangers. One of them was Morgan Rielly, who became his best friend. (He was the Toronto Maple Leafs' top draft pick in 2012.) His parents didn't see their son again until October.

"Notre Dame was the best time of my life," said Slater. "Being around the guys, living in the dorm, sitting up all night talking. There were no girls, no drinking, just fun. And we won. If I ever have a boy, he's going there." But, after his first year, when he came home to play spring hockey, he fractured two bones in his forearm so badly that an intern at the Hospital for Sick Children in Toronto looked the young boy in the eyes and blurted out, "You probably won't be playing hockey again." The kid was devastated until a surgeon told him the intern should not have said that, because "we have no way of knowing." To Slater, that meant there was a chance, and when there was a chance, this kid ran with it. During his first surgery, they put screws into the forearm. That didn't work, so metal plates were installed and moulded to his bones. This was followed by vigorous, painful rehabilitation.

Slater worked hard all summer, toiling daily to make not only his arm stronger but his body as well. He did sprints up hills, weight training, anything that would improve his conditioning. His parents were amazed by his training program and their son's determination. He returned to Notre Dame that August fully recovered, and he starred in the national championship tournament in Quebec, helping the Hounds to win the title. He was named tournament MVP. The Petes' Mike Oke, filling in until Reid was hired, had seen the boy's name in a scouting report and was in Quebec watching him. He instantly knew he was their man.

Even with all that he had achieved, the Petes were the only team that called Koekkoek about the upcoming OHL midget draft. Oke's scouting report on the six-foot, one-inch, 184-pounder was glowing: "Strong and powerful two-way defender. Poised beyond his age. Great shot, good hands/puck skills. Excellent physical play. He shows great puck movement and possession. Displays good mobility. He is a very active and involved defenceman who possesses an impressive collection of physical tools. He has legitimate size. He really likes to play a high-pressure, involved game in all three zones of the ice."

His parents said other people probably see their son "maybe as a bully, pushing his way through things, determined to reach his one goal, to make the NHL. Even when he was a little boy, and his grandmother babysat, he'd tell her he was going to play in the NHL.

"He is fixed on what he wants," said his mother, "and doesn't quit until he gets it. He wants to play in the NHL and has always wanted it, right from when he was a fan of the Maple Leafs. He has no backup [plan] without hockey. He says having a backup is setting [himself] up for failure." But they added that Slater is a "sensitive guy with a soft spot who doesn't like to see other people's feelings hurt.

"People don't understand what has gone into this. They have no idea. You just don't walk into this; it's tough, very tough. He's been through a lot. You have to give up so much to get there. His buddies don't understand and it frustrates him when he sees other teammates not doing what they should or could be doing. He has to be trying his hardest at all times."

And yet, he had a modest, shy streak as well. Whenever anyone discussed his talent in front of him, he shied away, and if it was his parents talking, he would tell them not to talk about him.

Slater remembered the OHL draft. "The Petes showed an interest, it was a good fit and excellent for me. My Uncle Tony [his dad's brother] had been living in Peterborough for 30 years." The Petes drafted him in the first round, seventh overall. That fall of 2010, at age 16, he began living with Tony and Mary Lynn Koekkoek. "It was an easy turnaround and I had no trouble adapting."

His first season, he scored seven goals and 16 assists, but it was his maturity and confidence that surprised many of the veterans, who jokingly called him their "rookie overager." He even hung out with them. Things were going well the next season, but after only 26 games he injured his shoulder and it required surgery. It was another spring and summer of rehabilitation with Ottawa-area fitness guru Tony Greco, who pushed him as hard as possible. Slater responded the only way he knew how: with everything he had, the same that he expected from everyone else.

He came to camp this season in the best shape of his life. For all of these reasons, Reid and Pelino figured he was their captain. "I wasn't expecting to be named captain, but I was hoping to," said Slater. When Slater was asked about the recent captain curse (the Watson and Puempel trades) and told that, in the past, Petes captains had stayed with the ship, win or lose, his response was different from what past captains would have replied. He said simply: "It's a two-way street. Winning keeps good players, losing is not fun."

He continued: "History shows that past captains were probably treated well and had teams good enough to win. I am hoping for this. When I first got here, they said I sure didn't act like a rookie. Being captain is an honour. [Jack] Walchessen was the captain when I got here and he took me under his wing, told me not to get excited about some things. The worst part is losing and the community knowing all about it. When I got here, it was supposed to be a good year, but they got rid of everyone; then last year, the same thing happened. It's time for management to step up and be buyers, not sellers. This is our year."

He was determined to succeed, but at 18 he had no training in how to lead, nor any instinct for it. He just picked up on what he had seen captains do in his past two seasons. He was driven, but his drive hurt his captaincy. "People don't know what we give up. They say it must be a good life, but we can't go to Halloween parties, New Year's Eve parties, . . . Our weekends are hockey. We give up a lot to get here and to be where we are. We are just normal guys. We want to have fun; a lot of people think of us differently off the ice.

"The best part of our day is in the dressing rooms, when it's story time [the guys talking with each other about things outside hockey] or on the bus trips. It's the best time of the year, and on the ice you forget about your life.

"When I'm out there, I never want to be off the ice. I want to outwork everyone. I refuse to be outworked. That's to honour my dad, who has always outworked people."

And he usually did.

"He's a good kid," said Wayne Clark. "A passionate hockey player who just wanted to win so badly."

Pelino added that selecting a captain is sometimes a compromise when a coach is trying to change the player by giving him more team responsibility. "Maybe it's a guy that was brought up in the 'me, me, me' [thinking only of himself] and maybe we think it will help him become a 'we, we, we' person [acting more for the team]. The added responsibilities sometimes bring out the best in the player. It's a fine line, though, and you're guessing. Sometimes it works, sometimes it doesn't.

"Leadership is the ability to influence others. The captain is just another dynamic in putting a team together. He has to be honest, upstanding, a great player. It won't work with lack of experience. The captain supplies leadership in the dressing room, sets the examples and needs the support of the team. It's very important for the team.

Saying this, though, a kid like Cornel, who listens, learns, goes to the weight room without being asked, could also have that leadership quality, but at that age he needs some experience. He is already setting an example, but he's the furthest from being a captain because he is young and has just arrived."

This year's choice was certainly honest, a great player and veteran. But a captain helps with team morale as well. Besides the captain, there also need to be at least a half a dozen other players who are willing to do anything for the team. And it was for this reason that the Petes' choice was mystifying. It was as if the coaching staff were utterly unaware of how many veteran players felt about Koekkoek. It was as if they had no idea how much he intimidated the younger players. It was as if they were unaware of what was going on in their own dressing room. It's not that the choice of captain was made without discussion. The names of Derek Mathers and Clark Seymour, ultimately named assistant captains, both came up in their discussion. But in the end, the coaches came to an agreement they could get behind.

While Pelino outlined the rationale for his choice, there was obviously another consideration that was left unspoken: it's likely that the move was meant to keep the player, a top draft pick, happy. This had been the justification for selecting Matt Puempel, and it had hurt the team, but they went ahead and did it again, convinced they had their man. And there were many people on the outside who applauded their choice.

The coaches and GM announced their selections in the dressing room following practice, then took the captain and assistants to a suit-and-tie dinner. Some of the players questioned the captain decision—not openly, of course, even though Pelino had encouraged players to ask questions. "Don't bitch and whine about something," he had told them, "but ask and get answers." They were teenagers, however, and mostly too intimidated to question adults and their decisions, especially in front of teammates.

Neither Reid nor Pelino had any idea their decision would cause a controversy unlike any other in Petes history. They knew there would be some disappointed players, especially among the veterans, but they could not have predicted how deep it would go.

Koekkoek knew the captain would get the blame when the team was losing but would also get the adulation when winning. He wished only for winning. Playing in the NHL was never far from his mind. Just as when he was small, he wanted to play with and against the best players. That's what drove him. "The quicker I get there, the better," he said. Twenty-five NHL teams interviewed him before the spring draft. They had followed his play not only as a member of the Petes, but for Canada's under-18 team. Some, like Tampa Bay, had been watching him since Notre Dame.

Koekkoek was happy, ready and excited to start the new season. He, like all the others, had high hopes. Unlike some of them, though, he wasn't willing to accept anything less than winning.

And then the first home exhibition game arrived.

CHAPTER 7

Fight or Flight

September 6 would mark the Petes' seventh consecutive day on the ice. That night, they were scheduled to play their second exhibition game—and their first at the Memorial Centre—and things were not going according to plan. Reid, a hands-on manager in every respect, was juggling questions from the board and staff enquiries while dealing with technical issues such as condensation dripping from the arena ceiling, opening-night logistical details, player agents calling about their clients' training camp experiences and calls from other managers looking to trade (or dump) players. There were so many distractions. An Elton John concert had forced the Petes out of their fitness centre; the national senior lacrosse championship was also going to be held in the Memorial Centre, displacing the team for another five days. The Petes, the Centre's main tenant, were being tossed out like buffet leftovers.

Exhibition games were rehearsals for the real ones, and now, 17 days before opening night, Reid was frustrated with his team's amateur-hour performance, which would extend to tonight's game. This latest rehearsal was against the Oshawa Generals—a bigger, stronger, meaner team that was winning more battles. The first period wasn't bad, ending with the score tied at one, but the second was, well, scary. The Generals were like an army advancing on a volunteer brigade: they took a commanding lead. Late in the second period, there was a power outage, the period ended early and some of the fans left. Only a few had noticed that, just before the power interruption, with fewer than three minutes remaining, the Petes' brightest light was dimmed. The newly appointed captain had gone to the dressing room holding the same shoulder he had injured last season, after taking a hit into the boards from Generals captain Boone Jenner.

Reid went from his perch in the Petes' staff suite to the dressing room downstairs, not because of Slater, whose injury had gone unnoticed, but to discuss with coaches a list of issues he had compiled, such as the Petes' difficulty winning the small battles. But before he could say a word, Reid was told the alarming news about Koekkoek. Fifteen minutes later, he returned to the suite, his face as white as the ice surface below. He whispered what had happened: "Slater has popped the shoulder, the same shoulder; he's gone to hospital." The season hadn't started, and their best player was out again.

"I can't watch this anymore," he said. The team was losing 5–1. "I'm going to the hospital." There were no team tweets, no announcements, no confirmations, nothing coming out from the organization until they knew what Reid was expecting: bad news. Pelino told the media following the game it was an "upper-body injury," employing the terminology that teams use when they don't want the public to know anything more than they have guessed already. The 18-year-old who was expected to carry the team on his shoulders, who had returned with the energy, passion and enthusiasm every coach wanted in a player, had been taken to a hospital emergency room. The physical and mental pain was unbearable.

The first reaction by a team after an injury is always about the team. Losing Koekkoek would be like losing the oil for the engine, the oar for the boat, the shine in the sun. That's the initial reaction, but quickly you check yourself and think about the poor kid, a teenager with such a great future ahead, who hasn't relaxed or sat out exhibition games as some other league stars do, waiting to see if the NHL might call them up (in seasons where NHL players aren't locked out). Koekkoek was a kid who had put everything into his return and made his debut with the C on his chest, who hadn't yet signed a contract with the Tampa Bay Lightning. His injury was also a multimillion-dollar concern.

Back home in Mountain, Ontario, though, there was only one concern that night, one worry, one thought: the boy's health. When Brian and Karen Koekkoek got Reid's call, they dressed quickly and headed toward the hospital three and a half hours away.

Reid stayed with Koekkoek until after midnight, trying to console his star, who was openly worrying about his future and the impact it might have on a possible tryout for Canada's world junior championship team. The GM couldn't help but think about last year, when Puempel, Seymour, Boland and Koekkoek were injured. And now this. Was there a curse on the Peterborough Petes?

Koekkoek was injured, they had lost two exhibition games and—in the minds of many onlookers—the Petes' season was in doubt. This was when Pelino, no matter how distraught, how frustrated, how depressed it made him, had to influence people and keep the team together. It was far too early to jump to conclusions, Pelino warned fans. He admitted the team had played poorly against Oshawa, their traditional rival and a division rival they would play eight times in the regular season. He knew there was a lot of work to be done, but there was time yet to turn things around.

Meanwhile, the injury list was getting longer. Matt Robson, the goalie, had a broken kneecap; Alex Robinson, a defenceman, a broken jaw; Francis Menard, a pulled hamstring; Chase Hatcher, a sprained ankle. Adding to their misery, Clark Seymour, another top defenceman, got into a fight with less than 10 minutes to play and was out for the next game (the rule in exhibition games). For Reid and Pelino, anxiously waiting to see what impact this would have on their team, it was like watching an elephant about to step on a field mouse—overwhelming, helpless.

Then, the afternoon after the loss to Oshawa, Reid and Pelino got some good news: Koekkoek would probably return early in the regular season. X-rays, and a trip to a Toronto specialist with his parents, showed there was no damage. For a week or two, he would have to endure rehab (which was turning into a specialty for this kid) and wear a Sully brace while playing to stop the arm from rising past the shoulder, but the prognosis was that he should be okay. Reid's face was a better colour after he got the news, although he and his staff had gone through more change than a slot machine in the past 16 hours. He phoned Slater's parents; Tampa general manager Steve Yzerman; Slater's agent, Murray Kuntz; board members (even Devlin had called from his vacation in Europe); the media; and some fellow GMs who were curious (or nosy) about the star's condition. He didn't reveal the injury's extent to media or rival GMs, saying only that it was bruising—he didn't want his player to become a target for shoulder hunters on his return.

All was well for now.

However, the Petes' next exhibition game, two days later in Oshawa's rink, had Reid even more concerned.

The game should have seen payback for what Generals captain Jenner had done to Koekkoek. Amazingly, however, Jenner was still standing after one period—untouched, unscathed and allowed to hit at will while chirping at whomever he wished. Retribution is a tradition in hockey, just as it is in baseball (the chin-high fastball in return for a spiked ankle, for example). The Petes' captain had been knocked out of commission, but tonight there was no equivalent response by his teammates. Oshawa dominated the first period, hitting every maroon-and-white jersey in sight, while outshooting the Petes 18–10. A fuming Reid, furious at the lack of physical play, steamed to the dressing room to talk with the coaches between periods, something he hadn't done much in past seasons but this year was determined to change.

Early in the second period, Jenner hit Steven Trojanovic. The two dropped their gloves, and four more fights erupted in a single stoppage of play, which is unusual in today's junior hockey leagues.

"It's about time," said Reid. Oddly, tough guy Derek Mathers, considered the league's heavyweight champ, was absent during all the scraps.

Tonight, there were so many fights that each team had only 11 skaters left for the rest of the game. The Petes were no better shorthanded than at full strength, however, and suffered their third consecutive loss.

Their goaltending and the lackadaisical play of Mathers, who hadn't made a hit all night in this western brawl, were both concerns. Board member Bob Neville even commented to Reid about Mathers's lack of aggression: "He's out there looking more like a chaperone than the tough guy." They had been outscored 14–4 in three games and had only one even-strength goal, but Pelino remained positive.

The Petes' woes continued with another loss in Brampton three nights later, but still there was no panic. Pelino was not coaching to win but still rotating lines, giving every player an opportunity to show his stuff. With a little more than a week until the regular season, he had not yet formed lines, there were no power-play or penalty-killing units, no shortening of the bench or matching lines.

Mathers finally got into a fight. The Battalion player should have chosen a different dance partner. The 17-year-old teen required plastic surgery, his tryout ending on the end of Mathers's punch.

Derek—or Diesel, as he was known to teammates—had once been a long shot to make the NHL. He had been drafted in the seventh round, 206th overall, for his six-foot, three-inch, 231-pound frame and his toughness. There was hockey in the family, although his uncle, Don Van Massenhoven, had taken a different route as an NHL referee. Size, too, ran in the family: his younger brother was six foot ten and weighed 295 pounds. Diesel was a defenceman until Reid asked him to come to training camp as a forward. By that time, Mathers was playing Tier II in Strathroy and gotten into his first fight, which he liked. Now he was the OHL's top fighter. Although he was the tough guy when he first came to the Petes, he, like so many kids coming to a strange city, team, home and school, was so homesick that he kept asking himself if he had made a mistake, but assistant coach Jody Hull had talked him through it.

The day after the team's latest exhibition defeat, every player had a one-on-one with Reid and Pelino, the GM and coach telling them what they needed to do if they wanted to continue to play—not only for the Petes but in the OHL. Goaltending was still an issue— Dagger was giving up big rebounds, but it wasn't clear that Giggy was ready to take his place. Defence, not supposed to be a worry for the Petes this season, threatened to become one. It still was early, but Pelino and Reid were surprised at the blueliners' poor play so far. Maybe Koekkoek's return would help. A week before the regular season was to begin, Koekkoek and Oke drove to Windsor to visit a specialist that Tampa Bay, protecting their valuable asset, wanted him to see before he played again.

Koekkoek's return to practice the next day was a reassuring sight. The familiar number 29 was skating freely and taking slapshots. It was a joy to watch Koekkoek skate—his quick strides took him away from others so quickly. But he was so intense, it was as if the team was on his back. He was so concerned already about the struggling club. He was expected to return for the home opener, an incredible recovery.

The next few days were intense for everyone. Hull said, "You don't know what you have. If the Petes played like they did in the first period [of one game], we have a team, but there are so many ups and downs. The way they played in the second period was a different team. It is a difficult two weeks. Last year, it was a little easier going, but this year we're not sure what we have and what's going to happen opening night."

The *Examiner* conducted polls—with no pretence of scientific accuracy—asking readers to vote on the question of the day: "Do you think the Peterborough Petes will qualify for the playoffs this season?" Sixty-four people responded, of whom 70 per cent voted no. It appeared that the hockey community, like Hull, wasn't sure what this year's Petes were made of.

Pelino said that when he first came to the Petes, he understood that the OHL was just one step away from the NHL for these kids, but also only one step away from where they had been . . . in youth hockey. Hull agreed, saying that you had to remember they were kids. But

Hull, too, saw the difference between these kids and his contemporaries when they were the same age. Some of the current junior players just didn't respect authority, whether it was rink staff or coaches. "Even sitting in a principal's office doesn't bother them anymore."

Above each player's wooden stall in the dressing room was a plate bearing the name of a former Petes player who had gone on to NHL glory. In the middle of the carpeted floor was a large maroon Petes logo. The current players could hardly escape reminders of the tradition they were expected to continue. Perhaps this is what overwhelmed them: it was a quiet dressing room, there were seven new faces among them, and they were not quite a family, not quite a team. The silence and lack of togetherness were mystifying and unusual for any hockey team. Some rookies would comment on it, months later, saying that they too felt it was strange. "We were new to this and thought maybe this was the way it was supposed to be."

Even during the game, the players who hadn't dressed, either because they were injured or benched, were spread out, not sitting together. One was in the Petes' suite, two others with friends in the stands, two others sitting alone. "I don't think we've hit our peak yet where we know each other that well on or off the ice," second-year defenceman Trevor Murphy told the media.

After the next exhibition game, on September 13—another loss—Pelino, calmly but with authority, told his players the last two weeks had been a day-by-day learning process. "We know every time we put on that jersey we want to win. I've said this before: even if the game is for shit, we want to win, we all do. You still want to win it because the thrill is in the winning, not the prize. We have come through a lot in the last two weeks, moving from our rink, adding a lot of new players, and some injuries. We have shown signs of being a good team. There is a Chinese proverb that says a teacher can't teach until the student is ready to learn. We have to be ready to learn."

Pelino asked the captain and assistants if they had anything to say. They reinforced what the coach had said, that it was the pre-season and they had to work harder toward the home opener. The exhibition games had been learning experiences, jammed into two intense weeks, and they had to learn from them and work even harder. Koekkoek said if they were expecting to achieve their goals and get to the NHL, they must step it up. Pelino asked who had won the Stanley Cup the previous season. Some replied correctly: the Los Angeles Kings. He then asked what the Kings' exhibition record had been. Without waiting for an answer, he said, "Nobody remembers exhibition games."

Following the game, Reid and Pelino had more one-on-one interviews with players about their progress. Three of their fellow players had been cut that day, including Cole Murduff, a fill-in player in 2011–12 who was dating Reid's daughter and would become an innocent party in a controversial storm later in the season. All three were told to report to the Tier II Lindsay Muskies. Their play, or Petes injuries, might determine whether they returned. The Petes' scouts would keep the team apprised of their play and attitude. The moves would also mean further cuts in Lindsay to make room for them. There were still at least two more cuts to make.

Over the course of the pre-season games, Reid had repeatedly found himself wanting to get involved in the coaching, but he always stopped himself. He knew what it took to win, and too often he hadn't been seeing it. He doubted that Pelino had allowed the players enough rest before the first exhibition game. He had been infuriated by the lack of pushback against the aggressive Generals and the repeated mistakes the Petes made coming out of their own zone. Time and again, he had been on the brink of barging into the coaches' quarters and giving them hell, but it had happened only that once. Later, he would wish he had done it more.

If Pelino was aware of the GM's doubts, and he probably was, it didn't change the way he went about his job. He was concerned that his two overagers, Francis Menard and Brett Findlay, hadn't had good games. Nor had Nick Ritchie. Eric Cornel was trying to make things happen, but he couldn't. Zach Lorentz didn't look good. However, Pelino thought the return of Alan Quine, Slater Koekkoek and Derek Mathers might pick the team up. He thought winning would depend on the players' work ethic and ability to listen and learn.

For the coaches and general manager, the day had begun at 8 A.M. and ended just before midnight—a long and exhausting grind. They had shaved and showered at the arena, changed into the suits, shirts and ties they kept there for game time, and changed again into casual clothes before heading home for a well-deserved night's rest.

Before practice the next day, the captain and assistants had a short players-only meeting to reinforce what had been said the night before. Koekkoek told them they had to have a good start to the season. He was worried about the talent on the team but kept that to himself.

The September 20 home opener was fast approaching. Everything would become more intense when the real season began. The coaches and veterans knew this; the others would find out. The players were itching to get into the regular season. Pelino had given them the weekend off to rejuvenate their engines, knowing it would be their last full weekend off until late October. In the next 35 days, they would have just four days off, all of them Sundays. They had no idea what was about to transpire. A season to remember? Or one they would want to forget?

CHAPTER 8

Burning the Boats

The bad news for the Petes continued as they prepared for opening night, when star forward Alan Quine found out he had mononucleosis. God, thought Reid and Pelino, when would the pain stop?

The five-foot, ten-inch, 160-pound forward was the Petes' most reliable goal scorer. Obtained in a trade with Kingston early in his second season, he had had a stellar first full year with the Petes, scoring 30 goals and earning 40 assists in 65 games, a record impressive enough to get him drafted in the third round by the Detroit Red Wings. But his pre-season performance had been disappointing, and now they knew why. Worse, he could be lost for weeks, even months. He went home to Ottawa to recover.

The team would sorely miss the Belleville-born teenager, who had been raised in Bedford, Nova Scotia, and Ottawa before moving to Toronto alone, when he was only 15, to play in a more competitive league. He lived with other players in a house that his father, Shawn, a pilot and former Junior B defenceman, would visit on his flights to and from Toronto. His mother, Gail, was the daughter of Ottawa junior assistant coach Stump Craig, the best friend of the winningest coach in OHL history, the retired Ottawa 67's legend Brian Kilrea, so the couple knew what it would take for their son to play in the OHL.

Thankfully, Koekkoek would be ready to play on Thursday.

Building a hockey team is like constructing a home: you need a good architect, a site manager, a plan, a good builder, a solid foundation and strong support to add the parts that will make it a home. None of it happens unless the right people are on hand and work is finished on time. Every GM and coach thinks he has a good team before the season begins, but the Petes would have to be patient, make some additions and amend their original plan to complete this season's house. They weren't sure what would be needed to make the house a home until they lived in it for a while. Quine's absence opened up a crack in the foundation, but all teams faced similar setbacks throughout the season.

Most coaches knew of teams that had great exhibition seasons but failed in the regular season and vice versa. The results of the Petes' exhibition games had concerned the Petes' builders, not because the team had lost but because of the way they had lost. "We know there are some missing pieces we need to find to go a long way," said Pelino. "We think our defence, with all the veterans, should be good, but are we hoping this or expecting this? I see some of the other teams and their defence units look stronger or as strong as last year. Are we just hoping ours is [strong too]? They should be strong, but are we really expecting them to be better or hoping this? Why will we be better?"

Reid and his staff evaluated the team after every game, but the big date in Reid's mind was November 1. If they were not .500 or above by then, changes would be made. "I won't panic if we lose our first four games, but after 10 we should be at .500 or better. We started out well last year, then the injuries hit and we went on a slide, but this year we will be on a tight leash, and I don't blame the board for that, if we don't have a good year." He figured the team would be in the top four of its conference.

The man under the most pressure to get them there, Pelino, guided the team through more intense drills—passing, rushing, going to the net and skating drills—and spent time on power plays and penalty-killing units during the week, while forming the lines he intended to start on opening night. Without Quine, the 16-year-old Cornel, with no OHL games under his garter, moved into a spot at centre on the top two lines.

Sports teams are big on slogans such as ALL IN! or OUR YEAR! The Petes' fitness and dressing rooms were full of inspirational phrases, such as YOUR ACTIONS DEFINE WHO YOU ARE: YOUR WORDS MERELY DEFINE WHO YOU'D LIKE TO BE; THE STRENGTH OF THE PACK IS THE WOLF AND THE STRENGTH OF THE WOLF IS THE PACK; and CHARACTER IS HOW YOU WORK WHEN NO ONE IS WATCHING.

The coaching staff wanted something more than this to start the season, something special. Two days before the opener, Clark presented their theme at a team get-together in the alumni room following practice. He told them the story of the Spanish conquistador Hernando Cortez, who sailed his 11 ships to Aztec country, now Mexico, in the sixteenth century on a journey to steal the precious treasures and claim the land so many had tried to conquer. When he got there, over his men's objections, he demanded they burn their own boats.

Cortez, who had also helped conquer Cuba for Spain, had only 600 Spaniards with him to attack the thousands of Aztecs. He took the position that they were there either to win or to die. There was no other option. He eventually won the land that others had failed to vanquish for the previous 600 years. Alexander the Great had used the same all-or-nothing approach to conquer Persia. The coaches bought into this story of courage and hoped it would give the players the inspiration to move forward and buy into the team concept. "We will conquer and sail home in the enemies' boats. We aren't going home without conquering," Clark told the players.

The coaches then shook each player's hand, wished him luck and handed him a grey tank top with the words BURN THE BOATS emblazoned on the back. The players liked the slogan, especially because outsiders wouldn't know what it meant. It would be the team's secret. Koekkoek joked that he was going to tattoo it on his forehead. In TV interviews the next day, some of the players mentioned the phrase, but nobody asked them what it meant. Months later, Toronto Maple Leafs coach Randy Carlyle introduced the same slogan to his team, told them the conquistador story and presented them with a blue-and-white boat. Clark and Hull were ahead of the NHL team on this point, too: they had a plastic boat (a toy obtained courtesy of Andrew Verner's seven-year-old son) ready to be presented to the team's best player after each win.

Pelino told them the shirts were part of being a team and to wear them with pride and believe in winning. "This is a special year. We want to be able to remember it. There is no turning back, no excuses and no other direction but winning. I believe this team has what it takes. You have to believe. I believed that last year and the year before. I believed when I was with the New York Rangers, I believed when I was with Team Canada. It didn't always work out, but I believed, and I believe if the team believes in the words in our dressing room like 'compete,' 'determination' and 'commitment,' we will win." And then he added, "I believe we will win the Memorial Cup."

Nobody cheered or applauded; nor did they roll their eyes, smile or show any sign of disagreement. They showed no emotion at all. It was as if they were afraid to do anything. They seemed to accept Pelino's speech, but not because they shared his belief; rather, they seemed willing to accept that if the coach believed in these words, then maybe he would teach them how to believe too. Or perhaps they just weren't listening.

Jody Hull stepped up next. He also spoke about respect and how they were not entitled but had to earn being there. He said no player should think he was better than anyone else. Hull—like former coach Dick Todd, Petes historian and former hockey scout Don Barrie, *Examiner* writer Mike Davies and many others—had found this sense of entitlement in players to be the biggest change in junior hockey during the last 10 years. Hull had personally seen it in the dressing room during the last three years.

He also told them that no matter where they went with hockey—even as far away as Korea, where three former Petes were playing—there would be a link to the team.

Verner, who played in Europe for 14 years, told them to enjoy the year, soak it up. Verner was a good addition to the team. When he was drafted by the Petes, he had also had the option of an NCAA scholarship, and that's where he was heading until Coach Todd talked him into coming to Peterborough. He was drafted into the NHL, played in the AHL and for Team Canada, and then took his wife to Europe, where they had three children and he won the gold medal while playing for Germany in the Spengler Cup. He was fresh out of the player circuit and could offer these players plenty of advice and stories. He knew they were young, mostly too young to be aware of the respect the Petes name carried in the hockey world. "I was like that at 18 and not appreciating it. I have every hockey jersey of every team that I ever played for after I left the Petes, but I don't have my Petes jersey and I wish I had kept that. It meant so much to me years later when I appreciated it more."

The coaches then handed the room over to the team's spiritual counsellor. The Petes have had a chaplain for a long time. Dave Fisher, a local man, and uncle to NHL star Mike Fisher, filled the role for 14 years before Tim Coles took his place. Coles introduced himself to the rookies and renewed acquaintances with the veterans. Coles was a Christian youth counsellor and the Youth for Christ Canada field operations director. He said he would be there for them if they needed or wanted him. He told them that when his son was five, the boy had prayed for two Petes tickets. Minutes later, a friend called offering him two free tickets for the game the next night. They had been season ticket holders for eight years since.

The thin, short-haired 41-year-old married father of two would meet every third week with any of the players who wanted to attend, usually over a meal as an added inducement. The meetings appeared on every player's schedule under the heading "Coles' Notes." The team, unlike many in the OHL that had similar Christian sessions, generally enjoyed an excellent turnout—seldom did the entire team *not* show up. Occasionally it was for the food, but at other times the spiritual offering was paramount.

Coles ended his short meeting by asking if anyone wanted to pray for anything. One shouted for a win at Thursday night's opener. Another asked for a prayer for Quine and another for Robinson, which changed the meeting's mood, bringing them closer, as it usually does when someone is asked to pray for fellow teammates, family or friends. They bowed their heads and Coles prayed, not for a win but for God to help them play good enough to win. He prayed for Quine and Robinson, and for Koekkoek to avoid any further injury.

Giggy wasn't there. He had been excused for the day to attend two funerals near Toronto. A friend had died on a high school football field; another friend's mother had passed away. It is the most difficult way of learning to put hockey into perspective. The worst part of living is the dying.

The team had some ice cream with Coles before breaking up and going home to work on homework, get some sleep and wait nervously, impatiently, as opening night crept closer.

The team was ready. Reid and Pelino had their lineup set. Teams could dress only 20 per game but usually kept 23. The defencemen would be mainly veterans: Slater Koekkoek, Clark Seymour, Peter Ceresnak, Connor Boland, Trevor Murphy, Steven Trojanovic and Steven Varga with rookie Alex Robinson. Fourth-year man Andrew D'Agostini would start in goal with rookie Michael Giugovaz as the backup. Other veterans were forwards Alan Quine, Nick Ritchie, Derek Mathers, Brett Findlay, Francis Menard, Stephen Nosad, Stephen Pierog, Zach Lorentz, Luke Hietkamp and Chase Hatcher. Rookies Eric Cornel, Greg Betzold, Jonatan Tanus and Josh Maguire were also on board. Koekkoek, Mathers, Ceresnak and Seymour had already been drafted by NHL teams. Boland, Murphy, Varga, Giggy, Betzold, Nosad and Tanus were all in their NHL draft year, while Pierog, Trojanovic, Lorentz and Hatcher had been passed over the year before, and Findlay and Menard were the overagers. The Petes were a veteran team on which many of the players had plenty to prove.

Among the unknowns that gave Pelino restless nights was the team's performance in net. Would Dagger finally prove, as he should, that he was a number one goalie? The coach would start him knowing there were as many reasons why he shouldn't. There was a feeling among the coaching staff that not starting him would send the wrong message to the team, that they weren't relying on the veterans. Starting Giggy, who was in his first OHL year, didn't, in Pelino's mind, send that message. However, Reid thought there were good reasons to think that the team would rally around the new kid, that he was a promising up-and-comer who had outplayed the veteran and deserved the start.

Giggy was an interesting study, a 17-year-old whom some sarcastically called Einstein behind his back. He was a long-haired teen in the type of baggy clothes more likely to be seen in a skateboard park than an OHL rink. The coaches didn't like his antics but tolerated them. His behaviour on and off the ice was an adventure, his schoolwork a disgrace. He wasn't a curfew breaker or problem player off the ice, but he had his own way of doing things.

He would be scheduled for an interview and then not show up. He had medical forms given him by B-Man that were three weeks overdue. He was chronically late for class.

But he was very good at stopping frozen pucks—or, as he said, "doing something crazy"—so some of this was tolerated. If he had been a mediocre forward, he would have been sent home to contemplate his future alone. But he was so good at his job, the Petes couldn't even score on him in practice. He had the ability to be one of the league's better goalies. Two of his mother's brothers and a cousin had also played goal when his mother was growing up and she hadn't wanted her son to play, but he "begged and nagged" until his mother had been talked into it. In his first year, he used a catching glove for the wrong hand because the team didn't have a righty and the family couldn't afford one. He fell in love with the position, and the family accommodated him throughout his all-star years, spending more than $10,000 a year on registration, fitness, instruction and camps.

"We always taught our kids to work hard and if they have a passion, to go for it," said Janet Giugovaz.

Many of his weaknesses or bad habits, which he shared with many teenage boys growing up in today's changed culture, were forgiven because of this potential. Pelino, along with Giggy's parents, encouraged him to do something about his frailties throughout the season. Giggy was conscious of their concerns. "I'm not stupid," he said. And he wasn't. "I'm just not applying myself. I want to work harder at school, but I'm really having trouble with time management. I know I have to get better at it, but time management has been the most difficult thing about living away from home."

His mother agreed. "Don't forget, he is only 17. He is slowly turning around. Rome wasn't built in a day. The criticism of others can be too much. It's not like when he has a bad game, he killed someone or is going to jail. We know it is a high level of hockey, but they are still teens and it hurts. All OHL teams are looking for an adult in a child. They are so young and have to give up a lot to get to the OHL, but going to the NHL they will have to give up even more. He has put his entire focus on hockey; which is not a good thing, we know that, but Michael has a dream." His dad's father had come to Canada from Italy with a dream of a better life, worked at a car factory, saved money and invested in apartment buildings the family still owned. The family oozed work ethic.

Reid also felt that starting Giggy would send the more important message that this was a new season, that last year had no bearing on the present, but he bowed to the coach's decision. Both Pelino and Reid knew, however, that everything was a gamble in hockey. Even if there was a shutout tonight or a 10–0 shellacking, Pelino still would be asked, "Was it the right move?"

Opening night was September 20 against the team's greatest rival, Oshawa. Before the game even began, some fans were complaining to anyone who would listen about the 33 per cent increase in parking fees, a city-initiated change. The Petes took the brunt of the complaints but got none of the revenue.

More than 2,000 fans (the official attendance was 2,731, but that counted season subscribers even if they didn't show up) pushed their way through the turnstiles, including a loud crowd from Oshawa, which was only an hour-long bus ride away. There were a dozen tweets from fans and former players wishing the Petes luck. Former Pete Pat Daley sent his best wishes but also added good luck to Oshawa's new general manager, Twohey, "in the house he helped build." Twohey told the media the game had no special meaning, but it must have; after all, he had played a role in hanging 11 of the Petes' banners in the rink's rafters. Brett Findlay tweeted, "Been waiting a long time for this," and added the hashtag "#boatsbeburning." Last year's fan favourite, Lino Martschini, tweeted from his home country, Switzerland, wishing them luck.

A half-hour before the game, Pelino had handed each player paper, an envelope and a pen and asked them to write down the name of the person or persons to whom they wanted to dedicate the season— something to keep in their stall. He said they could share it with others if they wished, but he wanted them to dedicate it to someone who had helped or inspired them to get here, someone they would play for all season.

All of them wrote their parents' names. These were the people who had opened their wallets to support them and driven them to countless games and practices over the years. Menard added his unknown birth parents.

Some remembered others as well.

Findlay dedicated his year to grandpa Delmar Bailey, who had had a heart attack. "I'd stay at his house when I was six, and he'd drive me to games or practice. He was my best friend growing up and we were always close. He went to every game, and when I got traded, he got the TV package, and even though he's a Detroit Red Wings fan, he would watch my games instead of the Wings."

Mathers dedicated the season to his grandpa "Slim," for whom he also has a tattoo. While seriously ill in 2004, Slim attended one of Derek's games, dying just days later.

Trojanovic wrote "Dedo," for his deceased grandfather, whose Serbian name was Dragoljub, or Danny in Canada. "Even after two strokes, he would still come to the games, but he never got to see me play as a Peterborough Pete."

Murphy wrote his recently separated parents' names. "It has been tough with them being separated, so there is a lot of tension, but things are getting better, and both have done so much for me."

Giggy dedicated the season not only to his family, but also to his past coaches and "to everyone who tried to put me down, saying I was no good or I couldn't do this or that, who thought I would or wouldn't make it."

Dagger wrote down not only his parents but also "myself," to remind him of all the hard work he had done (a regimented, year-round daily fitness routine) and would continue to commit to hockey.

And there were more reminders that these players were teens, just kids.

Hatcher wrote down his 13-year-old brother Kelton, "because he looks up to me and basically he was the saddest when I left home."

Seymour, naming his parents, sister and grandfather, also added his dog, Trooper, a black Lab he had had for 10 years—"my best friend."

And Stephen Pierog, the happy-go-lucky curly blond kid with the chipped front teeth and sandpaper voice, dedicated his season to his deceased mother.

Now that the regular season was starting, a familiar face turned up in and around the dressing room. Iain Norrie, a developmentally challenged 52-year-old, had been the Petes' honorary stick and water boy for 25 years. Iain had missed very few Petes home games, always wearing a team jersey and helping the training staff fill water bottles and make other necessary preparations. He even gave the players an occasional pre- or post-game pep talk, but usually he just shouted out "Showstopper!" The Petes had invited him to drop the puck at the opening-night ceremonies in 2011 as part of Community Living Night. The year before, he had received an award at the annual team banquet. The son of a deceased local doctor, Iain had his own small apartment and did well for himself.

As soon as he learned you were with the team—even in the dubious capacity of team chronicler—in his mind you were a team member and greeted as family. Whenever he saw me, he gave me a big smile, patted me on the shoulder and said hello. He made me feel at home all season long. Whenever I asked him to predict that night's score, it was always the same: "The Petes win 5–0."

The players had pooled their money a week earlier to buy him the latest hockey video game, *NHL 13*. Iain loved video games, the boys loved him and he loved being around them.

The last minutes before game time saw 20 anxious players fixing their sticks, fiddling with tape, tightening their skate laces again and again and moving their shoulders to adjust the pads until finally pulling on their helmets and gloves.

Four thousand, six hundred and ninety-four pounds of Petes bone, muscle and flesh was set to glide onto the ice for the start of the annual Showtime on home ice. There were two Americans, a Slovakian and a Finn on a team otherwise made up of Ontarians from towns and cities such as Kemptville, Manotick, Cobourg, Strathroy, Embrun, Tottenham, Orangeville, Stittsville, Maitland, Echo Bay, Brooklin, Scarborough, Brampton, Burlington, Newmarket, Ottawa, Guelph, Windsor, London and Waterloo. Twenty players, aged 16 to 20, were dressed for the game while four others were sidelined. They had all played all-star hockey while growing up. They had all been the top players on their teams. Many now playing defence had grown up as forwards; some of the forwards had played defence.

Their parents had spent, on average, more than $100,000 on everything from registration to ice time, power skating and figure skating lessons, hockey camps, hotel rooms, tournaments, automobiles, food, gasoline and more so that their sons could play at a higher level and chase their dreams. Their sons had given up a normal teen life for a more regimented one. They had adapted to new homes, cities and schools. Four of them had adapted to life in a different country; two acquired some proficiency in a different language. For seven, it was their first OHL experience. All admitted that their legs shook as the national anthem was played in the rink on Roger Neilson Way.

None had grown up in a world war or economic depression. Their world was defined by hockey rinks, hockey clinics, spring hockey programs, graphite hockey sticks, moulded skates and constant practice. They looked at hockey as a career rather than a game. They no longer played just for the fun of it.

Koekkoek got the loudest applause when the players were introduced. The kids of two former Petes skated out onto the ice, waving Petes banners attached to hockey sticks. Before the anthem, the team remembered those who had died since last season, including former scouting great Norm Bryan and original season ticket holder Roy Oddie.

The ceremonial faceoff was between the two captains: Koekkoek, wearing a shoulder brace, and Jenner, who had caused the injury.

There were about 200 Oshawa fans making more noise than the introverted hometown crowd. There was also mascot Roger (a dog named in honour of former coach Roger Neilson, who surely must have been laughing in heaven over that one). Inside the costume was Reid's son Alec, ready to shoot T-shirts into the crowd from an unreliable gun during breaks. Reid's wife and daughter hosted billets, players' parents and Petes staffers in the alumni room.

Reid, dressed immaculately for the game as always, sat in the last row of a team suite at the south end of the rink. It was during the play that he became most alert, leaning forward, moving only on whistles.

During the game, his voice rising and falling, he furiously took notes about bad plays and corrections he felt the team needed. "Dump it." "Shoot the puck!" "No, no—get rid of that lateral pass." "Force the play, damn it! Force the play!" "Don't let them come to you." It was obvious he was not happy with the team's play. And it was obvious that some members of the team—particularly newcomers facing the reality of the regular season for the first time—were surprised with the home opener. The energy, speed, flow and tempo they had seen in exhibition games had been raised even higher. It was like moving from swimming lessons in the shallow end of a pool to the deep end.

The game was entertaining and fairly even for a while, but the Petes had a 10-minute lapse in the second period and took some stupid penalties, and "Mo" (full name *momentum*) swung the game in Oshawa's favour.

After the first intermission, with impatient players pumped to hit the ice again, the lights went out and the game was delayed—surely a bad omen for the Petes. Reid wondered what his office staff had lined up as plan B to entertain the crowd—nothing, it turned out. After a few minutes, the arena's power came back on, and so did Oshawa's. Reid looked on helplessly.

Three of five Oshawa goals were scored on power plays. The Petes didn't have a match for Jenner or Lucas Lessio, both of whom had tree-trunk bodies, legs of lions and moves like squirrels in traffic. They were, barring injuries or lifestyle problems, NHL-bound journeymen finishing their apprenticeships. On the ice, they were men among boys.

Reid continued to call the game in muttered asides: "No, not a back pass, no! Move it forward. . . . Shoot the puck! . . . Got to have him, hit him, take the play, hit him. . . . No, don't let him walk out! . . . God! Move it off the glass when you're in trouble." He saw some good things, too, but the lack of discipline decided the game's direction. He scribbled more notes.

In a world that finds it necessary to erect signs telling people to stop at train tracks when red lights are flashing, these young players were having trouble picking up on signals, so many obvious ones. Findlay and Menard played like ghosts—only those who believed in them could see them. Their younger teammates outplayed, outhustled and outworked them. The two were being depended on for their experience, scoring ability and leadership, so this was not good. The overagers needed to be better if the Petes were to succeed. Out of the team's 219 goals last season, 118 had been scored by guys who had left the team. But the top teams, such as Niagara, had scored 291 goals in regular-season play and London had scored 277. Peterborough had to improve.

The defence and goaltending remained a concern. Dagger was pulled after four goals, two of them scored when he failed to recover the puck while down. Last year, the Petes allowed 281 goals while Niagara, for example, allowed only 169, and London 178. The Petes scored the second-lowest number of goals last season, and only six teams allowed more goals. The principle of winning wasn't complicated: score goals, stop pucks. The difficulty was in doing it. Former NHL star Steve Larmer had once said hockey was not a game of chess but a quick game of checkers. You need to think fast and not too much.

Menard managed a goal and an assist in the third period, but he showed up two periods too late. Defenceman Boland, who hadn't played for eight months following an injury, seemed lethargic, winded and out of breath even while walking up the arena stairs before the game. He looked like he was in good shape, but something was wrong. Giggy, who had no time to get nervous when he was thrown into the game in relief of Dagger, allowed just one goal on 14 shots.

Even with the team's poor display, many of the faithful fans, a group of about 800, remained to cheer when the players raised their sticks toward them at centre ice before heading to the dressing room.

***

Tanus's parents weren't at the game, but they watched in the early-morning hours on a computer in Finland. Betzold's had listened to the game from Maryland. Many other parents drove to see the opener. Pelino, however, was oblivious to their presence: after the game, he walked quickly past the two dozen relatives and friends in the hallway outside the dressing room. He was angry and frustrated but controlled, addressing the team. "That is not acceptable. That is just not acceptable."

Later, in his office, Pelino shook his head in wonderment, saying some veterans were missing in action. He couldn't believe what had happened.

Surprised at the lacklustre play of many of his players, he was impressed, as most seemed to be, with the intensity, work ethic, hits and checking in the first period. But he was shocked by the dumb penalties and disappearance of some senior players after that. Findlay was the object of his most serious criticism. He was a player Reid believed had the talent to be better, but Pelino thought he was soft as grapes and unable to keep the puck.

A frustrated Reid thought many of the previous season's problems were still there, including a lack of effort.

Board director Pat Casey, around for 53 season openers, knew it was early but wondered about the defence. "I don't think some of them are going to be around" by the end of the season, he said.

Dagger would have a restless sleep wondering what was next for him. It was only the first game, but he knew he had to continue to focus, train harder than the others and be even more committed, even though some, including him, thought his training was already "over the top."

He wasn't the only one Reid and the coaches worried about. The four rookie forwards—Cornel, Betzold, Tanus and Maguire—had only two shots among them. Cornel had gone through the entire exhibition season and now the opener without a goal.

For all their worries, however, the team and coaches stayed positive. Pelino was not an old-school coach who got into players' faces, yelling at them or punishing people for poor efforts. Even when players made mistakes, he seldom took away their minutes. He saved his criticism for video sessions, where he pointed out the errors. Many of the players wanted some traditional accountability and expected some yelling and punishment—like missing shifts— for poor play by them or teammates. They expected it, waited for it, but it seldom came.

Some fans were less sanguine. It was only one game, but the naysayers came out like blackbirds on roadkill. "Petes will end up in last place with Dave Reid in control," one anonymous fan commented on the web. Another pointed a finger at the "public ownership," a common theme over the years. There were 67 games still to play, 134 points left to be gained. Anywhere from 70 points and up should get them into the playoffs, and yet some people were already counting them out.

The good news was that their next opponents were the Ottawa 67's, who had also lost their first game. The Petes had 12 wins, 2 losses and 2 ties in their last 14 games against the 67's.

The Petes needed a win.

The bad news was, so did the 67's.

And the bad news took the form of those black clouds continuing to hover above the Petes, which would release more storms in the coming days.

CHAPTER 9

Storms Erupt, Koeks Unbound

The OHL and teams like the Petes are places where boys become men. And places through which hockey players pass, some on their way up, others on their way out. A season in the OHL is a constant challenge for the staff, who have to deal with kids leaving home, schoolwork, discipline and player attitudes as well as hockey. All season long, they worry constantly about the 23 young players whose parents have left them in their hands, on and off the ice.

Late on a Sunday night in September 2012, just days before the Petes' season opener, four men wearing masks and carrying pistols forced their way into a house on a quiet Peterborough residential street. A neighbour saw them and called police. Within minutes, a half-dozen officers in four cruisers had converged on the home, while heavily armed officers had taken up positions outside it. If the police were jumpy, they had reason to be: a year before, one of their own had been shot in an incident that began like this one. They approached the front door warily.

No shots were fired. The four suspects came to the door. Police, with guns drawn, ordered them outside to the ground and handcuffed them. It turned out they were members of the Petes—bored teenagers who had set out to scare a rookie who was staying in the house they had raided. Their pistols were toys and their motives comparatively innocent. Like virtually all team members, their intended victim was from somewhere other than Peterborough. The house was his billet, the home of his landparents, and the boys had actually alerted the family of their intentions. They had not, however, considered the possible consequences—which, in the worst imaginable case, might have involved gunfire. The kids, the family and their neighbours were terrified. The police were not amused.

The attempted punking of the newbie player was not, in itself, extraordinary. Petes of the past had pulled plenty of stunts in what was once standard rookie initiation, or hazing. Kids had been taped to telephone poles. Others had been obliged to streak outside hotel rooms or moon people from bus windows. And of course, many had undergone the traditional hazing procedure of decades gone by: shaving the genital area.

This latest adventure was different.

Police called Reid, at home that Sunday—his first day off in weeks—where the unbelieving and tired GM got out of bed and drove to the scene, about 20 minutes from his house. Upon arriving, he was told that the incident could have ended much differently. The police gave the players a lecture and Reid followed up, having a long chat with the boys and getting them to apologize to the police for their stupidity. The next day, the players returned to the neighbourhood to explain and apologize to neighbours. Their actions were received positively by the neighbours, many of whom didn't even know about the incident. Fortunately for the players, no charges were laid: they had learned a tough lesson. Neither the police nor the team released any information about the incident to the public.

A week after the home invasion incident, a reporter with the *Peterborough Examiner* who had heard rumours about the story left a message for Reid. The GM thought the best policy was to explain that it was a prank gone wrong, that the boys had told the billet about it before arriving, that the neighbours had no idea what was going on. He reminded the reporter that the players were minors and said that they had apologized to neighbours and the police. The reporter didn't dig too deep.

A day or two later, Reid read the paper's short story on page three. PRANK GONE BAD was the headline, and the text briefly outlined the incident. It didn't mention the number of police cruisers, police drawing their guns or handcuffing the kids. But even without the details, the reaction from fans, bloggers and other media was immediate. Some comments on the Petes' fans message board ranged from "they ought to concentrate on practicing they're [sic] hockey skills since they're [sic] record has been the real joke!" to "No one got hurt other than a few peoples' feelings. Seems like the definition of a prank," and another stating: "So that's the type of kids we have representing our city in the OHL! Ones that think it's funny to play a prank with a gun? That's embaresment [sic]." One online fan joked, "At least the Peterborough Petes finally scared someone."

By a happy coincidence, the team's annual educational visit to a police station took place the same day the story hit the media. It was here that the players learned the prank was no longer their secret but was in the daily paper and on websites. Sportswriters across Canada were tweeting about it.

Days earlier, Reid had told the pranksters to let their parents know what had happened, but he learned that only one or two had taken his advice. He reminded them again that it would be best if their parents learned about it from them directly. He also told them to direct any questions from the public to him. There were none.

Meanwhile, Reid had other problems with other players to deal with. Their school had called to report that there had been complaints that some of the players had made what might be considered homophobic comments heard by other students. Reid addressed this issue, too, with the named players. Neither the team nor the league tolerated such behaviour. Nor did they condone the use of chewing tobacco, another no-no that the GM had to address that day.

The Petes had mechanisms in place to try to combat or curb bad behaviour. Probably the most important was the annual meeting held at the police department to discuss issues such as chewing tobacco, drinking, drugs, fighting, sex and other traps and temptations.

The "chaw," or chewing tobacco, might seem minor but its persistence was disturbing. The stuff was banned in the OHL, banned by the Petes and banned in school, but some kids still used it, many of them openly. Sometimes, players on other teams could be seen, in the stands before games, chewing the chaw. Police warned the Petes about its addictiveness and the cancer-causing agents it contained. They were even told that some chaw had minute fibreglass pieces in it, which could cut cheek tissue and enter their bloodstream. You'd think this would be deterrence enough.

Still, players kept chewing, even after the police meeting, where the home invasion was a perfect introduction for the talk by Walter DiClemente and Detective Constable Rob Fitzgerald, a former OHL player with the Belleville Bulls. They spoke to the boys about the health and other dangers associated with unwise indulgence in sex, booze, drugs and social media.

Social media had had a major impact on players' lives. Pictures, videos and words could be spread instantly all over the world. Koekkoek told the others that he had been interviewed by an NHL team and had been asked about something he had posted on a Facebook page, something that had conveyed a wrong impression. It wasn't a big deal, but it showed that future employers—including professional hockey teams—were looking at what players posted online.

The police showed the boys photos of NHL players who had let down their guard. They found their photos on the Internet with bikini-clad women, drunk or in other embarrassing situations. They showed the boys newspaper clippings about junior players who had been accused of various crimes. They reminded them that, even if they were accused of something and then subsequently found not guilty, the story would be on the web and stain their reputations forever. Three OHL players in the Soo were charged with sexual assault that week. It wasn't until six months later that the accusations were thrown out of court, but the allegations would never be erased from the web.

Police took them through two hours of issues, showing them confiscated drugs and making them aware of all the possible damage from even being associated with drug users. They spent considerable time discussing and warning them about the problems that could arise from casual encounters with the opposite sex. They reminded them that "no" means "no."

"Always remember, you choose your behaviour," said DiClemente. "You choose the consequences. You are responsible for the life you lead. Your life is a product of your choices and the consequences."

They devoted time to a discussion of alcohol and its perils, reminding the players that bars were off-limits unless they had their coach's permission, and if they went into bars to remember there were web cameras and social media lurking everywhere.

They also touched on the danger and illegality of steroid use.

DiClemente reminded them that "the Petes are seen as celebrities and role models in our community. As a Pete, be prepared to handle the positive coverage with the negative. Everything you do is under a microscope. This is a great town, but like anything you do, be careful. We don't get rid of charges, but we will help you through the process."

It was impossible to say what long-term effect the session at the police station had on the players. There's no doubt that they left the station in a subdued state of mind, at least for a while. They knew, though, that getting back on the ice was their answer to most problems.

Reid no longer had the advantage of getting back on the ice to forget life's issues, and it sometimes seemed to him that the problems were endless—constant bumps on what was already turning out to be the long and winding road of the 2012–13 season.

As Mother Nature prepared to put on its new autumn jacket, making the beautiful Kawarthas even more picturesque, the Petes had unzipped their golf jackets to bundle up for another regular season of hope and high expectations, but the grey cloud that had lurked over the Petes' last season had reappeared with the staged home invasion.

On his way home, Reid wondered if this job was all worth it. He hadn't needed this off-ice behaviour problem; the on-ice issues were troublesome enough. He felt before training camp that the team had two good scoring lines to open the season, a third line that could score and another that gave them depth. He figured they should make the playoffs, and then anything could happen—the playoffs always were unpredictable. But the players were just teenagers, with so much to learn—not only about hockey but about life and living away from home. The life of an Ontario Hockey League player is full of ups and downs. It was all about chasing dreams and getting through nightmares. Reid worried about this year's team. He saw trouble brewing.

They were leaving at 1:30 for a 7:30 game in Ottawa, the team's second regular-season game but their first road trip—three and a half hours on the highway. There would be shorter ones, like the hourlong journey to Oshawa or 90 minutes to Belleville and two hours to Kingston, but there were also plenty of others that dragged them across Toronto or that required overnight stays, like those to the Soo, Saginaw and Plymouth. The trainers and rookies loaded the buses with sticks, the large standup toolbox, the skate-sharpening machine, glove warmers, and bagels and yogurt for pre-game snacks, while the other players packed their own equipment bags. There were no empty seats; all were taken by training staff, a stats man, a video guy, Mike Davies of the *Examiner*, radio announcer Rob Snoek, the coaches, the assistant general manager, players—and now me. Reid, who seldom rode on the bus, would leave later.

The bus drove directly from Roger Neilson Way to a Peterborough restaurant, where everyone had a buffet lunch. Pelino could have let the players eat at home, as they do before shorter bus trips, but he wanted them together for a healthy meal before most of their road games. Davies could remember when he first rode the team's bus, 20 years before as a student statistician, and the players "would have a bag of chips under their arms, chocolate bars, a litre of pop, and after games it was pizza or McDonald's." He says that changed in 2008 with coach Rick Allain, who introduced proper nutrition, carbo-loading and food diversity.

Generally, every bus trip was the same. Their bus driver, as usual, was Dave Beamish, who had been the Petes' driver more often than not for some 22 years, so good at the job that he was chosen to drive Team USA during the world junior championships in Ottawa in 2009. Players packed their bags underneath the bus; trainers loaded the team equipment; coaches carried their bags full of notes and laptops, with jackets and ties off for the trip; players in casual clothes carried their dress suits to change into later on the bus, fingers attached to iPods, iPhones, BlackBerrys and cell phones, earbuds in their ears. Garfat, on his phone, confirmed upcoming food orders and made sure that parents, friends and relatives got the tickets players had requested for them—each player was allowed two tickets per rink but could get more if others weren't being used.

The trip was uneventful, and unusually quiet, as most of the bus trips over the coming months would be. Davies remembered rides that were noisier, filled with music and chatter, but that was before players plugged into their own electronic devices and social media. The league and the Petes had a social media policy, warning players of the dangers and offering tips. (Avoid profanity and words that can be misinterpreted. Watch what you post. Don't post confidential information, game strategy or information about injuries. Don't complain about the OHL lifestyle, such as the long hours, uncomfortable bus rides and part-time schoolwork. Remember that "many of your fans and followers would welcome the challenge and opportunity to play for the Peterborough Petes.") As the bus rolled along the two-lane Highway 7, only two people read newspapers and, other than coaches, none read anything on paper. Some players played cards, which was allowed by the league as long as there was no gambling, a contrast to past years when players routinely played euchre, if only for a few dollars.

The seating arrangements were simple: senior players got the better seats near the rear, and some got seats by themselves, while the younger ones shared seats near the middle of the bus, closer to staff and coaches who occupied the first seats. (Former coach Scotty Bowman would often ride at the rear of the bus to observe his players.)

The bus pulled into the rink in Kanata, near Ottawa, at 5:10. The players gave no indication that they were excited as they filed out of the bus—not even a single "Let's get 'em, boys." Maybe other OHL buses were without this rah-rah, giddy-up noise too, but the silence seemed eerie for a team of teens getting ready to do battle. Or maybe it was just too soon. The team always arrived at least two hours before game time in a familiar hurry-up-and-wait routine designed to antici-pate the factors, such as weather and traffic, that could disrupt travel arrangements.

Ottawa's regular rink, the downtown Civic Centre, was being renovated, so this season the 67's played in the NHL Senators' rink at Scotiabank Place (later renamed the Canadian Tire Centre), a beauti-ful facility that put all other OHL rinks to shame, even the wonderful ones in London and Windsor. This might be the only time most of these players would get to play in an NHL arena. The game attracted 6,000 people inside the 19,000-seat arena, a healthy crowd for junior hockey, but only a few days earlier the team had hosted 11,000 for its home opener. Jody Hull had played for the NHL Ottawa Senators twice during his excellent career—a good thing, because he knew how to get around the rink. Some of the rink staff remembered him, and autograph seekers went after him and the rest of the team.

Once they had found their way to the dressing room and the play-ers had dumped their equipment, with rookies helping the training staff unload, they went to the bench at rinkside, where they joked about the rink that none had ever played in. "What? We have to play in this barn? What a dump!" they exclaimed and looked up at the giant Jumbotron that was "even in HD."

Before game time, the players changed from their suits into shorts, runners and BURN THE BOATS tops and then broke into small groups to tape sticks, do some stretching individually, sit in the empty stands, wander around, have a team stretch or run before returning to the dressing room, which shook with rap, rock or country music while they dressed.

Giggy was starting his first OHL game, and as would be his custom, he took a seat alone on the bench to tape his stick and focus in silence. When he wasn't starting, he jabbered, would sit talking with a few fellow players in the stands and was never alone.

Pelino took Josh Maguire aside to tell him he was sitting tonight. Josh just kept walking, replying, "Okay, coach." He was disappointed and hurt. No coach had ever sat him, not once, but he told me he "kind of understands" because he is a rookie. Still, it was difficult, as it is for any competitive athlete. While the others were in the dressing room, he was alone in the hallway, doing stretches, biking, walking around, but not getting dressed for battle. He gave 100 per cent to impress the coach, but on some nights it was not enough. He was an extra. The coach thought his skating was too slow. Maguire didn't disagree, but he saw others who were shying away from hits, not wanting to block shots and playing without discipline. After his workout, he dressed back into his suit to watch the game from the stands.

"I was blindfolded coming in and didn't know much about the league," said Maguire. "Everything was different, unbelievable, fast and skilled. In minor hockey, there were players who wanted to make it. I really wanted it. In the OHL, every guy here wants it and is willing to do what it takes to make it—not like in the minors, when it's fewer. There are some nights I go home at 6 P.M. and fall asleep. There are long days at school, then the rink," he said. "I also have to be in condition and watch my diet. It is more than I expected, but it is my dream. I have other dreams, but playing pro hockey is my career choice.

"There was so much I didn't know about the OHL, and so much more I still don't know. I'm excited, but know how much more work I have to do." He would keep his nose to the grindstone, continue to work hard and wait for his opportunities. That didn't mean he accepted sitting, which, as he said, "sucks."

The game was special for Cornel, Seymour and Koekkoek, all products of the Rideau St. Lawrence Kings minor hockey system, whose teams were there watching them tonight. Pelino knew this and started the threesome. Cornel was anxious, excited and nervous about playing in this arena before his family and friends.

The Petes got off to a good start, with three quick goals, but Hull knew that teams tended to let their guard down when they got an early lead. Sure enough, the 67's came back with two goals, one on a power play, as penalties again changed the Petes' Mo.

Giggy faced 18 shots in a second period that resembled Thursday's poor play, except that this time the goalie was phenomenal. His first OHL start was in an NHL rink, and he stood on his head, blocking at least nine excellent scoring chances as the Petes' defence fell apart. Ottawa had at least six scoring chances in just a single shift. Giggy turned them all away.

Reid, who drove his car for three and a half hours to watch a game that lasted only three hours, was fuming. At the end of the second period, he once again went to the coaches' room to express his disgust. He even thought about going into the players' room to give them a blast but caught himself. Pelino didn't like Reid even seeing the coaches between periods and had told him so in past discussions. He thought it was a distraction and believed it would be problematic for the staff, because players have to know the coaches are in control. Reid understood all this but felt an urgency this season that made him want to barge in regardless. Once again, however, he held himself back from the dressing room. When he returned to his seat at the beginning of the third period, you could almost see steam coming off his head. The Petes won the game, but it did not make Reid happy. He had a very short, curt meeting with Pelino, which would lead to a longer, more productive one on Monday morning. Reid was on the highway before the players had undressed.

Reid drove back home threatening to go on the ice at the next practice and thinking about replacing the coach with himself.

He got frustrated when he felt his staff wasn't listening and said that when he went to the coaches' room between periods, they didn't even look up; they just ignored him. Pelino was not developing the team identity Reid wanted and felt they needed. He vented during the three-and-a-half-hour ride home about his frustrations. He said things had better change. "I've been watching this for two years. We need an identity. We need a team with a work ethic, one that stops their silly mistakes, has a proper penalty kill and power play, gets the puck out of their zone."

Reid said the opposition didn't know what type of team the Petes were, and that was another bad sign. When you played Oshawa, you knew you were playing a big, strong team with two big, powerful forwards. When you played Barrie, you knew they were playing Dale Hawerchuk hockey—get the puck out, get it deep and keep it in the opposition's faces. Pelino and Reid both knew that to win, they needed the Petes to be a gritty, hard-working, lunchpail team and that the other teams had to know every shift was going to count. This wasn't happening now.

He knew the team worked hard, knew how organized and knowledgeable Pelino was, but he wasn't sure the players respected Pelino or feared his power over them. Pelino seemed reluctant to wield the ultimate weapon—the withholding of ice time. Players never seemed to miss a shift for their sins. He wasn't sure if they were even threatened with bench time. When the players made mistakes, Reid didn't think they were being held accountable. "Even if we are 5–1 after six games, but still playing this way, I'm going to make some moves," he said, threatening again to go on the ice at the next practice.

Reid didn't carry out his threat, nor did he even reveal the impulse to the coaches. Instead, he and Pelino had a long, frank discussion in which they agreed on what had to be done. Reid was a demanding manager, but when push came to shove, he was more noise than action, a loyal guy, too nice to make tough personnel decisions, too inexperienced to manage people and not willing to make moves that he felt in his gut were right.

Pelino knew the team hadn't played well against Ottawa. He told the media he was happy with the win, but "it wasn't a Picasso. It was more like a fence being whitewashed." After the game, Hull said, "It's good to see we finally got some goals." He was full of praise for the goalie: "Giggy doesn't feel like a rookie. When I watch him in practice, he hates to get scored against." The team had yet to score a power play goal, but Hull pointed out they'd had their chances. "It's just execution. It will come." But he, too, was concerned with the team not performing proper breakout routes and quick, smart passes.

The bus returned at 1:30 A.M. to Roger Neilson Way. It was another half-hour before players and coaches got home. The coaches' day, which had begun at 8 A.M., ended shortly after 2 A.M. The train-ing crew didn't quit until 3.

Pelino came up with an idea to strengthen their team's identity. He asked players what they'd like their team to mean to rival clubs and marked their answers on a chart, grouped under a number of differ-ent headings, on the dressing room board.

Identity: winners, relentless, tough, not pushed around, hard-working, consistent, competitors, determined, physical, disciplined

Adversity: facing something and beating it such as being benched, taking penalties, having bad games, bad bounces, getting over such things as nothing clicking, injuries, illness, draft ratings, program of excellence

Game Management: protecting the lead, dealing with the situ-ation, awareness, penalty-killing mindset, don't cheat on work ethic, pay the price, get shots through, get pucks out, short shifts, do the little extras

Following Game Plan: being on the same page, buy in, use glass to get the puck out, get it in deep

They were all things Reid said weren't being done and what the coaches had been preaching, but now the players had come up with their identity—at least on the whiteboard. It was like a classroom, and as in any classroom, some would get it and many others wouldn't. Players didn't want to know *what* to do, they wanted to know how to do it—and then be rewarded if they did it right and criticized if they didn't.

There was also a quote on the board from internationally known fitness trainer Terry Butts: "Every day, you have to test yourself. If you don't, it's a wasted day."

More words. Words stared at players everywhere, as soon as they arrived at the dressing room door: TRADITION, EXCELLENCE, PRIDE, PASSION, RESPECT, it said on the front. On the back, IT'S ABOUT THE GUY IN FRONT OF ME. Inside the dressing room were even more words, with the names of alumni so familiar to hockey fans across the world. More exhortations adorned the walls in even bigger type: COMMITMENT, DEDICATION, ATTENTION TO DETAIL; 212 ONE DEGREE MORE; TRUST; TO WHOM MUCH IS GIVEN, MUCH IS EXPECTED; and EXCHANGE ME FOR WE.

They were just words, though. Pelino wanted the boys to be big on action—to talk the talk but, more importantly, walk the walk.

On September 27, the Erie Otters brought their 0–2 record into the city, along with their number one draft pick, the kid who had received special status for the OHL draft and was nicknamed the Next One: 15-year-old Connor McDavid.

The Petes were beaten in almost every statistical category. After what appeared to be good practices all week, after discussing what the team needed to do to succeed, after writing down what they wanted to be, the players acted like they weren't there. They were a losing, awful team in front of an audience that, as it happened, included more than 40 pro scouts, a number the Petes hadn't seen in two seasons. Many were just curious to see McDavid, even though he wouldn't be eligible for the NHL draft for another three years, but there were also 13 '95s on the ice playing for the Petes and Otters who would be available that spring. McDavid was certainly worth watching. He created more plays than Shakespeare and got more ice than a cube machine. One 20-year veteran NHL scout said McDavid was the best he had seen, including Crosby, because "he's quicker than Crosby and makes plays that nobody in the league will make. He's just too bright for his age." McDavid had two assists and was the best player in the game.

There was a lot of head-shaking in the stands. Cornel had three shots, but all into the goaltender. Betzold, whose parents had made the nine-hour car trip from Maryland, had two of the best scoring chances. This would become his season trademark, earning him the nickname Two-a-Game Betzold among some scouts.

Clark, during an intermission, took his defencemen into "the woodshed"—actually, the weight room—and blasted them loudly enough to be heard in the dressing room next door. Someone should have told the Petes that hitting was allowed in the OHL. The veterans were ghosts. Pierog, who won a scrap, and Betzold, were the only physical players. It didn't help that Ritchie left the game with a separated shoulder. Quine and Ritchie were two-thirds of the Petes' power-play forward line. The team lost 5–1.

Following the game, the Petes' office was like a funeral home hosting a wake: visitors didn't know what to say or how to say it. President Devlin said the Petes didn't get any breaks, but Reid told him, "You make your own breaks, and we didn't."

Pelino thought he had some "pretenders"—pretending they were OHL players. He mentioned that Betzold and Pierog had had a good night. "The frustrating thing," he said, "is we aren't seeing guys at their best, even though we have good practices. It's like the golf pro who makes the good shots on the driving range, but in the tournament he can't do a thing." As for the absence of Quine and Ritchie, "we can't worry about what we don't have. It shouldn't matter. Other guys should step up."

"The Peterborough Petes won't win back many fans with efforts like Thursday's 5–1 loss," wrote Davies in the *Examiner.*

The Petes had played two home games, losing both, and the next night they were in Oshawa for the Generals' home opener. According to a national happiness survey released that day, 94.2 per cent of Peterborough's population were satisfied with their lives; the other 5.8 per cent must have been Petes fans.

After one month, which included 16 practices and 10 games in 29 days, the Petes were falling like the autumn leaves. The Generals pushed five goals past them. In two games, the winners had taken close to 100 shots on Giggy, who couldn't be faulted on any of them. Eggs had more protection. The good news was he had stopped 90 per cent of them; the bad news was he allowed 10 per cent to go in, and a 90 per cent success rating is not good enough for a goalie.

The injury list also got longer when Seymour suffered a sprained shoulder. The Petes' two best forwards and one of their top defence-men were now out, while third-year veteran Boland was a healthy scratch. B-Man and his training staff were earning their wages again this year as they tried to get ready for a trip to Oshawa.

Oshawa fans were louder, more boisterous, more willing to show their spirit than those in Peterborough. They dressed in team sweaters, hats, even capes to cheer, unlike the quiet fans at the church in Peterborough.

"Imagine bringing a recruit into this rink to try and sell him on coming to this team. Now imagine the same recruit going into another rink—say, the Memorial Centre," said goalie coach Verner, as he sat in the stands, marvelling at what the architects had achieved when they planned this mini–Air Canada Centre.

With the Oshawa result, the Petes sat in last place at the end of their first month.

The highlight of the night didn't come until after the game, when former Petes and NHL superstar Chris Pronger, whom Pelino had once coached on Team Canada, came to the dressing room to talk with the coach and Philadelphia Flyers pick Mathers. Even the six-foot, two-inch Ritchie had to look up at the lanky six-foot, six-inch Pronger, a tough, talented player whose meanness made him 10 times better than most players. Meanness was something the Petes were lacking, on and off the ice, on the bench—even in the office. Everyone was so nice. Pronger made Koekkoek, who some players complained was too critical of his own teammates, look like a marsh-mallow. His teams also won. You can get away with a lot when a team is winning.

On the bus ride home, the team ate pizza and was silent. The chocolate treats that assistant trainer Larry Smith passed around to staff and media during each road trip were the only sweet taste on the one-hour ride.

A blogger advised, "Fire them both [Reid and Pelino] before the season is lost." Another writer, The_Lone_Wolf, said, "It sounds like these guys are training to be Toronto Maple Leafs."

At the end of September, only four games into the regular season, the mood was grim. The team still had hope going into a new month, with the weekend off and four days of practice before the next game, but they didn't look strong. Yes, they were only teenagers, but so were the other teams' players, who had given the Petes' kids another hockey lesson.

No successful Petes team had started a season so poorly. Could Pelino solve the defensive and offensive problems? Was it far too early to judge the team? How long could Reid and the board ride the train without putting a new engineer in charge? Would the veterans ever wake up? The team had not burned the boats; it hadn't even struck a match.

The coaches had set up a team-bonding event, a nine-hole golf game, for September 29, followed by a players-only team party at a home outside the city. This too turned into a messed-up night, with some of the players partaking too much and many calling for rides at 2:30 A.M.

The new month started like the old one, with the dark clouds still hovering overhead. Boland, in his NHL draft year, spent a night in bed shivering, sweating, with pain under his ribcage. He hadn't been feeling great for a couple of weeks, and like Quine, he had mononucleosis.

The losses, injuries and illnesses all led to more panic in Petesland. There were signs that the level of anxiety was going critical at every level, from players to management, and especially among members of the board of directors, where it counted the most.

The air of promise, hope and expectation was slowly leaving the deflating tires of the maroon-and-white machine as the number of fans in attendance dipped by 700 to 2,100 after the home opener.

Problems before the next home game, on October 4, were a sign of things to come. One of the kids scheduled to carry the Petes flag wouldn't go on; he was too young, too shy. The person meant to perform the national anthem backed out, and a group of children from the crowd had to substitute at the last minute. In the third period, a piece of glass along the boards was smashed. The rink crew didn't have the proper replacement, so action didn't resume for 20 minutes. By the time the game resumed, most of the fans had left. There were still seven minutes remaining, but with the score 4–1 there was little to keep them there.

B-Man's MASH unit continued to be crowded. Seymour and Lorentz left the game. Ritchie, the media was told, was day to day, but in reality his separated shoulder would probably take three to four weeks to recover. Broken-jawed Robinson hadn't played a game, not even an exhibition game, and was at least a few more weeks away from doing so.

Pelino had to shuffle lines and player positions. The team statisticians—Terry Bowser, Larry and Adam Murray—hadn't seen such juggling since they were kids at the circus. Cornel and Maguire got far more ice time than expected, going up against other teams' top lines, which they couldn't handle because of their youth, lack of strength and inexperience.

The third period was painful to watch, with Sudbury outchancing Peterborough 8–0. It was no wonder the seats were emptying.

The coaches and players closed the dressing room door for an extra-long time following the game. Some strong words were spoken. After removing his suit jacket and placing it over a pedestal fan, Pelino, as was his habit, questioned the team's desire and passion. He asked if anyone knew the addict' or alcoholic's first step toward a cure. Koekkoek, usually the one who spoke up in the dressing room, said it was the realization they needed help. Pelino agreed but said the first thing was to recognize there was a problem, adding this applied to the Petes as well.

The captain, incredibly, in front of all the players, said: "I'm an honest guy. I'm not going to hold back. There are players in this room that shouldn't be here. There are players who are not playing up to their capabilities, and management is not giving us the players we need. This needs to change." Pelino, even more incredibly, backed him up. He told the team that Koekkoek's words were some of the most courageous he had ever heard.

It was an extraordinary statement coming from a player whose responsibility it was to speak up for his teammates. It was made even more extraordinary by the coach's endorsement. Both captain and coach had just told the players there were some among them who didn't belong, that they weren't good enough. Not a good motivational move for either.

Worse was to come.

The *Examiner*'s Davies, who had missed only one game in his 17 years covering the Petes, had never heard or seen anything like what happened after the game.

Captain Koekkoek was one frustrated, intelligent, aware and angry hockey player. When he walked out of the dressing room still in his gear for an interview with Davies, his frustrations poured out. With perspiration dripping from his forehead and down his nose and his hair soaked with sweat, Koeks made it crystal clear that he was not prepared to stay on a sinking ship.

He repeated what he had said in the closed dressing room. He told Davies that changes had better be made soon. This 18-year-old put it all on his own back, and the brutal honesty came out of him as he stood in a soaked BURN THE BOATS tank top, talking to the surprised but very attentive Davies.

"We have a problem and we need to get it fixed."

"I'm not sure what's going to happen in the future here, with regards to this team or certain players. Something has to give here or this is going to be the longest season ever if we continue like this.

"I'm not going to do the GM's job, by any means, but if there are certain players in here not willing to compete, then something has to happen. We're not good enough.

"It's pretty difficult to come to the rink every day. It's a negative attitude in the room. It's a negative attitude outside the room as well. We're losing and we don't see a light at the end of the tunnel. I know it's only five games, but it would be different if we lost in overtime or they were pretty close games, but they have not all been close.

"I've always respected our team meetings, and we respect Mike and Jody and Wayne. No, I don't think they've lost the room. I think they're doing the best they can with what they're given," said Koekkoek.

He was pointing the blame directly at some of his teammates and at Reid, warning him to get things done. He had made targets of himself, his teammates and Reid.

Koekkoek was not afraid to speak his mind. In his previous background interview with me, he had talked about loyalty being a two-way street. He had said that trades were needed, which he had also mentioned to Pelino. It was clear it wasn't the coach or even the GM that he wanted gone. He wanted players moved and better ones brought in. This kid wanted to win and wasn't going to wait any longer for management to do what he thought should be done.

Pelino, knowing nothing of the Koekkoek's interview with Davies, didn't hold back in his post-game interview, either. Without revealing what was said, he admitted to the public that the players and coaches' exchanges were frank and biting in the closed-door meeting, although he and the captain had done most of the talking. He said the players didn't seem willing to do what it took to be successful, nor did they know how hard it was to get there. Pelino seemed to be echoing the team captain's sentiments, handing a kind of ultimatum to management after only a handful of regular-season games.

CHAPTER 10

Panic in Petesville

The next morning, the *Examiner* headlined Koekkoek's comments. Team president Jim Devlin read them soon after the paper landed on his front porch. He had been following the team since 1956 and had seen a lot of captains come and go. Never in all those years had he seen something like this: an 18-year-old was telling the team's manager to do his job.

The injuries and illnesses had been legitimate excuses, but the team's talent and the skill level of the uninjured players didn't look good to Devlin. Neither did the captain's brutal public honesty. Devlin wondered if it was injuries, the coaching staff or the GM that was to blame. He had been questioning some of Reid's moves, and the tension between the two had been growing. First there was the Puempel trade, then some of the player selections, and now this. Reid was an inexperienced GM and relatively new to the OHL, but he was a seasoned and insightful hockey man who had made the trades and drafted the players. Was he the one to go? The experienced, knowledgeable coach hadn't been responsible for drafting, trading or bringing in the players. Should he be the one to go?

The board had hired these people; was it the board's fault?

At times, the board members, like many bosses, believed they knew more about hockey than the people they hired to do that job. They also tended to react in a knee-jerk fashion, just as the fans did, a worrying tendency if you happened to be the GM or coach. There were too many bosses, directions and thoughts about the team.

Board members had already scheduled a meeting for October 22, which was 18 days away. They had already made up their minds that if the team hadn't improved by then, changes would have to be made. But the captain's complaints and the story in the *Examiner* made the need for change more urgent. The board panicked and, at Devlin's request, called a secret emergency meeting for Thanksgiving Sunday, two days away.

Nobody asked the captain to sit down and discuss his words. Nobody in management asked whether the captain's behaviour was appropriate. Nor did they ask any of the players what they thought about his comments. They might have been surprised if they had. Neither the coaches nor the GM knew what really went on within that team. While Pelino called the captain's comments courageous, many players thought Koeks was an arrogant pain interested only in his own future. He was confident, yes; aloof, yes; and wanting to play in the NHL more than anything. But he also wanted to win more than any other player on the team. He knew winning would ease the team's pain and maybe puncture this bubble of negativity that he had helped create with his attitude.

Mathers described it best. "In the dressing room, there had been disappointment when Koeks was made captain. He was not a leader. He criticized the younger guys too much, yelling at them when they made mistakes. They were afraid of him, afraid of making mistakes, and certainly wouldn't go to him if they had a question, or he would make them feel like idiots. There is a line between the veterans and the rookies, but I would want them to come to me with concerns and questions [if I were captain]."

To many in the room, Mathers or Seymour should have been made captain. Mathers had wanted the role and was a natural leader. He was not the best player, as Koekkoek surely was, but he was more loyal to players and team, more about *we* than *me*. "When Koeks was named captain, I was disappointed—I wanted that—but I wasn't surprised. It wasn't until later—and I wish I had known then—that I found out they made him captain to keep him happy and from leaving.

"There were little cliques in the room. I love Koeks, he's a great guy, but he wasn't a good captain, and the room knew it. He wasn't inclusive. If there were any mistakes, he would be screaming at players."

Koekkoek had changed over the seasons. Last season, he had been the last man off the ice at practice, always trying to learn more from the coaches. This season, he was one of the first off. He had always had a touch of arrogance, as many great players do, and had never seemed like a rookie when he arrived with the Petes. He was so mature, he instantly became a veteran. "Koeks was a good kid, a passionate hockey player, and he made some of the guys uncomfortable with his honesty," said assistant coach Clark. "Sometimes the truth hurt—he wanted the guys to have more accountability. He just wanted to win and was a frustrated veteran. He just sometimes didn't know what to do as a captain. He was copying a past captain, Watson, who hadn't been a great captain." Clark remembered Koekkoek calling even *him* out once, saying after one game in front of everyone in the dressing room, "We don't need guys like Clarkie whispering instructions in Cornel's ears." Koekkoek thought the whole team should hear what players were being told. Some of the veterans had taken him aside after that incident, and Koekkoek called Clark at home that night to apologize, but Clark was okay with it. He understood his passion.

Meanwhile, it was more than the captain that was bothering the players. They were tired of seeing certain players repeatedly making mistakes and not getting benched. The veterans in the dressing room were waiting and hoping for Pelino to demand accountability. They were also worried about something that others weren't mentioning but that the statisticians had already seen: players were changing lines more often than runway models switched clothes. This season, nobody seemed to know whom they were playing with.

"We couldn't get used to each other," said many of the players. "There was no bonding. Some teams in our league had lines that had been together for three years, and we weren't together for three shifts."

"Coach had no respect from the players. We laughed at him," Mathers told me. "He was too lenient. By the time he realized this, it was too late—he had lost us, and we weren't listening. Last year was the same; we were losing, and we expected and accepted losses as if it was normal. Nothing was done, but when we won a game, it was like a Memorial Cup party, everyone was happy over one win.

"Coach was also showing favouritism. I was among that group, but it wasn't right. He knew his hockey, but he wasn't getting through to us. We were not scared. We were not scared of making mistakes, because nothing would be done if we did."

Many veterans wanted accountability. The rookies had no idea of what it was supposed to be like in the OHL, but by the second game they had a feeling things were not heading in the right direction. Even in exhibition games, they had seen similar problems. The coaches didn't see this, saying at that point in the season that the team was still together. Clark later would say that he thought the teens were just exaggerating about Pelino and were looking for someone to blame.

Pelino was technically sound, with great tactics and knowledge, "but the players were too powerful and people had already started looking for excuses," said one insider. The Petes' captain was already down and complaining in the dressing room and in public about the team's potential. Unknown to either Pelino or Koekkoek was that many players were not impressed with what was said by coach or captain—and this was before they had found out about their captain's remarks to Davies. Koekkoek had his allies, like Quine, Menard and Seymour, but the rest of the team wasn't as tight.

"The players did not respect the coach," said Cornel. "He let players do too many things. Koeks would talk back to him in front of players, stand up and say things critical about others. Us young guys couldn't believe it. We had never seen it happen before."

Because he was a rookie, Cornel didn't know any better. He thought maybe this was the way it was in all OHL dressing rooms. It was not until a month later, while talking to some players on other teams, that he learned it wasn't normal. It wasn't that the players all didn't like Pelino: he was a gentleman and a knowledgeable hockey guy, but he wasn't loud enough, strict enough. You couldn't earn your ice with him—he just kept playing his favourites. Findlay, who felt like he was the coach's whipping boy, tried everything he could but couldn't get the ice time he felt he needed to perform better. Behind Pelino's back, Findlay gave a rather good impersonation of the coach. It wasn't a flattering one.

***

A challenging week awaited the team as it headed to Barrie on Saturday, October 6. It was only the Petes' sixth game, but already the club was in crisis. Some players' parents were in disbelief at the team's failure and the captain's words. Some of their sons had described to them the mood inside the dressing room, and they worried about the team, but more importantly, about their boys.

There were 3,150 fans in the Barrie Molson Centre, which seated more than 5,000. At least a dozen Petes parents were present, there in many cases to take their sons home for Thanksgiving following the game. Four injured players had already been allowed to go home, while Ritchie and Lorentz (who was now showing signs of having suffered a concussion) met their parents at the rink.

Cornel, sliding on his knees and flipping a Hatcher rebound high into the mesh, finally got his first OHL goal.

Mathers moved back on defence because the team was short there and President Devlin had suggested that Reid use him, instead of bringing up the more experienced Cole Murduff, now playing for a Petes affiliate. The issue had come to the forefront that week at practice, when Devlin received an email from another board member saying Murduff was dressing for practice. Devlin had spoken with Reid several times about the 19-year-old Murduff. He said the board hadn't known that the locally born and raised Murduff was Reid's daughter's boyfriend when Reid traded an eighth-round pick to Belleville for him two seasons ago. Reid disputed this claim.

Murduff was a borderline player who had filled in for injured players in 2011–12. Devlin and other board members wrongly believed most fans knew about the Reid connection. The reality was that only the connected fan had a clue, and only the crass among them even cared. Nevertheless, the board and some of the Petes' scouts and coaches felt that Murduff's inclusion created an awkward situation for other players, management and even the player himself. This wasn't the only potential conflict of interest, either, because John Oke, father of the player personnel manager, Mike Oke, sat on the board of directors. These were all good people, but outsiders, and some insiders, insinuated that nepotism and favouritism were factors influencing staffing decisions.

Devlin was determined to put an end to that, and he went to the rink, where he told Reid that Murduff would not be stepping on the ice. Reid replied that he was the best defenceman left to call up and that the board had better tell the GM if it wanted to put a winning team on the ice or an economical one. Devlin suggested that Mathers be moved back. Devlin, backed up in a fiery telephone call between Dr. Neville and Reid, stuck to his guns. Reid, unsurprisingly, remained irritated by the interference.

Arguing with bosses usually meant trouble in paradise.

Both the president and the GM were shaking with frustration and anger after the meeting in Reid's office. Reid followed instructions, angrily pulling Murduff from the plan. This was the day the president began quietly asking questions of some of the staff members—even Davies and Pelino—about the GM. Their answers confirmed to him that it was Reid, not the coach, who was the source of the team's troubles.

Reid had read Davies's interview with Koeks but was leaving the following day on a long-planned, board-approved trip to Vegas with his family to celebrate his in-laws' 50th wedding anniversary. He wished ardently that he was with the team instead. The optics and timing of the trip were terrible. The team was suffering, the captain was calling out the GM and the president was on Reid's back. The holiday trip never did become public—a good thing, because the fans were in a foul enough mood without that.

Reid watched the Barrie game online from Vegas and was happy with the team's overall play, but he was still furious with his captain for throwing not only him but also some of the players under the bus. Some fans and members of the board of directors were impressed with the captain's courage and thought it woke up some players. Reid knew the criticism was being aimed at him, and to a lesser extent at Oke, since they were the people responsible for making trades, but he felt there was nothing out there for him to get or give. No team was getting rid of good players this early in the season. Reid said he wasn't taking Koeks's remarks personally—although he clearly was—and that he would discuss them with him after Thanksgiving. At the same time, Reid felt he was being micromanaged by Devlin, a development that inevitably made Reid more tentative in making any moves.

He was definitely frustrated and feeling pressured. The board had complete control over spending and was tightening the team's financial belt. The strain was having an impact on Reid's health to the point where he was beginning to think he wanted out.

Reid hadn't been sleeping well as the team struggled. He was having heart palpitations, worrying constantly about on- and off-ice issues. The job had been consuming his life. Everything else was playing second fiddle, including his family, which had always been number one. He longed to get back to broadcasting, a job he did well and that wasn't nearly as nerve-racking as this one had turned out to be. He was also aware his temper was becoming more volatile.

The on-ice product weighed heavily upon him. He had spoken to Pelino about the lack of a team identity. He hadn't mentioned the line-changing problem because line shuffling was common at this time of the year, but he had noticed and deplored other problems that the team couldn't seem to solve, such as its inability to move the puck out of the defensive zone or to finish checks. It bothered him that the coaches didn't listen: he was itching to hit the ice at a practice, something he knew the coaches wouldn't like. He had won two Stanley Cups and spent a career learning defensive coverage from some of the best players, such as Jarvis and Gainey. He thought he had something to contribute. He had tried to get through to staff, but the message didn't seem to be getting to the players.

Little did he or any of the coaches know how right he was. A pragmatic man, Reid was also wondering whether he was expecting too much from these kids. Maybe he was unfairly comparing them to their NHL counterparts. They were, after all, junior players—boys, really. But one thing was certain in Reid's mind: if his team was going down, he was going to get things done his way. Pelino might have to go.

The GM didn't want to coach unless he had to, even though such great ones as Todd, Keenan, Green and Bowman had. He was hoping things would work out. He had the right instincts, but not the intestinal fortitude to act on them. Unbeknownst to either Reid or Pelino, some veteran players were waiting and hoping for changes. If he had only known how some of the veteran players felt about their coach, he might have carried out his unannounced threat to replace Pelino.

There was a conflict between the coach and GM that reverberated into the dressing room. The watershed moment had probably come last season when Puempel took a teen rookie out and broke curfew. Veteran players wanted Puempel and the other player disciplined when they found out. Pelino gathered the team and expressed his disappointment, telling them that this was against the rules, it couldn't be tolerated and disciplinary measures would be taken. But Reid was also in the meeting, and instead of backing up the coach, he took out $250 and gave it to Puempel, saying, "If you're going to break rules, do it as a team." The veteran players went out and enjoyed a night of drinking, which did not surprise the coaches, but it came as a shock to Reid, who just thought they'd go out for dinner and some drinks.

When Puempel wasn't disciplined, the players took note and understood that Pelino was not in charge. Pelino was strict on the 11 P.M. curfew, which his assistants and Reid had questioned, wondering if it was too rigid, but the coach worried about the possibility of a player driving while under the influence or getting into some other kind of trouble. At the same time, imposing an 11 P.M. curfew on 19- and 20-year-olds seemed unreasonably restrictive. There didn't seem to be any sense of balance, and the players knew it.

From then on, Reid and the coaches were no longer on the same caboose on this train. "Pelino would set up structure and Reid would tear it down. You can't get your job done that way. He undercut the coaches," said one insider.

On Sunday, October 7, the afternoon following the Barrie game, the board held its secret meeting in the alumni room of the Memorial Centre. The topic under discussion was whether to let go of either Reid or Pelino or both. (It was doubtful they would let both go because of economic considerations: two contracts to buy out, two new salaries to be absorbed.) Usually, in these circumstances, it was the coach who was fired and the GM who did the firing, but the trouble between Reid and Devlin, and between Reid and Neville, altered the dynamics of the situation. The board decided it would be making a mistake to let the coach go. They thought, in their ignorance, that the players were responding positively to the coach and felt that the six injuries, three of them to key players, were hindering the team's chances. At the same time, they were worried that the Petes had only two points and were officially tied with Ottawa as the worst team in the OHL.

Devlin was especially perturbed by the lack of return the team was getting in Reid's trades (specifically those involving Watson and Puempel). He also revealed to the five board members the results of his quiet investigations regarding Reid. He told them of a two-hour conversation he had had with Davies of the *Examiner,* and of his talks with other insiders, including Pelino. Devlin mentioned the $250 dressing room incident he and the coaches thought had undermined the disciplinary structure they were trying to impose. He said his research had convinced him the problem was at the GM level. He said he thought Pelino and his coaches were doing everything they could, but they didn't have the players they needed.

He also recounted how he had listened to Reid telling his scouts on draft day that he would never take Jake Evans, the player they had recommended. Devlin wondered if Reid was paying attention to his own staff. What he didn't say was that Reid had been right in that dispute, because the player in question had stuck with his NCAA commitment. Devlin saw it differently.

The board meeting lasted two hours. They had a healthy debate, but surprisingly there was little discussion of the coaching staff's performance, only Reid's. The board voted 5–0, with one abstention, to give Devlin carte blanche to handle the situation. It was understood that Devlin's intention was to fire Reid, and it was for that reason that the one director withheld his vote, saying he had not signed on to fire people. Oke left the room when his son, who would become a figure in this controversy, was discussed as a candidate to temporarily replace Reid.

Devlin slept few hours that night or the next. He said he had been thinking about firing Reid for a week, beginning "when I went to the Erie game and couldn't believe how badly we played." The following morning's publication of the captain's interview in the *Examiner* added fuel to his internal fire.

"'Oh my God,' I said. It was all a gut feeling," he said. "The only effect Slater's words had was just another confirmation that it wasn't the coach's fault.

"Dave is a good person, but I knew it had to be done. I started rehearsing my opening line. The next day, I was at my daughter's for Thanksgiving dinner, but my mind wasn't there."

Since Devlin had become president, Reid had been more open and friendly with him than anyone connected with the team, openly discussing issues and problems and talking hockey as if he were on staff. Reid was a Petes guy, wearing the honour and loyalty badge proudly, defending and promoting them wherever and whenever he went, protecting the image as if it was part of his family. He even took players into his house when they had no homes, a service he had offered to Ceresnak and Tanus when they arrived in Canada, and most recently to Ritchie, who had left his billet and was still in Reid's home before moving to the Crowleys'. He invited players to his home to go waterskiing, entertaining them just as former coach Roger Neilson had done so often. (Pelino and Clark thought Reid's relationship with the players undercut their powers and relationship with the players.) Whatever Devlin thought about Reid's performance, he could not question the GM's dedication or commitment to the Petes. He tossed and turned in bed the night before the firing.

At 8:30 A.M. on Tuesday, October 9, Devlin was in the Petes' office talking idly with Pelino, who knew the presence of the president that early could only be bad news. Reid arrived at 9 A.M. after delivering

Ritchie to school. When he saw Devlin, he suspected the coach was going to be let go, but he also understood it could be him. Devlin followed Reid into his office, closed the door and told him he was being relieved of his duties.

Reid claimed the first thing Devlin said was that the Murduff issue was the final straw. Devlin, however, says he began with some small talk about Saturday's Barrie game and then said, "We need to talk about something more serious.

"Dave, we're going to let you go."

Then Devlin went over the litany of reasons: bad trades, bad player moves, lack of information to the board, and then the Murduff issue.

A shocked Reid couldn't believe Murduff was such a big concern. As Reid put it, Murduff was a ninth defenceman, was a call-up, available at any time. If the board thought that was a conflict of interest, what about Oke and his son? But Reid kept the thought to himself. The two men talked for a few minutes more before Reid got out of his chair, the one he had bought for the office so it wouldn't cost the Petes, and left the room. He told Pelino and Hull he had been fired and then walked into the dressing room to inform the nine players there, including Koekkoek. He thought he saw Koekkoek smile as he told them he had been dismissed. He reminded the captain that his words carried a lot of weight and to be careful what he said in the future.

Devlin was left stunned in Reid's office when the GM went to the dressing room. He feared Reid might do something stupid, like blame the players. Devlin followed him, but Reid was already finished. Reid left the office and called his wife and some friends. His shock was not at being dismissed, but that the Murduff issue appeared to be such a problem.

As he drove home, he still couldn't get the team out of his mind.

It was only minutes after his firing when he said: "I hope they look at the Green Bay Packers' setup [an idea to have the public buy shares of the Petes] because something should happen there. Maybe I will sleep now and be able to live with myself better. I think we [he kept referring to the team as 'we'] have a good team, but I guess the board thinks they have got rid of the problem."

When the board hired Reid, it was getting someone with no managerial experience and it didn't supply any training or guidance. Now they were blaming the team's failure on him. It didn't seem fair, but little in hockey does. It was a bad day for those involved. Nobody enjoyed being around when things like this happened. Nobody enjoyed giving or receiving such news. Devlin was devastated. Reid took the decision like the pro he was, but he was naturally upset. He didn't, and wouldn't, push anyone on his team under the bus; instead, he insisted, "There is a good team there." He had given two years to the Petes. He had gotten involved in everything from ticket sales to rink maintenance, dealing with the city, helping charities, schmoozing sponsors and greeting fans. He hardly had time for the hockey issues that were central to his job.

The business of hockey is just that, a business, one in which the bosses win and employees take the blame. In this instance, the board panicked and then exercised its prerogative to make a change. Someone asked, after the firing, whom did the board answer to? The reality was that the board, as the owners of the business, answered to their accountant's figures and, this being hockey, the team's position in the standings. These factors were also what mattered most to the players, parents and agents who looked at wins and team success as the necessary preconditions to getting the players drafted. If you're winning and the team is thriving, the scouts look longer at your players. If the scouts are looking and the team is going deeper into the playoffs, there is more chance of players getting drafted. Winning leads to the playoffs, which attracts more money. Winning creates harmony while reducing anxiety. It creates a better work environment for everyone involved. Winning keeps team captains, and board directors, happy. It prevents firings.

Reid was too nice a guy. Yes, he was demanding and wanted things done his way, but he was too nice to pull the trigger and act on his threats. He should have told Matt Puempel to sit on his ass until he froze. Watson should not have been traded for so little in return. Whether he was perceived as a team problem or not, Watson could downright play hockey. What Reid did was trade cougars for kittens. But it was all done on the board's watch. Puempel, after hearing of the firing, said Reid was not the problem. The GM had treated him well, he said—so well that he moved him without getting much back. The kid was right to express his appreciation, if only retrospectively.

The board told the public only that Reid had been dismissed for personnel moves. Reid told the public he was disappointed the team didn't do better, but he was convinced it was a good team and wouldn't change a thing. He did not cast aspersions on anyone else—even when he learned that Pelino had spoken about him with Devlin and other board members behind his back. He was miffed by that but didn't utter a bad word. Reid was loyal to the end.

In a press release, the team said the firing was a "business decision taking all factors into consideration." Devlin told the public that the coaches could only coach the players they were supplied with and that those players were not good enough. He moved the player personnel director, Oke, in to help Pelino do Reid's former job.

The cheering that comes when a hockey person is fired seems so archaic, barbaric and inhuman. But this is sport. Some, not all, fans excuse their vicious attitude by pointing out that they pay for their tickets and can damn well do and say what they please. It is wrong, and we know it, and yet we accept it and it goes on. Still, not all the comments in the aftermath of the firing were aimed at Reid. Some onlookers were shocked that it was the general manager and not the coach (or both) that was let go. The board was bashed for being "an old boys' club" that needed to be changed itself. Poor Mike Oke, whose father was on the board, but who had been hired by Reid, took a bashing as that conflict became an issue. One fan wrote: "Is it any wonder that the GM was undercut and replaced by the son of one of the Petes' board members. Something stinks worse than a Memorial Centre toilet." Other fans wrote on chat lines and message boards that the firing was "too bad," that Reid "was a good guy" and that "he ruined the team." Invariably, fans are a tough crowd.

Reid was now free. He would no longer have to make and take early-morning or late-night calls to and from staff, parents, agents or coaches. He no longer had to worry about the Petes or the close to $90,000 in annual salary he was paid. (The coach got a bit less; OHL teams, including the Petes, seldom, if ever, reveal what they pay.)

He was fired on a game day, so there would be no Dave, nor Kathy or Jessica, to look after and serve coffee and snacks in the alumni room, and no Alec inside Roger the Mascot's outfit.

The present assistant general manager, Aaron Garfat, was virtually passed over in the shakeup. He wasn't even told about Reid's firing until many others knew. Even Davies at the *Examiner* knew before Garfat. Pelino and Mike Oke now looked after hockey operations. Devlin took over business operations.

Devlin said the Oke-Pelino partnership would continue "for the entire year." Few noticed that he had said "year" and not "season," but Pelino and Oke took it to mean the balance of the season. Although the two were now in charge, neither knew who had the final word if they disagreed with each other—a strange situation for two staff members to be placed in.

Pelino spoke to the breakfast club players, the veterans who didn't attend school but showed up at the rink every morning, about Reid's departure. And then he addressed all the players that night. The young players said little, shrugged and whispered among themselves when Pelino left the room, but basically carried on listening to their music and going through their workouts. "When the GM was fired," says Mathers, "the players were pissed off. Sure, Dave might have made some bad moves, but he wasn't the problem—the coach was, not the GM. It caught us all off guard, but we also knew it was out of our control."

Before the home game on October 9, Pelino asked Oke to join the coaching staff for the pre-game meeting with the players. He wanted to let them know about the firing, as well as who was now in charge and how it impacted them.

"You never know what's going to unfold in life or what might happen or when something is going to be taken away from you that you cherish," was Pelino's message to players. Maybe some listened, but most said it had little effect.

The Memorial Centre was abuzz with talk of the firing and Koekkoek's interview with Davies. The rumours circulated among fans, ushers, rink crew, restaurant workers, scouts and even the team as the players tried to focus on the game.

They came out hitting, checking, winning faceoffs and blocking shots. Stephen Pierog (nicknamed Perogi) took over the game with his stamina, tenacity and determination. He blocked two shots on one shift and kept going. His play mirrored his progress. He had never expected to be drafted into the OHL, but that didn't stop him from wanting it, and he wouldn't give up. The Guelph-born player was better at lacrosse when he was a kid: American schools had been looking at him in his draft year for both sports, but he was generally thought to be too scrawny. His mother had died of a heart attack when he was only 13, and he dedicated his sports to her from then on in. He was cut from teams but kept coming back to prove people wrong—and to secretly carry out a promise to his mother to make it to the OHL, and then to the NHL. "I knew I'd be a long shot. I was five foot ten and weighed 160 pounds and had been drafted in the 11th round." He got cut his first year but kept the Petes informed of his play every week and made it the second year. He now weighed 180 pounds, a hundred of it all heart.

Giggy was incredible in net that night against Niagara. Koekkoek made a brilliant effort to join the rush and used his NHL-calibre wrist shot to put one in the top corner. They even scored a power-play goal and killed off three of Niagara's strong power plays for a 3–1 win. The hometown crowd of only 1,500 gave them a standing ovation as they delivered their traditional post-game salute at centre ice. A few fans chanted, "Atta go, Mike"; another shouted "Sign him for another three [years]." There was a good atmosphere as the players left the ice.

There were some powerful moments inside the dressing room when Pelino surprisingly invited in three executive members—Devlin, Bob Neville and Ken Jackman—along with Mike Oke for the team's first home win. The guys in charge were clearly exhilarated. Hull pumped the players up and then handed over the floor to Clark, who lauded their work. In addition to the Burn the Boats Award, which would be presented to the team's MVP after a win, the Petes had instituted a second private, internal team award.

The 212-Degree Award was a concept Pelino had reached into his past to revive. When Pelino was 12, his coach in Welland had told the team about putting water on the stove and heating it to 211 degrees. He asked the players what that did, and one replied, "You've got nothing but a pot full of hot water." The coach agreed but said if you add only one more degree, you got steam, and steam was powerful enough to send locomotives through mountains. The team could all move together with just that one extra degree of effort. The Petes would hand out a 212-Degree Award after a win to the player who made that extra effort.

When Perogi, who had won the 212-Degree Award in the team's first win of the season, presented the award for the hardest-working player, he said: "There are so many of you guys that deserve it. You guys were all awesome. Giggy in net. Koeks, you got a great goal, but I'm going to give this to Frankie—you were awesome, man." The players agreed and gave Frankie Menard applause as he accepted the honour. Giggy, the last winner of the Burn the Boats Award, presented tonight's award and said, "So many guys played great, making my job easier, but I've got to give it to Tanus for his first-ever OHL goal."

"I'm so proud of you guys, you met our expectations tonight," Pelino said. "I know you guys are getting criticized by the fans in the community, and I want you to know that when you are grinding it out, it is not only you feeling the hurt but these people [the directors] also hurt with us, so we wanted them to share some of the joy as well."

Devlin spoke briefly about their work ethic again. Board director Jackman turned to the captain and said: "We don't want you feeling responsible in any way for what happened earlier today. It was something that was happening without you. You were great in what you said. You were not responsible for a man losing his job. Speaking up for your team is what you should do." And when Devlin shook players' hands, he told Koekkoek, "The decision was made before your comments. Don't you ever blame yourself."

Dr. Neville, probably the Petes' most influential board member, told them: "I've been involved with this team for a number of years, and what I saw tonight was one of the most special moments. This was a special night and I'm glad to be a part of it."

Many of the players were astounded, both by the fuss that was being made over a single win and by the praise being lavished on the captain. "When [Jackman] walked into that dressing room and told Koeks that it was not his fault," said one, "we didn't even know what he was talking about. We hadn't read the newspaper, but afterward we thought it fed Koeks's ego even more. Nobody had even expected the GM to be fired." As Mathers remembered, "We all thought the coach should have been fired," and Reid and Hull would have made a good combination going forward.

The players were unimpressed. It was a good win and they were happy, but it was only one win. Unlike the adults, they kept it in perspective. Mathers said, "Every time we won, it was like we had won the Memorial Cup, but when we lost it just seemed everyone accepted it." Most of the other players shared this level-headed opinion.

Davies wrote a column in which he said it was time for the board of directors to change, that Oke should have stepped down when his son was hired and that new blood was needed. The biweekly newspaper *Peterborough This Week* picked up the theme on its editorial page.

The real problem, as far as the players were concerned, was left unresolved. As they saw things, nothing had changed: they had the same coach and captain, and the same lingering doubts about their future with both.

CHAPTER 11

The More Things Change . . .

The Petes' engine was missing some spark. Just when it was running smoothly or showing signs of moving forward, it would stall. The Petes were showing only flashes of promise and brilliance, of running on all cylinders.

In the October 11 game against Kingston, the Petes at least got some good news: they welcomed back Nick Ritchie, now recovered from his injury. He changed the look of the team with his size, toughness and shot. Two of his hard shots went off posts, and he earned recognition as the game's first star in the loss, but he wasn't in game shape yet and said afterwards that he had played no better than "okay."

Ritchie had to be the spark plug to ignite this team, just as he had always been in his youth teams. In his final midget year, he had scored 50 goals and 44 assists in 68 games. His scouting report was two pages long and full of praise for his ability to win battles and a "solid mean streak . . . the best player on the ice." But he was only 16, still developing on and off the ice. On the ice, he wanted to win and be the best. Off the ice, his behaviour was a bit dubious: he liked to be around the older boys, stay out late and wander with the veterans. Perhaps the real problem was that adults looked at his size and saw an adult, forgetting he was just a kid and easily influenced by others. He was sensitive to criticism, was hungry for compliments and wanted desperately to improve as a hockey player. He just didn't have the discipline that would probably come with age.

He was a great addition to the team, and if Alan Quine ever returned, Ritchie might have someone to play with. As it stood, the other teams, who usually had two or three great players, could focus on nullifying Ritchie.

The next road trip, the first overnighter, was not going to be similar to most. When the team got to Owen Sound, one of the team's better players would be disciplined.

Trevor Murphy had been getting to school late, skipping some classes and failing to pick up fellow players on time when they depended on him for a ride, and he was generally not doing well at school. This was not an uncommon problem in junior hockey circles, and each team dealt with it in different ways.

Pelino met with Murphy to tell him he was being benched for a game. It came as a shock; something like this had never happened to Murphy in hockey. The coach thought he had no choice, thought it was the only way to get through to the kid.

There were a couple of things bothering Pelino about Murphy. "You want to see the player develop on and off the ice. They go hand in hand. Some of the things that were creeping into Trevor's attitude I wanted to address. He's an interesting study. He has a lot of confidence, which you want. He plays with a chip on his shoulder. He's cocky, which is not always a bad thing, but maybe some of his success had made him more so and he was starting to think that being part of an OHL team was his right rather than a privilege."

Back in the early 1970s, under Roger Neilson, the Petes had asked an education consultant to join the team as a volunteer. They moved all their players to the same school and had them report to that consultant, a teacher at the school who kept the team informed of problems and sent report cards to the GM/coach. It was such a successful system for players, parents and the team that the OHL adopted it for the whole league.

"We have a good relationship with the academic counsellor and get reports," said Pelino. "We had indicated to the players that we know sometimes they would be late or absent, but they needed to tell the school and us if they were. Trevor wasn't doing this, so when all these little things were adding up, I decided to get him on board and let him understand what it takes to make it to the next level. It's not just about hockey. It's all part and parcel toward development as a player and mature adult."

Pelino discussed the problem with his coaches. He believed the Petes, with their rich education tradition, should start taking these matters more seriously, and he wanted to send a strong message to the kid and the team. "Sometimes you have to choose the battles to win the wars. We're talking about a good hockey player here who would be taken out of the lineup, but ultimately this would help him and the team." Concerned not only about Murphy's marks but also about his poor hockey statistics, Pelino was hoping for a marked improvement in Murphy's attitude to help him grow into a mature individual. He also hoped it would send a message to other players, "like when you're speeding and the cop has pulled over someone else, so you slow down because you don't want to be the next guy caught."

Pelino had told the captains, and word was passed on to the players. They were surprised by the move, but it seemed to awaken them. Most agreed that disciplining Murphy was overdue, but they also believed favourites were being played and that other players who deserved the same fate had escaped punishment.

"Does it set a precedent?" asked the coach. "Maybe for the next person that is late. I believe in fairness, which doesn't always mean equal treatment. There is a big difference between being equal and everything being fair."

Later, at the rink, when scouts in the media room asked questions about Murphy's not playing, they were told by those who thought they knew that he was a "healthy scratch." Pelino, however, corrected them, saying there were school and practice issues. Murphy, he said, needed to know more commitment was necessary if he was to realize his dream of becoming a pro hockey player.

The Owen Sound rink was built in the 1980s for durability rather than comfort, and exclusively for hockey and lacrosse. There were no video screens, no luxury suites—in fact, no luxury—but it looked, felt and acted like hockey rinks all across Canada. It was October 13, a Saturday night, and by 6:30 P.M., a little over an hour before the opening faceoff, 3,100 of Owen Sound's 22,000 people were jostling cheerfully into the front of the arena in a scene familiar to residents of small communities and typical of OHL rinks across the province. They were carrying paper and plastic cups full of beer, pop or coffee, eating popcorn from bags or boxes, munching on warm pretzels, holding wrapped, steamed hot dogs, French fries in boxes, pizza slices on cardboard platters. There were children wearing team jackets and ball caps; women with shoulder bags strapped over woollen sweaters or ski jackets; a few men in suits, but most in jeans and hockey jackets; teens with ball caps worn backwards, forwards, sideways, pulled down to their eyes or ears, pants below their hips. Some carried foam hands or homemade signs. They bounced along to the beat of loud music from country to rock, interrupted by shouted-out injunctions such as "*Welcome to the jungle! . . . Put your hands up in the air! . . . Where did you come from, Cotton-Eyed Joe?*" and those damn trumpets, sirens and car horns that blasted your eardrums.

Ritchie played well in the game, but then he took a spill, slamming into the boards and skating off the rink holding his shoulder. He knew immediately, as did B-Man, that it was serious. There were no tears from the 16-year-old, even though he was in obvious pain. Hockey players are told early in life to "suck it up," that tears are for the weak; besides, Ritchie was feeling more anger and frustration than pain when, arm in a sling, he returned from the hospital that night to join a team that had lost in overtime.

It didn't get any better for the Petes the next night in Guelph. It was the Petes' fourth game in six days, and yet the team came out with energy and got an early lead thanks to two goals by Francis Menard, who was confronting the team that had traded him. Late in the second period, Josh Maguire took a vicious hit that sent him to the nearby hospital. Incredibly, once again nobody rallied to deliver payback.

Guelph tied the game in the third, forcing the Petes into their third overtime in four games. They lost, but they had earned five of a possible eight points on the trip. After returning from Guelph, Pelino gave the team the day off, their first off the ice in seven, and learned that both Ritchie and Maguire (who was suffering from the first injury in his life) would be out for at least a month.

The team needed help.

Mike Oke had heard about an overage right-winger for the Regina Pats who might be available. Andrew Rieder had played for the Pats for three years and didn't have spectacular numbers, accumulating 25 points in 52 games in 2011–12, but Regina had committed to its full complement of three overagers. Rieder cleared Western Hockey League waivers, so the Petes claimed him for $500 and the price of a plane ticket. Rieder's previous season had ended with a dislocated shoulder, a problem that might require surgery before or at the end of this season. But Rieder reminded hockey people of what junior hockey players in Ontario used to be: tough, talented, team-oriented and willing to do whatever it took to win.

Born and raised in Regina, Rieder saw a big difference between the Ontario and Western leagues: there was more accountability out west. "The WHL is less scrambly, more system-oriented," he said. He thought the WHL was also rougher. "The players are probably more talented here, but the west is more aggressive and does whatever it takes to win. There is more discipline out west, more respect for all the coaches. They don't seem to have the same respect for coaches here. Players fooling around, throwing water at each other on the ice, wouldn't be tolerated there."

There were other differences. Western league road trips could last from three days to two weeks. He also noticed players were assigned to give others a ride to school here, but in the west most players had cars—and if not, "you had to ask for your own ride." In other words, he saw that there was too much coddling in Peterborough.

Rieder had insight into what it took to win, but the Petes' leaders pushed him away. The players hadn't had the same experiences as Rieder had: teammates being held accountable and doing whatever it took to win. Pelino and Oke were looking for some grit, work ethic and commitment—qualities right winger Rieder possessed—so they signed him to a tryout, well aware of his shoulder problem, although the public wasn't. He hadn't played a game all season and was rusty, but he didn't look out of place. There was nothing flashy about him, but he was a good player.

Quine, who had been itching to get back into a game, was expected back, but that turned sour. While Ottawa and Peterborough doctors had cleared him, his agent consulted the Detroit Red Wings, who didn't want him playing without their doctor's okay. His parents agreed with the Wings. Quine broke into tears. You couldn't blame Detroit, which owned his rights, nor his parents, whose main concern was his health. He was back to wearing an orange jersey. Others not playing because of injuries or health issues included Connor Boland with mono, Ritchie and Maguire with shoulder problems and Alex Robinson with the broken jaw.

Jonatan Tanus's parents and young brother had flown to Canada in October from Tappara, Finland, for 10 days to watch four games. It was a change from getting up at 2 A.M. to watch Jonatan on the computer. The Petes brass made no effort to entertain or even meet the family—not that they expected special treatment—and they were on their own, sitting in their son's inexpensive corner seats, just like parents from Ontario. It was a strange way to treat people who had travelled so far, but neither the Betzolds nor the Hatchers nor the Ceresnaks were treated any differently when they visited from Maryland, Philly and Europe. Pelino, however, welcomed the Tanus family and invited the younger brother for a breakfast club skate and later included him in a team community practice.

Pelino played Tanus quite a bit in the October 25 game against the London powerhouse, sending him out on the power-play and penalty-killing units in what turned out to be a David-against-Goliath contest. David almost slew the giant, but not quite: the Petes lost 5–4, with Findlay scoring his first goal as a Pete after 11 games, the longest he had ever gone without scoring in his life.

B-Man's life got busier when Stephen Nosad left the game after a brutal boarding that would keep him out for a couple of weeks, putting three of the club's top six forwards on medical leave. The London player got only two minutes. Not a single teammate went after the player who hit him, which Rieder said would not have happened in Regina. "I knew if I got hit from behind, someone was going to get that guy." The OHL later suspended the player for six games.

The Petes had only two wins in 12 games.

The following day, Pelino had a "whipping session," showing replays of some of Koeks's bad plays and short, soft passes, as well as bad plays by Steven Trojanovic and Trevor Murphy, who were being asked to look in the mirror. It was a tough video session in which only the bad plays were featured. Menard's two goals and Findlay's first were not included. Trojanovic was aware he had made some mistakes, but he did not appreciate being called out by the coach so publicly. Pelino was losing confidence in him, and he was losing confidence in the coach. Pelino knew Trojanovic had a major offensive side to him and was a good skater with a good, low point shot on the power play; but defensively, he wanted more from the Burlington boy who had been drafted by the Windsor Spitfires in 2009 and then traded to the Petes in January of 2011.

Two nights after the London loss, Tanus got a goal, won key face-offs in front of his visiting parents and blocked a shot with his instep. It was a performance that should have earned him a game star, but he was not even named the hardest-working player by the media. The players noticed, though, and he got the Burn the Boats Award inside the dressing room.

The anti-doping squad paid a surprise visit after the game. They took Menard and a Saginaw player aside and demanded a urine sample from each. Neither result was positive. Maybe someone should have checked the team the next day, when they walked into Oshawa and beat the hometown crew in a 3–2 shootout in which Betzold, now with a four-game point streak, scored the winner. Menard scored another two, making him fourth in the league in goal scoring and first on the Petes in every offensive category, a Reid trade that worked well.

After the warmup, Tanus said he couldn't play because of the bruised instep; this was an injury a Canadian player might have played with, but the Finn wouldn't. Goalie coach Andrew Verner had witnessed this unwillingness to play hurt while in Europe for more than a decade. He said many Europeans don't have the same attitude as Canadian hockey players when it comes to minor injuries. In Canada, if you're only 90 per cent, you can still play and give 100 per cent. Tanus would learn the Canadian way as the season progressed, but his absence tonight was a blow to the lineup and a disappointment to his family, who had followed the team to Oshawa before heading to the Toronto airport and home to Finland.

Alex Robinson, recovering from his fractured jaw, had been practising and travelling with the team, but shortly after this game, Pelino learned that his contract—including a $15,000 education package—kicked in if he played even one game for the Petes. So he was sent to play Tier II for Kanata. The team's explanation was that it wanted Robinson to get into better shape, but the main factor driving the decision was financial. Reid had signed Robinson, under board pressure, in favour of Murduff, and now the kid was paying for it. Robinson knew there was still a way to return to the Petes, and that was to play better than ever before, so that the team would have to bring him back. He was not a quitter. He was never told, however, the real reason for his demotion.

In the next game at home, against Oshawa, Andrew Rieder left in the second period with an injured shoulder that probably couldn't take another hit. This was confirmed later, when a surgeon told him to quit. He would make the next road trip and then head home for an operation, take four months to heal, and attend university in the fall.

The next morning, another Petes player was gone. Luke Hietkamp was in his father's car heading home, never to play for the Petes again.

Hietkamp had been an ongoing issue for a month as he became less and less happy with his role and ice time. Pelino told the media that if the team could make a worthwhile trade, it would, but other teams had access to the same statistics as he had: Hietkamp had scored only 15 goals in three hockey seasons.

Just a few weeks before his departure, the London-born Hietkamp had said he was a Pete forever and would "do anything for the team." In fact, he had already asked for a trade.

In his final game as a Pete, against Oshawa, he got into a fight and played well, but his dad was there, timing his minutes. The next morning, they told Pelino he was heading home.

It took more than a month to move Luke, and only then after a call from the OHL telling the team to hurry the process along. He was dealt to Kingston for a fifth-round pick in 2013.

The month of November was starting no better than October had been.

On the fourth, the Niagara IceDogs should have been primed for a loss after playing the night before, doing a bit of Saturday night partying and then getting on a bus at 8:30 A.M. and travelling three hours across Toronto for a 2 P.M. Sunday game. But by game's end, the Petes brass were wishing Nick Ritchie's older brother, Brett, hadn't shown up.

Brett's team upset the Petes 6–4, and the six-foot, three-inch, 230-pound forward scored five of the IceDogs' goals. The night before, he had six points against Guelph, making a total of 11 points, nine of them goals, in less than 24 hours. This was more points in two games than all but four Petes had recorded all season, and more goals than all but Menard had scored in the Petes' 16 games. If not for Giggy again making some sensational saves, Brett could have had eight goals before another small crowd, announced at 2,100.

Quine, a welcome addition to the Petes, got his first and second goals, but that was the only bright spot for the home team.

Pelino blasted his troops following the game, and in the next practice he took them through a two-hour on-ice session before conducting closed-door meetings in his office with individual players who were still wearing their skates. "You're either in or you're out," he told them. Unaware of how bad it really was, he thought: "There are signs of a split in the team, natural problems when part of the team goes to school and others don't, when some are older. Some guys bond together better, but those players have to make sure there is inclusion of everyone. There are times when the team comes first and the individual person second."

Koekkoek was on the edge. Somehow, he had heard that one of the hockey staff had told Tampa Bay GM Steve Yzerman he wasn't working as hard as he should be. He blew up in a confrontation with Wayne Clark. In fact, Clark wasn't the one who had talked with Yzerman. Koekkoek later met with the three coaches and Oke to make the same complaint. He never did discover who had talked with Yzerman.

Meanwhile, Pelino asked an underproducing Murphy if he wanted a trade. The young lad replied, "Whatever you think best." Pelino had told the team repeatedly to let him know if they had anything to say. No one had ever come forward, but their frustrations were seeping out in public. Mathers told the *Examiner* the team had to be better. Murphy tweeted, "Frustration builds up too fast here," and Ritchie tweeted, "Things need to be different." The coach had lost the team, but neither he nor his assistants knew it.

A few days later, Koeks told a television reporter that the team needed to keep plowing ahead and "the big guys [needed to] keep getting good minutes." Some players privately disagreed. Koeks was logging close to 30 minutes a game, which meant others were getting far less—and the team was losing. Lack of ice time caused more frustration, anger and hidden drama than any other issue, inside or outside a losing hockey team.

Hull, too, showed his frustration, angrily leaving the Petes' office after one loss, swearing and saying tersely, "I'm sick of losing." An

F-bomb may have been dropped in the conversation. He spent a lot of time in the dressing room and couldn't have missed the problems inside it.

Pelino was grouchy, and so were the players, so Pelino gathered the team to have what he described as a "State of the Union, come-to-Jesus meeting or whatever you want to call it." But he did all the talking.

"It's important we stay together. We have to move forward, stay positive, as tough as it is. We have to be together; we have a challenge. We have had some things not go our way, little things that add up, like referees not being up to par, but we have to do our best not to let these things get in our way.

"We have to learn how to deal with this no differently than lessons in life. We have to ride things out, battle harder; we can't give in or give up.

"We have to believe in each other. We have no choice but to come together, really believe in each other. We're not in a place we want to be. Everyone goes through this. How do we deal with it? We stick together. We can't let the negative frustrations creep in."

The coaches were on board. Now the 23 players had to get on the wagon and drive it over some rough terrain. Teenage boys must learn to become men. But in this case, time was running out. As Clark said, "It's like death by a million paper cuts."

After a three-and-a half-hour trip on Friday, November 9, to St. Catharines, the team booked into its hotel and ate before heading across the border on another two-hour drive to Erie, Pennsylvania.

Erie was putting $45 million into renovating its old rink, now popularly dubbed "Connor McDavid Arena" after its young superstar.

Ritchie would miss the game and Boland didn't make the trip, but Nosad and Maguire had returned. Pelino, grasping for anything, threw away the chalkboard, the *X*s and *O*s of the pre-game talk, giving them instead the "family speech."

"Tonight we start to turn our season around with energy, discipline, the best of our ability. We will drive forward, no stopping and with physicality. We will not give up; we will have no quit. If we give up, we're dead. We will all climb on board. There will be no excuses; we will rally around each other. Everyone needs to be that guy that says, 'I'm going to go for it.' All 20 guys must say, 'I'm going to carry each other on our backs.'"

The team clapped lightly, and in the hallway after the speech Pelino said, "The hockey gods better be with us after that one."

The Petes took a 2–0 lead on their fourth shot less than five minutes in. Erie took a time out. Mathers and Erie's tough guy McGuire duked it out. Mathers crushed him. The hockey gods seemed to be with the Petes, but it turned out to be an illusion. The Petes got two power-play opportunities, but Erie scored shorthanded on both of them to take over the game. Ritchie walked by in the second intermission, muttering, "This is a joke."

Their team's Jekyll-and-Hyde syndrome continued. The mood was not happy following the game. The players said they had listened to the Pelino speech but that it had little impact. Most thought his game talks were "always rehearsed." Most of them were.

After breakfast on Saturday morning, the bus left on a team shopping trip. They also toured Niagara Falls, where an unknown player, to our dismay, threw a plastic water bottle into the maelstrom below. His brain was on, but the lights were out. Betzold asked where all the water came from, and when someone putting him on said "Lake Ontario," he jokingly wondered, "Wow, what if they run out?"

The St. Catharines rink was another throwback, with wooden benches and cracked concrete floors. It had no luxury boxes or Jumbotron, just a siren that blared when the home team scored and periods began. Just as in Owen Sound, it was a rink made for hockey and nothing else. Built in the 1930s, its hockey ghosts would have plenty of stories to tell about NHL greats Bobby Hull, Stan Mikita and Red Sullivan, among so many others who had once played here for the junior St. Catharines Blackhawks. Soon it will not house an OHL team, because a new rink is being built nearby at a cost of $45 million for the start of the 2014–15 season. Peterborough was falling far behind, both on and off the ice.

The arena was jammed with some 3,100 excited people every game this season; a good team does that. It took Niagara only 58 seconds to score, leading Ritchie to comment, "It's getting uglier every night." In fairness, the Petes hit three posts and a crossbar and actually outplayed the home team. Pelino made a good point as he watched his dejected team after the loss: "*We're* taking it this bad; imagine teenagers trying to handle it."

The next morning, Pelino stopped Dagger on the way to the bus to tell him Giggy was starting that day in Mississauga. Dagger emailed his parents to let them know (they showed up anyway to support the team). Dagger hadn't lost his confidence, but the coach was losing confidence in him. He felt his veteran goalie was letting in weak goals at the wrong times in games. "I was happy with my play, but not happy with the outcome," said Dagger. "I wasn't sure what was happening, but clearly we were finding a way to lose. I never looked for excuses. Giggy was winning and I wasn't."

The team made the hour-long trip to Mississauga for an afternoon game, their third in three days and second within 24 hours. Koeks was yelling at the team and at the refs, his frustration building with each game, each goal allowed and each loss. He was putting the team on his shoulders and trying to carry it, making desperate rushes, trying to be both forward and defenceman. He was a rover on a team that couldn't afford rovers. The Petes lost 2–1.

The Petes arrived home after their three-game road trip knowing they were the worst team in the league. The weekend had cost the Petes $10,000 for rooms, food and transportation, but it had also cost them their confidence. The good news was, they couldn't go any lower in the standings.

The team was looking at three more games that week. Pelino gave all but two players Monday off. Ritchie, expected to be back for their next game, and the still-ill Boland would skate. And while the coach worried about the team's terrible showing, some of the players' school results would bring him even more concerns.

CHAPTER 12

An Education

There was so much more to playing for a junior hockey team than lacing up the skates to get on the ice. So much happened behind the scenes during a season to make sure these players grew into better adults. One of the most important duties for the coach and GM of the Petes was the players' education, and this was why Mike Oke and Mike Pelino went to the high school to meet with their education consultant after learning about several players' poor school results.

The Petes had always taken a leadership position in the way they looked after their players. Student players began their school weekdays at 8:45, took two classes, had lunch, then had another class before heading to the rink. The team's school expectations were simple: if you came to Peterborough with an 85 average, you were expected to maintain that average. If you had a 55 average, you were expected to at least keep that up. There was a policy that if you missed assignments, you didn't play, but the team had not followed through on that threat very often since Jeff Twohey's departure. Management and parents were still informed about grades as the season moved along, and there was good communication.

Petes education consultant Janet Wylie had seen a slackening of academic concern by the team in the last few years and had been in constant contact with former GM Dave Reid. She said the players needed a "plan B in case hockey doesn't work out," as it wouldn't for most. "I tell them they will get out of it [better marks and learning] what they put into it."

In the past, the Petes had had an enviable record: only two Petes had failed to get their secondary school diploma since at least 2005. Interestingly, one just couldn't handle school, and the other missed by one credit. Both were now playing in the NHL. But this year, as if mirroring their on-ice record, the players' scholastic results were the worst in all of Wylie's seven years as the team's consultant. At least four players were on their way to failure.

"We always get total support from the Petes," Wylie said. "They are as concerned about the players' education as they are about hockey. That has never changed." But still, it was the first year that overall marks had declined. "It's not because they aren't smart, but they are not motivated. I have access to their past marks, so I know they can do it, but they just aren't.

"There is not a lot of opportunity for the kids to interact with other students. They do go to the assemblies, but they don't have much time, and now the Petes do a lot more community work, leaving even less time for extracurricular school activities. I'm not painting them all with the same brush, but their marks are not good, and in some cases [the decline has been] drastic."

She said students in the past had usually turned it around when they got their first progress reports, but this time at midterm, nothing had changed.

Education issues and player attitudes had led the Petes to make adjustments. One of the first things that Roger Neilson, a high school teacher, did when he took over the team in the 1960s was enforce the schooling requirement. If you weren't going to school, you were working—never sitting around doing nothing. Coaches who came after Nielson, such as Mike Keenan, Gary Green and Dick Todd, and GM Twohey were similarly strict about making sure the players got an education. When Todd managed the team, anyone who missed school was barred from practice and games—that woke the kids up. If they were too sick to attend school, then they couldn't play or practise, and he got monthly, sometimes weekly, reports from the school.

There was no such discipline this season.

Since the Neilson and Todd days, Ontario had dropped Grade 13, and some of the players, with parental approval, were dropping out of school for a year before attending a post-secondary institution. A few years earlier, the team had loosened its strict mandatory schooling rules, and this had led to quite a split within the team between those attending and not attending school.

The biggest change, though, was in player attitudes and behaviour, which in the minds of many experienced people also had an impact on schooling results.

Trainer Brian Miller had been in junior hockey for several years before leaving for pro and returning to the Petes in 2003. When he came back, he found that junior hockey had become a big business with multimillion-dollar issues, but that wasn't all that had changed.

"This is not a blanket statement, but generally, players' agents are more hands on. With NHL players making more money, there is a push on these players to get somewhere. More promises are made to the players; players are told things that make them think they are great. They are pampered, coddled, and a great percentage of them are coming in with an attitude that 'I'm special.' There have always been players like that, but there are more who think it is more of a right now than a privilege to be here. They are too focused and anxious about getting to the next level instead of appreciating and enjoying where they are.

"I really think minor hockey and minor sports in Canada are in big trouble. It is not being run right or existing for the right reasons. I see it in players' attitudes, morals, and I'm tired of hearing adults say it is all about the kids when you see that this is furthest from the truth."

He wasn't alone in his disapproval. There wasn't one adult involved with the Petes this season who didn't agree. It was a familiar refrain in the OHL.

Miller also heard language that used to raise the referee's arm for a penalty but now raised little but eyebrows.

The *Examiner*'s Davies has seen the same changes. "When I arrived, the players had to earn their ice: now they show up and just expect to play. There seems to be a lot more involvement with agents, and parents are more plugged into what goes on."

Jody Hull, who played back in the 1980s, says he found there were striking differences in the junior game from when he played. "We had passion and a willingness to work hard every day for the organization. A lot of it today is individually driven, driven from outside voices. It was definitely more of a team-first [attitude] then."

Hull had an agent when he began in junior, but it was "more for logistical stuff. I never, and didn't have to, call my agent to ask the team, 'Why isn't Jody getting more ice or playing with this guy or that guy?' I never complained and always worked for the team first." The present-day prevalence of players who feel entitled instead of privileged "is the biggest problem in today's game." Agents negotiate contracts now that even include what type of sticks the kid has to use.

Even the pro scouts, like Ian Laperriere, the Philadelphia Flyers' director of player development in 2012–13, had seen the change. He said he was so tired of what he called the "Yeah But Generation"— players who don't listen to their coaches.

"When I talk to coaches about our prospects [Derek Mathers was one], the first thing I ask is 'How is he in the room? Is he the problem or the answer?' We don't want any bad apples. That Yeah But Generation is driving me nuts. You can't act like you know everything."

The Petes had relaxed their regime from Neilson's time. Even so, today's agents and many players knew Peterborough was still one of the "pickiest" teams when it came to discipline, school, curfews and team policy, but they questioned whether this was old-school thinking or as attractive to parents as it once was.

Years ago, parents brought their teenager to Peterborough knowing about and wanting this strictness and dedication, but players and parents were changing.

Only about half of the Petes' players were in high school. Another 10 were supposed to attend college and university, as Petes players traditionally had done, but surprisingly, this season they weren't. Several weren't attending school (with parental approval) because players said they had wanted to sign up at Fleming College or Trent University for some courses, but the team was too late in registering them. Reid agreed that he had dropped the ball on this.

The team had started the 9:30 A.M. breakfast club a few years ago so that players not in school could meet at the rink for light workouts and occasional on-ice work, but normally they spent a few hours of socializing and then ate breakfast at a nearby restaurant before the full team's afternoon meetings and practices, which usually began around

2 P.M. It was no longer mandatory to have a job or even volunteer if you weren't in school. That attitude of wanting to do little but play hockey afflicted the players who were still attending school.

"I can't believe guys like Nosad and Giugovaz, [student players] who have a chance at an NHL contract, don't come and give it everything," Pelino told me. "They, and all the others, have an opportunity others don't have, and it's beyond me why they don't realize or that it always has to be reinforced that they have to work. Why wouldn't you come to practice prepared to work as hard as you can to learn something to work on that will help at the next level? Why wouldn't you just love to get to the rink and work on things that will help you? I just can't comprehend that."

Teams around the league faced similar issues. Former Petes captain Mike Martone, now an elementary school teacher, joined in the general lament. "My mother said I'd have to keep up my school marks if I went to Peterborough, and if I didn't, I'd be coming home. The Petes were high on education. Had it been another team, I might have picked the NCAA route."

After the meeting with the education consultant, Pelino, Oke and a teacher spoke with each student player individually, taking 5 to 10 minutes to discuss his school reports. Pelino and Oke would contact the parents and either talk with them over the phone or meet with them about the grades. The players might have had excellent education packages, but they wouldn't get to post-secondary schools if they didn't have the grades. Wylie had hoped this would concern the players, but she saw puzzling lackadaisical attitudes.

Following the meetings, Pelino started a new program called "study hall." The coach and high school players would gather weekly to do homework. The Petes didn't have a players' room for studying, as some of the newer OHL rinks did, so they used the upstairs alumni room.

***

The meetings with the consultant disturbed the former teacher Pelino. At practice the next day, he felt the players weren't listening and couldn't or wouldn't do drills that he asked them to do. Some were talking when they should have been working. Some were just not ready. It was almost like school: they were not trying hard enough to move ahead.

"I guess my attitude has always been to treat them like men and get them ready for the next stages as hockey players, to grow and mature and turn them into men," said Pelino. "If I treat them like men, I expect them to be able to respond, and I think it shouldn't have to be necessary to motivate them in practice, treat them like little kids and skate them.

"They should come prepared to work to learn. At the pro level, the players come ready. These guys have to learn to get themselves motivated and not waste a day." Today, they were wasting time and were not motivated.

He stopped practice.

"You're not listening; you aren't doing what you can do. Since you can't, we will skate." He put them through 10 minutes of suicide skating drills: up and back, stop and start. It was this burning of the legs and lungs that hockey players dreaded the most at practices. Near the end of practice, he gave them a 10-minute talk, facing them as they knelt before him, alone in the rink.

"You can blame the coach, blame the injuries, blame the lack of players, but we are in last place, and you're better than that. We are 20 points behind Barrie, and we're as good [as they are]. It is not insurmountable, not impossible. It is a long journey, but we have a good team here. You just have to turn it around. You can't come to practice giggling, horsing around. When you get to the next place, whether it's Florida in the NHL or Oklahoma or the next Petes training camp, you can't just come expecting to turn it on. You have to work for it. You have to motivate yourself to get better. You come to practice to learn, to work hard and take advantage of the time to work to improve.

"Jody Hull had average skills and talent," Pelino said, although he obviously knew the former Petes 50-goal scorer was better than average. "Jody played three years here in Peterborough, where he worked at it. He didn't come to practice to fool around. [He] got drafted to the NHL and became a superstar in the working area. He worked at it, and every game, every practice, he came with his game face on.

"You have to want it," Pelino told them. "It's not impossible, but you can't come unprepared to work at practice. I shouldn't have to skate you [to wake you up]."

He skated off the ice, leaving the other coaches in charge of a non-mandatory shooting practice that most stayed for.

What the staff could never forget was that the players, despite their size, strength, skills and ambition, were still teenage boys, and as such, likely on occasion to be lazy, resentful, inattentive and difficult. Sometimes they did dumb stuff, and sometimes they got into trouble. The fans, however, didn't even know about players' marks or attitudes, and it certainly wasn't the players they were blaming for the poor season.

CHAPTER 13

Desperate Measures

On November 14, the *Examiner*'s fan columnist, Matt Campbell, ripped the Petes for not making any trades, especially after "firing Reid but not the coaches." He wrote that Albert Einstein once defined "insanity as doing the same thing over and over again, and expecting different results. He may well have been talking about this year's Petes, on and off the ice." Campbell asked what direction the team should take: building around the young players, trading veterans for a strong future or adding veterans at the cost of some future players to get into the playoffs. With Mike Pelino fighting for his job, Campbell figured the Petes would add veterans and give the fans some hope this year. "I believe the players on this team are better than their results to date," he wrote, "but they need to turn it around quickly."

He was not alone. Fans believed leadership, better power-play and shorthanded units and better defence were missing, which didn't leave much else. They also needed a single tenacious guy who would do anything for the team, a guy every team loved to have and hated to play against, a guy who played on the edge and put fear into others with either his size or ability. The Petes had had players like this in the past: Steve Downie, Tie Domi, Dallas Eakins, Doug Evans, Stan Jonathan, Bob Gainey, Doug Jarvis, Shawn Thornton and many others. These were players who would lift the rest, encouraging them with their grit and determination. Derek Mathers was the toughest and biggest, but Stephen Pierog, whom the players nicknamed Perogi, was the closest they had. This kid had sandpaper for nerves. He never quit on a shift, feared nothing and was what Pelino called a junkyard dog. He wanted the bone and would do anything to get it. And yet, before every game, while the national anthem was performed, he did something nobody knew about: he prayed and talked with his dead mother, who had died of heart disease only a few years earlier. He dedicated every game to her. With guts, compassion and heart, and the ability to compete constantly, Perogi was the prototypical Pete and a coach's dream.

The Ottawa game on November 15 would be one of the most important to the fans this season. Ottawa was just ahead of Peterborough in the standings, and the Petes were playing on home ice. There would be no excuse. A win was expected.

Game day started well when Cornel was named to the all-Ontario team for the world under-17 championship in Quebec next month. Wayne Clark was named an assistant coach, as he had been last year.

Pelino said the team was now basically the season's starting lineup. More important in terms of expectation and pressure was the return of Ritchie. He hadn't played in four weeks, but the team thought his presence would be a boost. He was itching to get back after missing 14 games. "The Big One" hated losing and wanted to be better than his brother, who had scored 14 goals in the last three weeks. He intended to show Brett who was the best hockey player in the Ritchie family, just as he had tried to do in their backyard rink when they were kids. It took Nick just 4 minutes and 36 seconds to bring the Peterborough fans happiness when his hard wrist shot slid off the crossbar and into the net.

It was incredible what a 16-year-old could bring to a game, not only in terms of competitive intensity but also with his size and physical attributes. In this game, he led the team in hits with six— only big Mathers had as many—while playing 21 minutes. Only Slater Koekkoek and Clark Seymour had more ice time. It was the way Ritchie played that was most impressive. Ottawa tested his shoulder. After one check, Ritchie shrugged the player off, bumping him six feet. His opponent was like a kid hitting a trampoline.

Ritchie got away five shots, scoring three goals to lead the team to a 5–2 victory. Recognized as the first star, he was a man playing hockey among boys. The fans, more than 2,200 of them, rose in exaltation when the final whistle was blown. The mood in the rink had changed; the crowd treated the team as though they were parents of a bad child gone good. One fan yelled again tonight, "Give them [the coaching staff] a three-year extension!"—the same staff that had been so ruthlessly maligned by anonymous so-called fans in social media. An unconvinced onlooker joked that the parade for the Memorial Cup was now being planned, while still others were unimpressed by a victory over a team that was almost as bad as the Petes. They muttered their negative comments, but the feeling of the crowd was so positive as the stands emptied that, for the first time this season, the critics' words were all but drowned out.

"In all my years, I've never heard of a bad win," said Clark, smiling after the game. This was a good win, but after the game, Ritchie was in B-Man's MASH unit, getting a pack of ice on his shoulder. His was a face full of smiles, however, because the players had named him the Burn the Boats Award winner.

"I think I did all right. Do you?" Ritchie asked. I looked for signs that he was kidding but quickly realized he was serious. He was looking for confirmation of his achievement, as if three goals, six hits, a win and the first star were not enough. "You're out of shape, kid," I joked before telling him he had done just fine. I was worried that he was in the MASH unit being treated, though. Was he okay?

Winning was like sinking a 40-foot putt or your first French kiss; you wanted more of these experiences and hoped they would lead to better things. Not everything was good, of course. How could that be the case with the Petes this season?

Tanus was benched in the third for indifferent play. The coaches felt he had hit a wall, thinking he was not used to playing so many games, but he had participated in close to 100 games last year on three different teams in Finland.

The coach now had a healthy team with extra players, giving him the opportunity to use the fear of the bench to motivate better play. Play well, or don't play. The players were aware of the threat but had watched as others around them kept making mistakes, ignoring the coach's directions and yet never missing a shift. Was this going to change? It was this perceived favouritism that bothered players the most.

While the fans went home happy, there were players who didn't because they were getting less ice time or were scratches. They were happy with the team win but unhappy because they weren't part of it.

The glow of a win didn't last long. After another loss, the sun disappeared back behind the clouds. The Petes were nine points out of a playoff spot after a third of their strange roller-coaster season was over, the team having experienced more downs than ups and show-ing signs of going off the rails. So finally, on November 22, Mike Oke and Pelino made a move, one that would relieve them of a player with a suspect attitude and, with luck, shake the team up to positive effect. They traded Trevor Murphy and Zach Lorentz to Windsor for overage right winger Derek Schoenmakers and defenceman Brandon Devlin. The trade was meant to add size, physical punch and more defence to replace Murphy's risk-taking offence and Lorentz's lack of physical oomph. Murphy, eligible for the NHL draft this year but no longer mentioned as a big-league prospect, would be returning to the Windsor Spitfires, the team he grew up wanting to play for. He also would be near his family, his school and the friends he had missed since going to Peterborough. It was a change the young man needed.

Schoenmakers, at six foot two and 189 pounds, had only three more points than Lorentz, but he had 38 penalty minutes while Lorentz, who shied away from the rough stuff, had only four. Devlin was six foot one and 204 pounds with a goal and five assists in 18 games. Murphy was three inches shorter, 31 pounds lighter and had only four points in 23 games. Both were on struggling teams, playing plenty of minutes. The two new players were to meet the Petes in London.

Both teams were trying to shake their teams up with the trade. Petes management also aimed to appease the captain's desire for new players and maybe get the upcoming road trip started in the right lane.

The bus ride to London on November 23 was quieter, tenser and more difficult than usual. The traded players were missed and the others were nervous. They were teenagers under a great deal of pres-sure, and they got little advice from the team on how to handle it.

The trading of teens, which teams rarely enjoy but which some do without blinking, is a topic few parents or players want to hear about. Petes director Pat Casey remembered when the team generally traded only because of disciplinary problems. Nowadays, trades were getting to be as common as coffee orders at Tim Hortons. He believed an age cap should be implemented, allowing trades only of final-year or overage players unless there were special circumstances. Some thought the number of trades one teen could be subjected to should be capped.

Schoenmakers's trading history illustrated the point: the Petes would be his fourth team in a year. The Kitchener-born player was drafted in the 14th round by Mississauga in 2008. He had spent a few seasons with Mississauga. Sudbury had picked him up midway through 2011–12 and then traded him to Windsor before this season. This kind of movement didn't help the OHL with recruitment.

It was the 18-year-old, Brampton-born Devlin's third team and city. The muscular son of a six-foot, six-inch former high school quarterback, Devlin wanted to come to the Petes. Granted, his only alternative was to quit and go home. The trade gave Devlin an opportunity to help the Petes get into the playoffs and moved him closer to his Brampton family. He was yet another Petes defenceman who had grown up playing forward, a top point-getter until a year before the draft. He was leaving behind a coach who was "in your face, yelling, screaming, calling you names with instant accountability" and joining one who emphasized "positive communications." He said, "Both styles are good with me."

So that was Pelino's plan, to give two underachievers a last chance to excel with a new team.

And then Schoenmakers decided not to report.

The Petes had called him the night before to welcome him aboard.

They told him how excited they were to get him and that they were looking to add a more experienced, older player to their lineup. The kid had been emotional, hurt, surprised and shocked at being traded. Neither the Petes nor the Spitfires had placed any conditions on the trade, relying on trust from both sides. The deal was official and there was no compensation rule.

Schoenmakers called Oke the day of the trip to London to say he was leaving the OHL. Pelino called Schoenmakers and his father, but the kid wasn't coming. He'd had enough. He was going home to Kitchener to think about enrolling at university there. Koekkoek reached out to him (at Pelino's request) in an email, but to no avail. An overager knows when he's had enough. The trade stood: the Petes had moved two good players for one.

The OHL did not allow either team to talk with players before a trade unless they had a no-trade clause and had waived that right. The Petes had little way of knowing about Schoenmakers's thoughts, although their scouts might have put an ear to the ground and found out.

Pelino was in touch with the family all weekend, still trying to talk Schoenmakers and his father into becoming members of the Petes family. It was a lost cause. He wouldn't be in London tomorrow, nor in the lineup for any game for the Petes.

Budweiser Gardens in London gave the Knights what they needed: money, something small-market teams like the Petes didn't have and couldn't get.

Their star centre, Max Domi, who chose the Knights over the NCAA, was one example of London's recruitment powers, but the team's European players were even more illustrative of what small-market teams couldn't afford. Brothers Dale and Mark Hunter, former NHLers who had slyly pieced together a team through drafts and trades, operated the team. Some ascribed their success to the money, but the Hunters were wily, hard-nosed hockey people who knew their stuff—Dale behind the bench, Mark from the GM's office, although both could do either job.

The Petes wanted to set a tone, so they started Mathers. Pelino also knew more than 100 of his family and friends were in the stands, some wearing Petes jerseys and holding "Go Petes Go" signs. (One sign, in an allusion to rap singer Eminem, boasted, "Mathers is the Marshal.") Mathers was from nearby Strathroy, and many of his family and friends would follow him to Sarnia the next night.

The rink was packed with 9,000 people because London won games and played in an outstanding facility. Tonight, despite Dagger's incredible effort, the Knights beat the Petes 2–0. (Except for the London broadcaster, no one noticed that when the London goalie was skating off the ice, Dagger made sure he got the game puck for his first shutout—a nice gesture from one goaltender to another.)

Dagger started again the next night in Sarnia.

Mathers's bigger but younger brother and two others stood out in the crowd, wearing Petes jerseys and with signs held high, cheering him and the team on. Betzold's parents had driven from Maryland for the game, still in awe of these western Ontario inks.

Sarnia was playing its third game in three nights and should have been tired. It was 3–0 for the home team after one period. Pelino switched goalies, more to pick up his team than to blame Dagger, but Giggy missed the first three shots, making it 6–0 for Sarnia. Was this kid sending a message to the coach? All the shots looked stoppable. Dagger went back in.

Mathers's brother and his fellow supporters stripped off their jerseys in embarrassment, but they put them back on when Ritchie scored. Cornel had some chances but couldn't capitalize.

There was so much fan-generated pressure on Cornel to perform. Other players in the league who had been picked later in the draft— Jared McCann, Spencer Watson, Samuel Bennett, Michael Dal Colle, Josh Burnside, Blake Clarke, Josh Ho-Sang, Robby Fabbri— all were ahead of Cornel in the stats. But those players were with more talented teammates, on better lines and getting more ice time. Until this weekend, Eric had been getting only five or six minutes a game, but now Pelino placed him in a better line while Quine sat for two periods for indifferent play.

Cornel said he didn't pay too much attention to the other rookie stats at first, but then "I put pressure on myself. As the season went on, I just tried to outwork and outplay the 16-year-old on the other team we played. I focused on playing well on other parts of my game, not just statistics." He was one of the team's hardest workers, on and off the ice; unlike other rookies, he was the last one, besides fitness fanatic Dagger, to leave the weight room, and he was not a concern to anyone internally.

The Petes were throttled by Sarnia, 8–2. And their coaches were angry. Pelino left the dressing room after telling players to carry all the trainers' equipment, from the skate sharpener, tool kit and sticks to glove warmers. The players hadn't helped themselves on the ice; they might as well help off of it.

After these two losses, it was official: Peterborough was the worst team in the league. Sudbury, with a tie, was eight points ahead for that last playoff spot. It was November 24 and Ottawa was two points ahead. After a third of the season, it was safe to say what was on the minds of most fans and many players: the season was over, their playoff hopes dead. It was not something players or coaches would dare to utter. They would not quit, but something drastic would have to happen for them to start winning. They didn't seem to have the horses to haul the wagon. The team was a sulky stuck in the mud, spinning its wheels. The boats weren't burning, they were sinking.

It got worse. Dagger was in net for two road games because Giggy had been late for or missed a meeting, was arguing openly with some veteran teammates and didn't help other rookies do their duties. He had apologized, but the kid didn't get it yet. If word leaked out about his attitude, he could find his name sliding down or even erased from the NHL's Central Scouting rankings. Scouts and teams didn't want a player with those kinds of problems when there were so many options.

After the Sarnia game, before the coach and others got on the bus, there was a high-octane verbal battle between Koekkoek and Giggy. It was short but filled with some salty language from Giggy, whom Koeks accused of not working hard enough and of not doing his rookie duties. Both charges were true, but too many other players were present—this was not the time or place for a dressing-down. Other rookies, tired of the captain's controlling ways, bit their tongues, even though they wanted to shout at him too. It was a telling scene.

Pelino and Oke, who never knew about the brouhaha, later talked on the phone on the bus about blogger chatter. They were disturbed by a tweet that a Petes player was reported to have sent after the game. Pelino jumped angrily from his seat—without actually having seen the tweet—and stalked back to the players. He reminded them quietly but firmly that they should not be tweeting about the team. Then he had Garfat check the messages. There was one from Mathers saying it was nice to play before family and friends and be close to home. There was nothing wrong with that message, but the blogger had interpreted it to mean Mathers wanted out. There was another tweet from Quine, who was not happy about sitting, saying he was "mapping out my ending." He would later say they were only words from a song. A storm in a teacup.

Pelino had bigger worries than the blogosphere. Still on the bus, he was on the phone with Oke to talk about where the team was headed. He wondered if it was time to talk with the president and maybe the board, to see which way they wanted to go as they moved forward with the rest of the season. The options were: make trades to improve immediately, trade veterans to improve in the future, or stand pat. The Petes had lost 11 of the last 12 games and were no better than when Reid was fired. They might have been worse. Was it because of Reid's drafting? Maybe they didn't have the players they needed to win. Or was it because of the coach?

It was 2:30 A.M. when the bus got back from London. The coaches were not unhappy about the hour; Saturday night had turned into Sunday morning, but at least the bars were closed. Coaches had a responsibility not only to hockey fans but also to these young players and their parents.

On the drive home on this below-freezing winter night, a bare-armed teenaged girl could be seen staggering in the main downtown street, held upright by a teenage male, maybe a stranger, probably a friend, as they both tried to walk without falling. Only steps away was a group of five other young adults, also staggering, also stepping from the protection of the sidewalk onto the street. Police were nearby because almost every weekend at closing time there was trouble, usually involving young people whose minds were clouded by alcohol, drugs or both, their parents unaware they were staggering, lost, drunk and unprotected.

While the Petes players were losing and missing out on some things in their young lives, surely their parents would rather have them on a bus with Pelino, Hull and Clark, out of harm's way.

It wasn't only Pelino who was mulling over the bigger picture. A couple of weeks earlier, on November 12, both Pelino and Oke had attended one of the regular board meetings, those long, drawn-out monthly ones without an agenda. They had been asked some hard questions: Had the coach lost the players in the room? Did he need any support on the bench? Oke told them the coach still had the players. Pelino told them he'd coach anywhere with his present staff. Of course, they were hardly likely to denounce one another when both were in the room.

The board discussed other issues after Pelino and Oke had left. John Oke had resigned; with his son now attending board meetings, he wanted to avoid the apparent conflict of interest. Now the board was looking for as many as three new members. Already they had reached out to a few possible candidates, but they had also taken the more public step of placing ads for applicants. After this and some other items, including budget and personnel issues, had been dealt with, the board went back to talking hockey.

Fans were calling for the heads of the board members and Pelino—and not the players, who they believed were leaving it all out on the ice and doing the best they could. In fact, inside the dressing room there were individual agendas, contracts, agents and even Team Canada pursuits. For Koekkoek, it was his third straight losing season, and fans wondered whether another captain would want out and how long Ritchie would be content in the losing den. These were difficult times, and the mood among Petes fans was getting ugly. The board members were aware of what was being said, but they decided to stick with their present coach and co-managers. They would tough it out.

More than wins and losses were eating up the attention of Pelino. Team Canada didn't invite a disappointed Koeks to camp. Pelino had a one-on-one with him to console him, but also to make sure the kid was still with the group. Koeks replied he was. After this last bus trip, there were more concerns about team bonding. The coach and Oke also met with the assistant captains—and got another shock.

Although Pelino had asked throughout the season that his players be honest with him, the frankness of one came as a surprise. Mathers told the two that Pelino had lost the room. It was a private conversation that would later have serious repercussions. Perhaps provoked by Mathers's comment, Pelino called another "come to Jesus" meeting before the next practice.

"I want to make sure nothing is falling between the cracks and we are all going in the same direction," he told me. "With our start, there is tension, finger-pointing, assessing of blame, and I want to make sure we aren't falling off the wagon, basically, and make sure the players are still trusting the coaches. I want to tell the players we are all in this together, that we're the solution to the problem.

"[Right now] it is not fun being a Petes player, coach, board member, fan or parent. The biggest challenge is that the players have to rally around each other, follow the coaches and leaders."

He was right. Many of the players had given up. Hull was so frustrated he couldn't sleep and was thinking of leaving. Board members were taking the heat and didn't enjoy coming to the rink. Parents were hearing, and seeing, the problems. Although many of their sons didn't share their worries with them, they were seeing the losses, reading the papers, listening to the fans and wondering if their sons could survive, never mind improve, in that environment. It was not fun.

Pelino told the team: "When a general says go into the river you do it. No one is absolved from the blame, no one is being traded, nobody has asked out. Even if you want out, you won't be traded unless it is beneficial to the team. What has happened in the past [trading marquee players at their request] will not happen here again. There is no escape. As a coaching staff, we are not going anywhere; we have the board's support. They believe in us. There is no easy solution, but there is no escape."

The players asked no questions, made no comments.

Pelino was frustrated and wondered why bad things continued to happen, why they had been this way for the last two years—last year with all the injuries, this year with more injuries and then the trade that didn't work out. "It's like a cloud is hanging over the Petes."

That day at practice, Giggy took a shot on the knee and fell to the ice, writhing and screaming in pain, but a few minutes later he was back in the net. Practice hadn't even stopped.

Pelino received an email from Giggy the next day—game day, November 27—saying his knee was swollen and he wouldn't be able to play against Oshawa. He was at school and hadn't seen the trainer; he had made the determination on his own, putting the team in a terrible position. Dagger had already been told he wouldn't be playing. Luckily, even though he had yet to win a single game, Dagger had the best attitude on the team and was glad to get the opportunity.

Dagger outworked every other player. He spent at least two hours a day on mental and physical workouts, always preparing, watching video, fine-tuning. Even the players agreed his regime was probably over the top, but they were mesmerized by his dedication and commitment. Before and after every practice and game, he worked with weights, stretched, did yoga and looked after his diet. It wasn't a new thing. His father, Tony, remembered always having to get him to his youth games or practices two hours before their scheduled start; once, when he didn't, at his son's request he wrote a letter apologizing to the coach.

"I take no days off from fitness," said Dagger. He was Giggy turned inside out.

The backup goalie would have to be the injured Giggy, because the Petes had no time to call in someone else.

The buzz in the building before game time was all about the Schoenmakers trade going sour and how a team could screw this up by not writing in a conditional clause. The Petes, like most teams, had not commonly taken that sort of precaution before because trades were based on mutual trust and usually worked out. The Petes had scouted the trade heavily (or thought they had) and never believed a player wouldn't report.

The Petes could have, and probably should have, won half the games they had lost this year, but they hadn't. Nothing could change those painful losses. But today was tomorrow's yesterday; they had to concentrate on what lay ahead. That night, November 27, they could have hung their heads and given up after the Generals took a 3–0 lead, but instead, something different, something special, happened. The Petes slowly took the game back. They pushed Oshawa into making mistakes, forced them into their zone, knocked them on their asses, put their work boots on and, as one fan said, "outplayed the piss out of them."

Maybe it had been the week of player tension, the rifts that had divided them, that now suddenly and unexpectedly brought them together. Families usually get closer when they have gone through tough times. Maybe it was because they learned how dark and dingy it was in the basement. It could have been the line of Cornel, Maguire and Hatcher that made the difference when they shoved a couple of hard-working shifts down the Generals' throats, sending a message to them—and to their own bench—that they weren't going to give up, that the others could hang their heads if they wanted to, but they were not quitting. Maybe the other lines saw this energy, fed off it and agreed it was time.

Maybe it was Captain Koeks saying, "The hell with this, let's get these assholes," or maybe, just maybe, when Quine got that first goal, they saw that Goliath was no better than them, was not a giant after all, and if David dug down deep enough he could slay him.

The Petes fought off five consecutive Generals power plays—five of them! How dominant the Petes were when they outworked and outchecked and got all those loose pucks, as they did in the second and third periods of this game, just as Reid and Pelino had wanted them to do.

But only in stories do the Davids win. In the end, the Petes lost, 3–2.

Losing resulted in no points, rewards or celebrations. It brought no relief to their pain. Oshawa knew they had been in a close game, that they had been lucky. If two pucks hadn't hit goalposts, the Petes would have come out of it with a victory. They outplayed, outdug, outhit and outsimplified the game, each player taking his man and dominating the action. Wave after wave after wave. Boone Jenner and the boys were happy to win, knowing they had just played a team they wouldn't want to face again.

Yes, the Petes had been through this before, winning a period or two, only to play poorly in the second or third, but this time it seemed different. The Generals had made their own mistakes, got lazy and weren't playing as a family. They were not ready to do battle against hungry warriors.

Maybe, just maybe, this was the spark that would ignite the Petes' fire and they could look in the mirror and say, "You know what? If we play every shift like that every game, those pucks are going to hit the mesh instead of the posts, and the hockey gods will start working for us."

The fans did not go home happy. But they did go home feeling like something was changing.

The Petes got their first break two nights later. Two of the better Bulls players had been suspended for a few games after a brawl. The Bulls, playing their second game in 24 hours, had coach/GM George Burnett looking at a chance to give their backup goalie, Charlie Graham, a start over superstar Malcolm Subban. The hockey gods were aligned for the Petes on Christian Faith Night as Toronto Maple Leafs goalie James Reimer, brought in by chaplain Tim Coles, met the fans and team.

Giggy got the start after having missed the Friday and Saturday games for disciplinary reasons and then Tuesday's because of the bruised knee.

The Petes' dressing room was noisier than usual, and players seemed looser before going out for the warmup. Clark's quote on the dressing room board was simple: "Be quick but don't hurry."

With attendance officially pegged at 2,776, there was an uneasy feeling in the stands. Which team would show up? The faltering, failing one or the tough, grinding team they saw Tuesday? It didn't take them long to find out. The Petes hemmed Belleville into their own end for the first two minutes and then the Bulls scored on a broken play. But the Petes rallied, and Perogi tied it up using that great shot of his, the shot that was so often seen in practice. It was not a lively game in the hitting category. If two things lost the OHL fans, it was the lack of hitting and the lack of excitement, items that went hand in hand. You could see non-physical hockey in beer leagues. The fans weren't paying big bucks to see games without hits, without fights, with little individualism and only systems. They needed to be entertained.

Belleville took the game to the Petes and at one point were outshooting them 21–10. Pelino leaned on Quine's line, with Menard and Ritchie. He was surprised to see that Koekkoek had logged only 12:30 in the first two periods, a low amount for the horse. Hull explained he was saving the captain's energy for the third. The Petes regained their composure after coaches watched some video clips during intermission. Regulation time ended in a tie.

Koekkoek played 12 minutes in the third for a total of 24:30, his lowest of the season, but this was still plenty of ice time, even if it was not enough for his liking. He added almost three minutes in the five-minute overtime, playing more than any of his teammates. Quine dazzled the Bulls and fans with his dipsy-doodle movements. Ritchie looked like a man playing against kids three years older than him and hit two posts. The rink came alive for the first time this season, with chants of "Go Petes Go!" There was applause for their efforts, yells and screams for close calls. People were clutching their seats.

Overtime was a thriller. Steven Varga fell at the blue line and the Bulls came in on a breakaway, but Giggy made a sensational save. One enthusiastic fan said, "Can you imagine if it was this exciting all the time and the team played like this?" An NHL scout jumped into the conversation. "If they played like this all the time, there wouldn't be overtime."

Quine scored a highlight goal in the shootout. Belleville missed, Menard missed, Jordan Subban—goalie Malcolm's brother—scored, but Ritchie, with the insouciance of a surgeon, put one by Graham, and then Giggy stopped the third shot and raised his hands in victory. Euphoria, relief and noise, not heard in the building all season, filled the arena.

The players gathered onto the ice, embracing each other and then saluting the cheering crowd, which gave them a well-deserved standing ovation. The final score was 4–3. There was joy in Petesville. The team needed the win. The fans needed it too. As Pelino said later, "Sometimes it is better to win an overtime shootout like this—better for morale, excitement and getting the juices flowing." Indeed, it gave the fans a more exciting Showtime.

As Giggy left the ice for the dressing room, the excitement overtook him. Before he could reach the privacy of the room, out of earshot of children, adults and some nearby Christian faithers, he yelled, with that alligator smile on his face, "Fucking right, boys!" Everyone understood. All was forgiven.

When the team finally got settled together, the noise was electric. It was their best win, only the second of this long, dreadful month. Pierog got the Boat, Giggy the 212 award.

Pelino spoke for two minutes. "This is traction, boys. Let's use this as a starting point. Let's get this going. Enjoy this, bottle this feeling and let's use it for the new start." A few F-bombs were thrown in, and the team slapped their sticks on the floor. Stick boy Iain then shouted, "Showstopper!"

Brought in by Pelino and Coles, Reimer congratulated the team, which presented him with a signed jersey. When all the adults got out of the way, the music was jacked, the players joked and the dressing room's jocular mood continued like a high school party. Tampa Bay's Steve Yzerman, the former Petes star whose banner flew in the rafters above the ice along with those of Murphy, Gainey, Bowman and Todd, waited in Pelino's office to see his draft pick, Koekkoek, for a 20-minute update.

Yzerman had been barely noticed during the game, certainly not by the media, keeping that low profile he preferred. He talked with Koekkoek about his play, told him not to worry about not being picked by Team Canada because he also hadn't been picked several times, and encouraged him to stick with the Petes. He asked about Koekkoek's shoulder, his willingness to keep learning, and said Tampa Bay just wanted to assure him they were still with him. He took some time to remind Slater to be a team player and leader, but generally, it was a keep-up-the-good-work meeting.

Koekkoek and a few other veterans went to a pizza place after the game without inviting some of the younger guys.

There were always reminders around the team that hockey was a game and should be put into perspective. Mike Oke continued scouting, putting 70,000 kilometres on his vehicles, or his "other office." Two days after he returned from one scouting trip in Ottawa, his mother, Mary Ellen, died at 65 after suffering from cancer for a year. It was the first time the general public, and some of those people who were so harshly and personally critical of his board member father, would learn of the family's pain. Mike took only two days off to mourn his mother's death.

He kept busy to keep his mind off the loss. There had been only six days in November when he hadn't watched a hockey game. In a typical month, he watched as many as 46 full or partial games in arenas large and small throughout Ontario and the United States. Some tournament weekends, he watched some or all of 20 games. And after seeing the Petes in November, he and his scouts were wondering if the players they had drafted were good enough.

CHAPTER 14

Nightmare on Roger Neilson Way

Even though the Petes had won their last home game in a thriller, November had been a disaster. The Petes played 14 games and won only two. They had allowed more goals than any other team while scoring the second-fewest. Not one of the Petes was in the top 20 in league scoring. They did not have a single player with a positive plus/minus rating. Koeks, their best player, was minus-23. Their best offensive forwards, Quine and Menard, were minus-18.

December started ugly, too, with a 5–2 loss to Sarnia on Saturday the first. Pelino, grumpy again on Monday, had yet another session with the players, but they had tuned him out. Their habit now was to bow their heads when he talked, not daring to look at each other for fear of laughing. The players had given him a secret nickname, Video Guy, not because he was always showing them videos but because the exercise seemed so pointless. When he ran the videos, he said things like, "There are two things we need to do," and then he'd list three things. Or he'd say he didn't have many points to make and then verbalize 20. All they heard were his mistakes. And even though these were often minuscule, they struck the kids as funny.

"We didn't care who would be the head coach," said one veteran. "We just wanted that guy gone. The team lost respect. Players weren't showing up at meetings on time, the rookies were immature, not getting to practice on time, and Coach wasn't doing anything about it. Players were trash-talking him—not to his face, but he had to hear it. Koeks would argue with coaches in the dressing room. Pelino had let the players take over and wasn't getting anything out of them. All the bad things we said about him didn't really make sense; even if they weren't true, we were saying them, but no matter what he said, we were not listening. There was no accountability, no discipline. People would screw up and they kept playing. He changed lines every game, every period, every shift. It made no sense."

Pelino never admitted it, but he likely knew by now how divided the team was. He did what most coaches do in a tough situation: he continued to hope that his veterans would turn the season around for him.

The next game, in Belleville, featured so much bad luck for the losing Petes that assistant coach Jody Hull, shaking his head in wonderment, said after the game, "I might sacrifice a chicken at centre ice."

A hurt and disappointed D'Agostini, after stopping close to 40 shots in the 3–2 overtime loss, overheard Koeks tell Nick Ritchie in the dressing room, "Had Dagger stopped that soft one, we would have won." It hurt, but the goalie kept his mouth shut. The point they earned helped them inch to within 10 of Sudbury for the elusive playoff position, but it didn't unwind the emotional tightrope on which the players were precariously balanced.

The coaches shook their heads as they watched video of the Belleville goals before getting on the bus. It was another "could have, should have" game. It was what office staff were now commonly calling "another day in paradise."

Ritchie turned 17 on game day, December 5, and the team didn't say a word. He got a goal and assist for his birthday, but no attention from the team or media. The next day, the reliable B-Man would have a cake for him in the dressing room.

On December 8, the team left Peterborough, where sprinkling rain splashed on green grass, only to hit snow-covered highways, blowing wind and bitter cold five and a half hours later in Sudbury.

To break up the trip, the team had stopped at a restaurant in Orillia. It didn't matter that the team had eaten breakfast sandwiches and wraps only two hours earlier. They stopped to eat pre-ordered chicken parmesan and salads and to welcome newcomer Brandon Devlin with the butter-on-the-shoe trick, performed this time by rookies Eric Cornel and Josh Maguire (one distracts, the other spreads it).

Back on the road, assistant coach Wayne Clark called Brett Findlay, and then Greg Betzold, to his seat to show them video of Thursday night's game, pointing out the good things, reminding them to improve on the bad ones. During the trip, the team watched the video of the F-bomb-filled television documentary *24/7: Road to the NHL Winter Classic,* which followed the first half of the New York Rangers' and Philadelphia Flyers' seasons.

It was too early to go to the rink when the team got to Sudbury, so the bus stopped at a Tim Hortons for refreshments. When they were wearing their team sweats to a game instead of their suits and ties, as they were today, they were supposed to zip them up, remove their ball caps or toques, and wear team shoes in public. That was the rule. Giggy went into Tim's wearing Superman pajamas, an unzipped jacket and runners. New man Devlin told him he should clean up his act. "You're representing the Petes, for God's sake." Giggy just smiled and told him to relax. Devlin just shook his head. It was not the new guy's place to say anything more; besides, the captain had given up trying to reform Giggy's dress habits weeks ago.

They had travelled for almost six hours for a 7 P.M. game to be played in a hockey barn that was built out of concrete and wood in 1951, another throwback to what used to be. Once they got to the rink, they shed their track clothes for warmup shorts and shirts and limbered up by tossing around a football.

Steven Trojanovic was back, but he didn't really want to play because he felt his groin was strained. Steven Varga played with a soft cast, while Peter Ceresnak had Slovakia on his mind: he was leaving tomorrow to join the national junior team's camp for the world junior championship.

The Sudbury rink seated more than 5,000, and in a winning season the team nearly filled it, but this year the team was playing so-so. They were still in the playoff hunt, however, and 11 points ahead of Peterborough in the standings. Attendance was just more than 3,000. It helped the fans' energy when the Petes didn't show up for the first period and Giggy looked as shaky as the last leaf on an autumn maple tree. In the first five minutes, the Petes were outshot 10–0, and Giggy didn't handle a single shot with confidence. It took Peterborough 12 minutes to get its first shot. Even when Sudbury took the first penalty, the Petes didn't manage a shot on net. And then they took a bench minor for too many men on the ice, and the

Wolves went ahead on their 13th shot. "Woo, woo, woo!" yelled a fan who had had too many pops while the upholstered wolf, the team mascot, was propelled across the ice in the team's customary celebration of a home goal.

Tanus did what he could to energize the team, making a big hit on a much bigger Sudbury player who went down like a deer in hunting season. Koeks fired a floater that went off Tanus's stick and into the net on only the team's second shot, but Sudbury got that one back and, after the first period, had outshot the Petes, 16–5. Giggy and the team might have played their worst period of the year, but the score was still only 2–1.

When the Wolves scored on their first shot of the second period, only two and a half minutes in, Giggy was pulled. Dagger gave the rookie a glove shake as they passed on the ice and then gave the team some life, doing what those who study, practise and train hard do: come in from the cold and perform well. The Petes started to take over.

Quine put a wrist shot past the Sudbury goalie as Pelino started switching up the lines and using Cornel more. Cornel was getting better, stronger and faster and he was playing with more confidence and tenacity. He was a coach's dream; he listened, learned and strove to get better—like a 16-year-old Dagger.

Sudbury was ahead 4–2. Ceresnak went heavily into the boards. He complained that his head was sore, and after he tried for a few more shifts, Hull sat him for the night. Peter worried about leaving for Slovakia with a concussion, but he would be okay.

Brett Findlay knew his family and friends were in from Echo Bay, about a three-hour drive, and maybe that played a role in his game—or maybe, as he said, "It's the northern air." Whatever it was, the Petes hoped he bottled it for future games. He played like his personality: vibrant, fun and competitive. Finner scored two highlight goals, one a backhander after deking two players, the other a creative passing play from Quine and a goalie deke to tie the game with seven minutes left. The goals were what Quine and Koeks called "sick, disgusting"—meaning wonderful.

Dagger took a shot to the mask behind his ear that floored him. Maybe he should get hit every game.

Overtime was needed again, the Petes' third extra session in as many games. The scoreboard showed that it was the fourth period, that the teams had taken 40 shots each and that the score was 4–4. Adam Murray had never seen that on a clock before and thought maybe the fourth Petes shooter would decide the game, but he would have to wait longer than that. Dagger made two unbelievable glove saves and Cornel, the 16th shooter, ended an entertaining game.

There was no more "Woo, woo, woo!" from the Sudbury stands.

Outside the bus after the game, players worked their phones, finally able to talk with others about positive team-related things. Ritchie, whose mood had changed in the last few days from a jovial kid to a more focused, silent one, said little. Clark said the kid was not happy with the way he had been playing. Ritchie was happy for the team, but he wanted to be far better, to dominate and be the best player every game. It was not happening, and he had become sullen. Stephen Nosad boarded the bus smiling, holding an ice pack to his shoulder; Frankie Menard had an ice bag on some leg bruises; and Varga held a bag to his wrist. Ice was the frozen magical medicine of hockey. Hull got his hurting back prepped for the long ride home with a cushion, although winning helped alleviate the pain.

Koeks was even smiling. He missed Clark Seymour, nicknamed Seabiscuit, his suspended partner, on the ice, but Seymour was now laughing, slapping people on the back, knowing that even though he hadn't played because of the suspension, he too believed the team was turning a corner. Trojanovic had played 30 minutes and, when asked about his groin, smiled, admitting, "It feels good now." Cornel, the shootout hero, was still grinning as he performed his rookie duties, loading equipment with the training staff and fellow rookies Maguire, Betzold, Tanus and maybe Giggy, if he was in the mood.

As we pulled away from the rink, unfamiliar sounds emanated from the back of the bus: teenagers shouting, laughing, farting, burping and basking in the joy of winning.

There were bodies all over the place on the bus heading home. Pelino was stretched out in his seat, softly snoring, his head hanging into the aisle. Hull was leaning forward with his face in a pillow. Some of the players were lying in the aisle, not daring to sleep for fear of missing something—or worse, being the victim of a practical joke. The players were loud, laughing, happy, enjoying this time together as they had on no other bus trip this season.

Assistant GM Aaron Garfat was wide awake beside me, complaining about the noise. Noise? Noise on the Peterborough Petes bus after a game? Shame! Shame! For the first time this season, stories were being told by players; there was girl talk, requests for a movie and shouts to the new bus driver to step on the pedal, while various gases emerged from bodies that had swallowed pizzas, wings, power drinks and water. For most of the five-and-a-half-hour journey, there was noise punctuated regularly by Ritchie's unique and loud laugh.

"Shut the hell up," the tired Garfat, who could not get to sleep, whispered halfway through the trip. "They haven't shut up since we left."

"I love this," Clark said, smiling, before he too dozed off.

***

Several players were late for the early skills competition on Tuesday, December 11, so Pelino sat them on the bench for 10 minutes before the real practice began. Pelino worked them hard, although in the last few weeks he had been ending Tuesday practices with fun competitions. It was probably not a coincidence that the team had been coming together at the same time: humour sometimes does that for a team. Fun was expected tonight as the players, directors, staff and spouses had Christmas dinner at a local golf club.

Two players joined the adults at each table in the dining room. At some point in the night, rookies, coaches, directors and staff all went to the front of the room to sing a carol. Giggy and the other rookies also had to tell jokes. While most told simple knock-knock jokes, Giggy broke out with a show-stopper: "Why doesn't Santa have many children of his own?" Answer: "He only comes once a year." Koeks had been asked to speak by a director, but the captain, who had won public speaking contests in grade school, declined, surprising and disappointing the board. Nobody asked why he didn't speak, but he wasn't a happy member of the family.

The players got new winter jackets, but few of them took the time to thank the board; some even told others they would rather have had cash. It was the first time the board had invited the players to this annual affair—they usually had their own functions. The players probably didn't want to be there, among the "old folks," but some enjoyed the night. They still were teens among adults. They got out as soon as it was allowed, some going off to a downtown movie, wearing their black jackets with the Petes logo on the front.

There had been Christmas chuckles during an enjoyable night, reminding everyone that the Petes were a family, but there was a trade deadline coming up, bringing fear and anxiety with it. Teams had until the following Wednesday to trade before the Christmas trade freeze, and then, beginning a few days after the holiday, they had until January 9 to make trades. The players suspected that some of their teammates, the same ones who had been praised and thanked at the dinner by President Devlin, would soon be gone.

The practice on December 12 was one players remembered as another turning point, one that pushed them even further away from their coach. Pelino had them bag skating: this was a strenuous, sweaty exercise, up and down the ice, tiring them out on the day before a game, something that hadn't been done all season.

Just before the gruelling skate began, the players said sarcastically that this should be good for the next night, and Pelino replied, "I know what I'm doing, guys."

"Then we'd go out and lose," said a veteran.

And they did.

In between periods of the next game, Koeks appeared to be pouting, his head down, muttering that he wanted out.

Rumours had been circulating in the blogosphere at least since early December that Quine and Koeks wanted out. The team and media, incredibly, paid attention to these blogs. Koeks worried Pelino the most because his mood rubbed off on Quine. The coach now thought that Koeks wasn't a good leader in the dressing room, that he didn't have a team attitude and certainly didn't treat the rookies as part of the team, all the things most of the veterans had known when Koeks was named captain back in September. Pelino thought his captain should also be working harder in practice, doing the extra things he had done during the last two seasons, like hitting the weights to improve the bad shoulder and taking extra ice time after practice to work on his hockey skills. Now he was usually one of the first off the ice. However, he was also one of the hardest-working players in practice, if not *the* hardest-working, and a better listener than most.

Pelino thought he wasn't playing as well this year, either, and wondered if that was the reason for the poor plus/minus stats. The coach had had several talks with him that sometimes brought tears to the 18-year-old's eyes, but the talks didn't seem to change his play. Koeks was frustrated, but so was his coach. It made for an even worse atmosphere in the dressing room.

Many of the players said that whenever the team got down, Koekkoek lost heart: he didn't believe the team could come back. "Koeks was very negative, always thinking there could be no comeback."

"Captains of the past were positive, pushing us on," said one veteran. "He talked back to coaches, yelled down to rookies who were intimidated by him and wouldn't say anything back, but behind his back they didn't appreciate his honesty or openness. He was always talking and thinking about the NHL instead of the team."

Koekkoek had privately unburdened himself about whether he wanted out of Peterborough. "I've tried to make it work," he said. "They keep telling me they will do something to better the team, and I keep asking Mike [Pelino], but at what point . . . something has to give at some point, and I'm not quitting, but I want to win. We all want to win and I don't see anything that shows me any different. I haven't asked to be traded or asked out, but if I don't see it happening, I will. Two months ago I expressed my frustrations and told everyone we needed help, but [we] didn't get it. "

It had been a tough year to be captain, and while Koeks knew he owed Peterborough a lot, as he had said after the NHL draft, he was not sure how much he owed. "There has been a lot of pressure with the Petes not doing well and struggling again this year. Everywhere you go, someone in the community has a solution. The adults can think whatever they want, but we are on the ice doing what we can. We all know how frustrating it is. Nobody has to tell us. We are frustrated. We want to win too.

"Every time there is a win, it's a new hope, but it doesn't happen. The team doesn't make the trades; they could have, and they made some bad trades lately. I've talked with Mike several times about it, and they say they will make some trades, but they don't. They have the draft picks; what are they waiting for? Or they say there is nothing out there, and then [Jake] Cardwell and [Brock] Beukeboom [players traded by other teams] come up.

"The hardest thing, probably, for the team are the fans here. I know I'm trying to do too much on the ice because of the team. I try to do everything and anything to win. I want to win. Everyone has advice on how to do it, but you can't listen to everyone. As far as rumours about me leaving, I don't get involved. People are going to say what they want; I can't take that too serious. I know what the truth is. We're trying here."

He was disappointed at not getting a call for Canada's national junior team, unlike his buddy Morgan Rielly, but Yzerman had met with him. "He's a good person and told me what he had to go through and that I have to go through all the ups and downs. It was a good meeting. I really have a lot of respect for him. He said not being named to Team Canada wasn't the end of the world; there is always next year. It hurts, but you can't cry over it. They told me they were going with veterans. I know people are talking about my plus/minus, but like he said, it doesn't matter. I know what I can do, and yes, I am the type that will prove them wrong."

Koekkoek had blamed Oke and Pelino for his not getting a Team Canada invite. The Petes certainly weren't promoting their players like some of the other teams in the Canadian Hockey League, but Koeks hadn't been invited because Team Canada had enough good defencemen.

Whether he would continue to play in Peterborough or on another OHL team, this was one determined hockey player. Koeks, blamed by some of the players for the bad dressing room atmosphere as if nobody else could lead the way out, was just an 18-year-old kid who believed in himself and wanted more for himself and his team. And he couldn't see it happening in his present job.

The upcoming stretch of three games in four days could decide the Petes' fate. The team would likely be blown up if they lost all of them. If they won at least two, there would probably still be trades to try for a playoff run. If they won three, the coaches and Oke knew they were still short a player or two to make a real run. Trades seemed necessary, just as the captain had said all season long.

Hull had bought horseshoes and new sleeveless black T-shirts with the words HOW HARD DO YOU WANT IT? on the front and TAKE NO DAYS OFF on the back to try to change the team's luck, but it hadn't worked. Some of the players were still wearing BURN THE BOATS shirts; others, the new ones. It was confusing. They were confused.

Giggy and Dagger had been singled out by some fans as if they were responsible for the team's losing ways. That's huge pressure for two teenagers already under a lot of stress as last man back, trying to backstop their team, impress scouts and stop every shot aimed at them. As Giggy said, "It is a crazy thing we are doing," getting in front of blazing black pucks coming at their heads. On December

14, he let in a softie over his shoulder that turned the game in favour of Ottawa, who won 5–2. The Petes returned to their dressing room as if to a funeral.

A change of T-shirts and slogans hadn't helped. A visit before the game from former Petes captain Jack Walchessen and forward Joey West hadn't helped. Nor had the horseshoes. A looser atmosphere, stricter coaching, continued line changes and greater use of the rookies had not helped. They would somehow have to win six more games than Sudbury to make the playoffs. "This team started heading downhill when they let Jeff [Twohey] go," said Garfat, his maroon-and-white blood boiling after every loss. "I hate to say it, but Todd Vandonk [the sports reporter for *Peterborough This Week,* who, a week earlier, had written that the team just wasn't good enough and wouldn't make the playoffs] is probably right." Garfat's best guess on what would likely take place in the next few weeks was "I have no idea." Apparently, no one did.

When the bus returned to the Memorial Centre, 12 hours after leaving, Giggy's car was covered in toilet paper. Life went on.

The players held a Secret Santa present exchange in their dressing room the next day, drawing names and buying gag gifts for one another, such as women's panties, various toys and children's games. They were thinking of Christmas and the holiday now. School was over until January and they were going home after Sunday's tilt against Barrie. Betzold and Hatcher would fly, courtesy of the Petes, to the U.S., Tanus to Finland and Findlay to the Soo, all driven to the airport by Garfat.

The players couldn't wait to get home. They were still children who needed to be hugged and told they were loved. They also wanted to get away from this miserable season.

On December 16, Pelino had a big decision to make: which goalie to start against Barrie for the last game of the first half of the season. He started Giggy, and Dagger was disappointed.

"I started wondering, 'What am I going to do?'" Dagger said. "I was in my fourth year of my dream and needed to get things going, get some exposure, get in the playoffs, needed to be seen. I didn't have much time left in my junior career. Christmas was coming and I didn't play that last game.

"I thought I had given up my spot to Giggy. I couldn't believe it. I worked so hard.

"I was confused. Pelino had lost my confidence and I lost my confidence. Giggy didn't work—he goofed around—and not playing against Barrie made no sense to me. I was pissed off."

Giggy stopped two penalty shots, something nobody had seen before, but he didn't stop the ones his coach thought he should have, and Barrie won 4–1.

Hull was so frustrated and angry when he returned to the Petes' offices that he punched a half-mannequin displaying a Petes jersey, knocking it eight metres into a wall. Unbeknownst to the staffers who witnessed it, Hull had just told Oke that if something wasn't done soon, he would make his own change and leave the team. Oke put it down to frustration, but he knew the team could not afford to lose Hull. Oke told him not to do anything too drastic. Jody's wife, Kelly, had left right after the game. "He was beyond upset," she said. "I just left him there." She knew he was a competitive guy, so much so that he had to win at everything, even at games of cards and back-gammon at home. And he didn't take losing lightly.

"During the first part of the season, I was worried about Jody, worried he might snap. He was so frustrated. He knew it could be better, but as an assistant, you can only say or do so much. I was getting really worried about him. I thought he was going to lose it, and then he beat up the mannequin," she said, laughing at that memory months later.

Hull went home hours later, so upset he wanted to cry. He bled for this team and knew changes had to be made—and had known for a while. If they weren't made soon, he planned to go to the board to tell them before he quit. He knew the coach had lost the dressing room. Pelino had even lost *him.* He knew that Koekkoek was not the right captain for that dressing room, and that neither of these prob-lems could be allowed to continue to ruin the season. The team was in flux, but there seemed to be little direction. Nobody seemed quite sure who was in charge. Everyone was just shrugging, wondering what the second half would bring.

More rumours were circulating around Peterborough about the changes that might come after the trading freeze was lifted. Had this player or that player demanded to be moved? The team denied that any player had come forward, but the fans remembered when Puempel had also said he didn't want out. Many of the players didn't want to leave Peterborough; others didn't want to leave but wanted to be on a winning team. The veterans, especially the overagers, knew they were possible trade bait. Other players thought a trade might be better for their own futures. They'd go home and discuss it with parents and agents and maybe approach the team when they returned to tell them they wanted out. Petes management claimed they would no longer let stars leave easily. They had been soft in the past and were getting a reputation for letting players run the ship. Trading either Koeks or Ritchie would be a public relations disaster and send all the wrong signals to players and fans alike. Quine would probably want out if others left, and as Koeks had said, who would blame him? The players had expected trades to improve their team long before this, and again, in Koeks's words, "They have assets; they have draft picks," so why not use them? (It was notable he was calling the Petes *they* rather than *we*.) The failure to get Schoenmakers in that trade had been frustrating and laughable, but Koeks still hadn't officially said he wanted out.

Since August 30, the Petes had won only eight games, losing 22 with four overtime losses for 20 points. That put them 22 points behind division-leading Belleville and 38 behind league-leading London. The London Knights ended their first half on a 21-game winning streak, only four games short of the record held by Kitchener. The Western Conference teams had taken over the league, with London and Owen Sound considered two of the top 10 teams in Canada. Barrie had also made the list, and Plymouth wasn't far behind. Peterborough, meanwhile, had scored only 85 goals, tying them for fewest in the league with Belleville, and yet the Bulls were in first place, the Petes in last. Belleville had allowed only 81 goals while Peterborough, at 140, was the third-worst behind Ottawa and Erie.

Menard was the team's leading scorer, with 14 goals and 16 assists for 30 points. Koeks was second, with only 5 goals and 20 assists for 25 points. Only Menard had broken the 10-goal mark. By comparison, Niagara's Brett Ritchie had 32 goals and 27 assists. The Petes had no one leading the league in any category. One of their rookies

(Betzold, with 4 goals, 10 assists) was in the top 20 in rookie scoring—he was 18th. Included in that rookie top 20 were seven of the top Ontario midget draft picks, five of them selected after the Petes' number one pick, Eric Cornel.

The rumour mill seldom stopped this season, fuelled by team leaks, blogs and tweets. It continued after the players left for Christmas.

Someone calling himself or herself "the Petes Insider," illegally using the Petes logo and OHL logo to look official, wrote that Koekkoek, Quine and Ritchie had asked for trades and wouldn't be back after Christmas. This anonymous, unconfirmed comment spread like oil from a beached tanker, reaching the media, agents and the NHL. Oke had to spend an hour dealing with calls and emails responding to these claims, which were simply not true. The three players were not demanding trades and hadn't approached the team. Even Koeks, who had muttered privately that he wanted out, had not made the request officially. CHEX-TV's Tyler Calver saw the rumours, checked with the team and told the public that the Petes had said none of their players had asked for trades, but the point was they shouldn't have had to deny rumours. The media had given credence to anonymous rumours and helped spread them, but at least Calver had denials on the record.

Little did Calver or anyone else know they were barking up the wrong rumour tree. On December 18, the board held another special secret meeting. It was called by Devlin, not to talk about players who wanted to be traded, but about the team's future. Devlin wanted Pelino fired, just as he had suggested a few weeks earlier, after hearing about Mathers's comments that the coach had lost the dressing room.

This time, the board listened. Arguments were presented and a debate about firing the coach took place. They liked Pelino, respected him and believed he was knowledgeable, but the bottom line was that the results weren't there. In the board's opinion, the team had lost its last three games miserably. Devlin reminded them of Mathers's comment (he had heard about it indirectly, although only three people were at that meeting) and said there was only one way to find out if the players they had now, and for next year, were really any good, and that was to get a new coach to see if he could win with them.

The board decided to fire the coach.

Firing someone who had worked his ass off and done no wrong as an employee was routine in hockey. It was not something anyone savoured, especially when, as in this instance, the people doing the firing had previously decided to keep the coach while firing the general manager, and had also announced to the public that the coach had their full support.

It didn't help that Devlin said he had read Mathers's lips on the bench after a Pelino tongue-lashing during a game, and the player's response was an F-bomb. Mathers had also told the media after the final 2012 game that the team needed to change its attitude and that everyone, including him, had to look in the mirror before the second half began. The directors didn't want their star players leaving and hurting their reputation once again, and they thought a change might also stop that movement.

The board also decided it would not trade Koekkoek without getting major assets, such as a number one draft pick, and that Quine and Menard would be traded if they got the right assets back. Ritchie wouldn't be traded: he was the milk on their cereal, the honey in their tea, the gold in their ring.

The board meeting made it clear who was making the decisions:

the directors. And they had just made two major ones. They would announce the coaching decision in three days.

On December 20, five days before Christmas, Devlin entered the Memorial Centre and fired Mike Pelino. "This is hard, Mike," he said, "but we're going to have to let you go." He told Pelino about the "grumbling player" who told the coach he lost the dressing room. The surprised coach, thinking his firing was premature, took the news professionally. As one staffer remarked, "If everyone was as professional as him here, maybe we wouldn't be in this situation." He thanked the staff for everything they had done, packed his stuff and walked out, still proud of what he had accomplished and confident that he had done his best with what he had been given to work with.

A good man had been given his walking papers. His goal of winning a Memorial Cup with the Petes would not be realized.

Staff felt like they had been kicked in the stomach. There was a sombre mood as Christmas approached, and any joyful spirit left the building. Wayne Clark, who arrived at the office a few hours after the firing, felt a double whammy. A friend, his school's 48-year-old principal, had suddenly died. Tears welled in his eyes as he thought of his two friends and bosses. "I was in a fog."

Pelino had known he would probably not be back next season if they didn't win, but he thought he had the remainder of the season to try. He thought the board should have held off on any decision until after the trade deadline, when he and Oke could move disgruntled players out and new ones in. He believed a few disenchanted players had caused the board's reaction. He wondered about the identity of the "grumbling player" that Devlin had told him about and guessed wrongly that it was Koeks, not knowing the president had somehow heard about Mathers's comments. He also wondered what might have happened if Dave Reid's attempted trade for Brett Ritchie had been successful; the season might have been different had there been a stronger veteran voice in the dressing room to keep Koeks in check and perhaps put an end to his pouting.

Here's what Pelino told the *Examiner*'s Davies, who broke the story of his departure: "It's easy to look around the league and look at someone like the London Knights as the neighbourhood kid with the shiny bicycle. They have everything going their way, have won 21 in a row and you can be envious. The bike I was riding was the Peterborough Petes. We weren't in a good situation for whatever reason, but that was the bike I was given and it was my job to pedal it as hard as I could and get whatever I could out of it.

"I loved my bike, even though it wasn't as shiny as some of the others in the league."

Pelino said his greatest mistake lay in not holding players more accountable, but even so, there was a reason for his behaviour: "If anything, I should have done things where 'it's my way or you're not going to play.' When I look at some of the leeway I gave players in terms of allowing them to get their game back or to try to find themselves—had I possibly said, 'That's not good enough and you're going to play the way I want you to,' maybe it would have made a difference."

If only he had known how right he was.

"Junior hockey is probably the most challenging level to coach because you have a hierarchy of entitlement and guys who are clearly better than others on the team. You get yourself convinced [that] by playing them more, they'll get out of it and start doing the things they're capable of, rather than playing them less because the pieces underneath aren't capable of taking their place. Sometimes, to live by those convictions, you don't know if it makes it better or worse."

Pelino said he understood his was a results-oriented business, but his greatest disappointment was not getting to finish the job. "When I was hired to coach the Peterborough Petes, my desire was to be a difference maker. A difference maker to my players in their hockey lives and personal lives, and a difference maker for the Peterborough Petes.

"I've never considered myself a victim and never will. I'll survive this."

Pelino sent an email to his friends and acquaintances, telling them not to feel sorry for him. "As Forrest Gump says, 'It happens.'" He was a class act.

Strangely, some board members who had supported the decision to fire Pelino emailed him to say they were surprised at his firing. Pelino kept those emails, along with the company car, and continued receiving his pay until his contract ran out in June. Reid was also still on the payroll, that issue still not settled.

When the news of the firing got out, Ritchie went public, saying he would miss the coach and had never asked for a trade. Koeks said he too would miss the coach, who had given him so many opportunities. He wouldn't dignify rumours that he wanted out and complimented the coach for all he had done for him. But Mathers said it was about time, that the team had been losing and it needed a change. It was an honest statement of a kind seldom heard from athletes. Mathers had played only two years of junior but had courage and maturity enough to tell the coach to his face that he had lost the room. It was his claim, never investigated by management, that led to the coach being fired. "The Petes needed to get away from what Pelino had done: his favouritism to some players, including me, allowing people to be late for meetings; allowing mistakes without getting angry, not benching players were all problems that needed to be addressed," Mathers said privately.

Merry Christmas. It looked like the new year would start with more upheaval.

CHAPTER 15

Changing of the Guard

The board appointed Jody Hull interim head coach and Mike Oke interim GM for the remainder of the season. It did not tell the public about its new trading strategy, but it had to be obvious to everyone that this season was done like a lobster in boiling water. Only Hull demurred: to him, the season wasn't over until the schedule ran out.

Hull and Oke knew it would be better for their futures if the team went on an incredible run. They also knew Devlin was searching for their replacements. Although the coaches did not know it, even the players were aware that former Marlies midget coach and one-time Pete, Ken Strong, had been approached by Devlin about the coaching position. He had declined because he was in Europe on a two-year deal. Devlin told Hull that if the team improved, his name would be added to the list of prospective coaches for next season. Hull, 43 when appointed, was the quietest of the coaches and the only one who had been through the hockey grind as a junior player before spending 16 years in the NHL and six more as an assistant junior coach. He was so dedicated to the Petes that he really meant it when he said, "If I could put that jersey on and play for the team, I would."

Hull was born in Petrolia in 1969, but it was in Stratford and Cambridge that he played most of his minor hockey. Representatives of various OHL teams, including the Petes' Dick Todd and their superscout Norm Bryant, who found more good Petes players than Cortez found gold, interviewed Hull during his midget draft year. Peterborough was interested but was picking almost last in each round and didn't think the six-foot, 180-pound high-scoring forward would be available. The black-haired, calf-eyed Hull didn't think so, either. "When I heard the Niagara Falls team announce, 'From the Cambridge Junior Bs,' I thought it was me, but it was Dan Tanko, one of our defencemen. Everyone was a bit surprised that I was still there when Peterborough picked me."

Hull went to camp in 1985, and how things have changed over the years. He went into coach Todd's office and was told to get into a car with goalie Kay Whitmore. They drove to a nearby high school track, ran 12 laps "as fast as we could, came back and did some testing and started on the ice."

Hull was a learner who had listened to coaches as a child and as a 16-year-old with the Petes, and this ability put him ahead of others. "I paid attention. I listened and took every little ounce of information I could get and used it to my advantage.

"Was I the best player every night? Probably not. Was I the hardest-working player in practice every day? Probably not. Or the hardest-working player every game? Probably not.

"But 90 per cent of the time, I probably was."

He credited Dick Todd and Roger Neilson with "getting me over the hump" on his journey to become an NHL player. Neilson had been fired by the Chicago Blackhawks and returned to Peterborough, where best friend Todd had invited him to participate in practices. "We always did extra stuff after practice," said Hull. "He [Neilson] would take me aside to show me about working along the boards, shooting, helping in whatever way he could. Whether he had an understanding that the potential was there, I don't know, but he taught me a lot and I learned the game here, and because of it, there wasn't another learning curve when I moved to that next level [the NHL]."

And move on Hull did, to an excellent 16-year playing career. The Hartford Whalers drafted the now 18-year-old, six-foot, two-inch, 195-pound winger after he scored 50 goals and 44 assists in 1987 and won a gold medal with Team Canada in the world junior tournament in Russia. In 831 regular-season games, he scored 124 goals and 137 assists while also appearing in 69 playoff games. His career as an NHL player ended in 2004. While the big guy isn't known for showing emotions in public, Hull admitted that he cried the day he left the game as a player. He was not alone among retired players who feel the pain of leaving a game they had played and loved since they were four.

Hull had married Peterborough's Kelly Downer, whose father, Ron, had coached the Peterborough Junior B team.

"When we were dating," she remembers, "he never said he was going to play in the NHL; he always said he was going to be a gym teacher."

After Hull retired, they returned to Peterborough with their son and daughter. Immediately he started wondering about helping the Petes as a coach.

"I was a student of the game when I played and watched how the coaches did things on the board with systems and drills. I'd sit in meetings, whether I had to be there or not. I sat in on PK or PP meetings, to observe how they killed penalties or did power plays, so I'd know how to play for or against them."

Now he was in charge of teaching these young players.

As for Oke, Devlin wasn't sure about him and was looking at more experienced OHL GMs. He told the board members Oke wasn't their man. The board still didn't know whether the coach and GM should be combined or separate roles. The name of Mike Kelly, Guelph's GM, was being tossed around, and like many board secrets, it was already being whispered in the wider community.

Hull deserved a chance. He had already said he wouldn't be the mirror of the last head coach, and players would have to be far more accountable. His NHL experience, and his years as an assistant coach, had given him plenty of opportunity to study what was needed to turn the team around. Hull was a nice man, but he wouldn't hesitate to make tough decisions.

He got to work immediately. He and Wayne Clark met at the Memorial Centre on December 24 to plan the future. Clark was leaving for the world under-17 championships for a week, so Hull moved goalie coach Andrew Verner behind the bench. He later retained Verner as the new defence coach. This was a bit of an awkward move because Clark, as the senior assistant, wanted to be defence coach, but Hull wanted Verner back there and wanted Clark to coach the forwards, looking after special teams. It wasn't an arrangement Clark was happy with; he had been told the defence position was his before he left, but he accepted the special-teams assignment when he returned.

The likelihood of trades undoubtedly preoccupied many of the players while they were away on their Christmas break. Some worried about being traded, others hoped for a move, and still others focused on the team's future and its impact on their own career. It was hard;

they were teenagers who had become commodities. The two overagers, Francis Menard and Brett Findlay, might be attractive to teams looking to add some seniority for playoff runs. The other veterans, such as Slater Koekkoek, Alan Quine, Peter Ceresnak, Clark Seymour, Derek Mathers, Andrew D'Agostini and Steven Trojanovic, were obvious trade bait, but the directors said they would be let go only if the team got value in return. The rookies were probably safe, especially Eric Cornel and Greg Betzold, but nothing was really safe in hockey.

Dagger "went home pissed," still upset at Pelino for not playing him in that last game. But then Hull took over. "Jody called me up and he knew I had been working my ass off. He said I'd start the first game back and that it was a new start. That meant a lot to me. I was going to come back with new energy."

Koekkoek, Quine, Menard and Seymour—"the Ottawa group"— vacationed in Mont-Tremblant in Quebec, not skiing but relaxing for a few days. It was during the Christmas break that Koekkoek decided he definitely wanted to be moved.

Hull was busy on Christmas Eve, going over proposed changes with Clark, when more bad news came sweeping into his office. Nick Ritchie would be out until the end of January. His shoulder injury had apparently not healed. The training staff had never heard a peep out of him about it, but he and his parents had gone to a specialist in Toronto during the holidays. Now, for at least 14 games, the team would be without their power forward.

Hull didn't think many changes could be made in the present system because it would take the team 5 to 10 games to adapt, and it didn't have the time. He had only 33 games to prove himself to the board or any future GM, but he was determined to put far more emphasis on three themes: attitude, respect and accountability.

On December 27 he met with Oke and the team captains for 10 minutes to tell them, and then the team, about his priorities. "We were uneasy at first with Jody coming in," remembered Mathers. "He had a different personality than Pelino. He had been our friend and was always joking in the dressing room. Now he was the head coach, and head coaches had to be separate, but he addressed it and we knew he was in charge. He was going to make all the players accountable."

Hull told the players he would still be close—his personality wouldn't change—but there would be no favouritism. Hull wanted more emotion from the players. Instead of telling them what they should be doing, he wanted to rely more on them to know what they should be doing to change attitude and show respect. Accountability would come from him, Clark and Verner, who would start benching players for their mistakes. Most players hoped those promises would be kept.

Hull created a team-oriented motivational system, which he told players about before their first game in Kingston—where Luke Hietkamp of the Frontenacs would play against the Petes for the first time. If the team met five of nine motivational goals, Hull would reward them, not with big financial incentives, which the league did not allow, but with something put toward a better meal or party for the end of the season. These were the objectives they'd strive to attain in each game:

- allow 5 or fewer odd man rushes against;
- take 35 or more shots on goal;
- allow 25 or fewer shots against;

- win 60 per cent of faceoffs;
- convert 25 per cent of power-play chances, or better;
- be 85 per cent or better on the penalty kill;
- finish plus or even in the first and last minute of each period;
- take no penalties for direct retaliation, abusive or unsportsman-like behaviour, or too many men;
- score the first goal of the game.

The list was something for the players to digest, to analyze the day after games were played, to improve upon, to get excited about and even to have some fun with.

In their first game of the "new season" after the break, on December 28, they played three excellent periods, taking a 5–2 win in Kingston's rink and fulfilling five of the nine objectives. Hull had seen Jekyll and Hyde trade places all season, so there was no celebration after the game, just a short word of praise.

It didn't take long for Hyde to reappear. The Petes lost the next night to put them back in last place to end the calendar year.

On New Year's Eve afternoon, Hull told his team at practice he still believed they could make the playoffs, "if you are willing to work hard and do the right things. You have to give up some things and replace them with the effort needed to get this accomplished."

That night, while millions of North American teens were ringing in the new year, the players were at their billets by 12:45 A.M., a modest extension of their regular 11 P.M. curfew, phoning the coach from the billet's number to let him know they were home and getting ready for their new beginning, the next game. The team had been in virtual playoff mode for weeks, and the grind would continue. There would be 13 games in January, only five of them at home.

The new year started with a beautiful sunny winter's day, and it didn't take long before Hull got his first opportunity to send his accountability message. A short meeting was scheduled for 9:45 A.M. on New Year's Day. Connor Boland arrived late. He apologized, but Hull sat him for the first 10 minutes of the game. The player understood, accepting his fate. Accountability for their actions was something this team had needed—and wanted—for some time.

When the game was over, the Petes could say they had not lost a game in 2013. They beat Belleville 4–3. Boland, whose father, Sean, had played for the Toronto Marlboros in the 1980s, was a plus-2 and Dagger was steady in net. For the third consecutive game, the team had accomplished five of Hull's nine objectives.

The team knew that no matter what happened, there was always one supporter who had never let them down. At practice the next day, Hull called the team over to the bench, where Iain was filling up water bottles. Hull acted as if he meant to draw up a drill on the whiteboard, but instead he announced that it was Iain's birthday and the players, on cue, broke into the song. Their number one fan, possibly the only one who never criticized them, the one who always predicted a Petes 5–0 win, broke out in the biggest, goofiest smile, like Fred Flintstone getting a kiss from Wilma.

Although they were often forgotten in the dismal season, there were so many positive little things team members had been doing, such as Mathers going to the local hospital that morning to visit a longtime season ticket subscriber who had had a limb removed while fighting diabetes. Or Seymour and Mathers carrying a little boy around the ice at the Petes' children's camp so he too could participate in a game of British bulldog. Or Koeks rubbing a little boy's head before warmups and offering him his stick. Or assistant trainer Larry Smith looking for a child to give a new Petes puck to before every game. Or Verner giving Iain a souvenir pin from his own collection after every home game. Or Clark driving Iain home following each home game and sometimes taking him out for hot chocolate. Or Dagger helping a little boy with cystic fibrosis.

Dagger, the kid that everyone cheered to succeed, had a night to remember on January 3, stopping 42 shots and collecting his first shutout of the season in a 3–0 win over Belleville. The Petes were still undefeated in 2013. "I came back with new energy that I didn't know I even had, but I took it to another level," said Dagger.

Hull knocked Koeks's ice time from 30 minutes a game to 24:30—Koeks was still on the ice the most, but the time was now shared more equitably. Boland scored his first OHL goal and received the team's Burn the Boats Award. The 212-Degree Award, a Pelino idea, was dropped.

Playing the Rangers in Kitchener was always difficult. The NHL-like atmosphere at the Memorial Auditorium, where more than 7,000 fans regularly showed up to cheer for their team, was intimidating, and Maguire, Tanus, Betzold, Giugovaz and Cornel had never experienced it before January 4.

Kitchener was the other OHL team that an NHL squad—in this case, the New York Rangers—had left in community hands. They had sellout crowds whether they won or lost. They even had a waiting list for season tickets. The arena had its own RangerVision TV, an incredible pre-game light show, a players' lounge, a weight room that would put some pro teams' facilities to shame, and a tradition not much less impressive than Peterborough's, as NHL stars such as Larry Robinson, Scott Stevens and Bill Barber had played on that ice.

Kitchener also had a population base almost triple the size of Peterborough's, but it didn't take long to learn that the community believed it was their team and supporting it was a civic duty. The two teams had been heading in different directions in the last few years.

Tonight, Dagger started in net and a new player, 17-year-old Tyson Baker, the Petes' 10th-round pick in the midget selection draft, joined them. The kid with the long blond hair gave up any chance of an NCAA scholarship by dressing tonight. If not a hockey player, he wanted to be a firefighter, so a university degree was not mandatory. The players didn't know he had won championships in kick-boxing. (His mother was an international champion, as was his father.) Tyson had given it up for hockey. He got two minutes of playing time and was sent back to his Junior B team in time for their game the next night.

Puempel, who was Public Enemy #1 in the eyes of Petes fans, was injured and did not play. It was doubtful he would be back in the lineup for the return game Thursday in Peterborough. Incredibly, he sat in the stands with Ritchie. Things certainly had changed in the hockey world over the years—there was a time when players from different teams would never dare to do this, or even think about it. Puempel even visited the Petes' dressing room afterwards to say hello to his former teammates. They greeted him with friendly hugs and handshakes.

Even though the Petes had lost in overtime, the bus ride home had a different mood than the Pelino trips. There was constant chatter, some laughter and even a movie, something Pelino never allowed after a loss. Hull enjoyed hearing the sounds of a team coming together, as teams had done during road trips in his junior career. He also looked forward to getting some sleep on the weekend before preparing for Kitchener again Thursday night.

The NHL and its players' association finally reached an agreement on January 8. Junior hockey GMs waited to see which of their players would be called up by their NHL teams. Niagara had three players invited to NHL training camps, Barrie had two and Oshawa two. If they were called on, the moves would change those teams dramatically. As it turned out, only Niagara lost a player—Dougie Hamilton, to Boston. The others were all sent back to junior.

It all made for a busy week in the Ontario Hockey League with trade deadlines, players leaving for NHL camps, and coaches and GMs trying to rein everyone in amidst all the distractions. Oke took calls from various OHL teams but tried to quell the fans' high expectations, telling the media that teams had been offering only bad players for good ones. He told Davies, "We've had some success since the Christmas break. We'd like to build on that momentum and try to reel in some teams and earn a playoff spot. At the same time, we'd like to do it in a way where, if opportunities are presented to us where we can move some players with an eye on getting players in return who are going to be here next year and beyond, that's something we'd seriously consider."

While a few Petes said they would move, the words of the junkyard dog, Perogi, echoed in my mind: "I never want to be traded from this team. I want to stay and help them. They've done everything for me. They picked me in the draft. I owe them. My work ethic is what got me here, what will keep me here and the only reason I'm here. I absolutely want to be here."

Inevitably, with deadlines looming, the rumours continued. The most rampant had Koekkoek going to Owen Sound, but three days before the deadline, the Attack grabbed Ottawa's defenceman, Cody Ceci, in return for rookie defenceman Jacob Middleton. The Petes had been involved in negotiations with Owen Sound for Koeks, but Middleton had made a list of the teams he would go to, and Peterborough was not on it. Despite the rumours to the contrary, he never explicitly refused a trade to Peterborough.

Koekkoek was the only Pete who had actually asked for a trade, through his agent, Murray Kuntz. Kuntz, who had been telling hockey people throughout the league that he had to get Koeks out of Peterborough, had also advised other former Petes stars Ryan Spooner and Austin Watson—a strange coincidence, and one the Petes organization was well aware of.

The board of directors met with Oke to discuss trade possibilities, and they expected to get a big rookie first-rounder with two or three years left in the league in exchange for Koekkoek. In 2013–14, Koekkoek would be the highest-drafted defenceman in the OHL, and he might fetch even more in a trade in the off-season, but a betting man had him gone by the deadline at noon Thursday. The dressing room had become too volatile to keep him around. His discontent was affecting others, and he wanted out—as did another player.

"Quine was getting as bad as Koeks," said one player. "The more Koeks wanted out, the more Quine did too, but we were winning with them after Christmas, so maybe that hadn't been a reason we were losing."

Clark said, "I was sick of Koekkoek getting blamed for everything, and that's what was happening. He was a passionate hockey player who made some guys uncomfortable with the truth."

Reid was the problem when he was fired. Pelino was the problem when he was fired. Koekkoek would be the problem when he was traded. It was the way the hockey world worked: blame the guy who's not there anymore.

Meanwhile, it was official that Schoenmakers would not come to Peterborough. All hope had been abandoned. You couldn't blame him. After all, he was an overager who had never been drafted by an NHL team. He had, however, been traded three times in eight months and had heard every lie and compliment from each new team's coach and manager. His dream might be over. He would go to university—unless, as he hoped, his hometown Kitchener Rangers traded for him, as he had requested.

Nineteen-year-old Zach Lorentz, sent to Windsor in the Schoenmakers deal, was traded before the deadline, this time to Plymouth, his fourth team and second country since the end of last season.

Shortly after Christmas, the Petes had identified the players they wanted to get and had assigned scouts to watch them. The team also acquired video on some of the players. Oke had an hour-long conference call with staff on the Sunday of trade week. "We talked about the different scenarios and shared as much information as we could about players," Oke said. "We wanted to acquire players to fill potential holes this season and future years. We would consider new players and acquire assets [and] draft picks we can use as selections in future drafts or for future trades to get other players. We had an idea of the players we'd like to give up—the older ones, mainly. This season is different. We'd like to get stronger for both this season's run and future years."

One player was London-born Michael Clarke of the Windsor Spitfires, cut out of that same cookie-cutter as so many of today's average Petes forwards—five foot ten, 180 pounds. Some NHL scouts, and even some Petes coaches, thought he was soft, small and a bit timid. He was inconsistent—so good one night, disappearing the next. He played defence for his first competitive youth teams but didn't like the lack of action, so by the time he was 13 he had switched to centre. Unbeknownst to the Petes, most of their defence-men (Trojanovic, Devlin, Varga, Ceresnak) had played forward for most of their minor hockey careers until about two years before being drafted.

At the practice on Tuesday, December 8, at 2:30 P.M., Oke came to the ice surface near the boards. "Nobody liked to see Okie come to the ice surface," said Mathers. "It could only mean one thing, and you hoped it wasn't you."

Oke talked with Hull, who skated to Menard. Menard left the ice.

"When Frankie got called over and left, we knew. Everyone knew. The atmosphere was tense on the team. The players who wanted to leave weren't motivated in practice, and everyone knew it."

While the practice resumed, Menard, still in full gear, went to Oke's office, where he learned that Brampton had traded for him in exchange for a third-round pick next spring and a sixth-rounder in 2015. That was it. The team's leading goal scorer, with 15 goals and 33 points in 40 games, who had never wanted to be traded by the Petes, went to the dressing room, got changed and quickly headed to his landparents' home to pack, have a meal and drive to Brampton.

"I would have liked to have finished what we started here," said a teary-eyed Menard, alone in the dressing room after hearing the news. "These things happen. I'm going to miss the guys."

But he was happy knowing that Brampton was going to make the playoffs. Menard was an overager with three months left in his junior career. The Petes had made a move for the future; Brampton had made one for their playoff hopes. Menard had been one of the friendlier and more professional Petes, and he was still searching for his biological parents. His shoulder tattoo commemorated his biological father, a man he had never met, forever reminding him of that journey. He moved on. The others waited.

The Petes finally dealt Schoenmakers to Kitchener for another overager, Nick Czinder, a six-foot, five-inch, 230-pound winger from Michigan who had scored the tying goal against the Petes on Friday night. There was also $5,000 involved, but not announced. Czinder had only three goals and six assists in 31 games this season and was moving to his third team in two seasons, having played in Windsor last year. He was also the third American with the Petes.

Walter DiClemente contacted Menard's billets and asked if they'd be interested in keeping Czinder for the rest of the season. Menard had left their home at 7 P.M.; Czinder arrived two hours later. Goodbye, Frankie; hello, Nick.

Oke and the coaches met after practice with the remaining players to tell them of the Menard trade. The Czinder-Schoenmakers deal was not mentioned.

Koekkoek shook his head. Although he had told the coaches in private meetings he understood trades would be made, he was surprised at the move of his friend, a fellow Notre Dame graduate, the team's leading scorer and a member of the "Ottawa group."

Oke told the team, "At the end of the day, moving forward, we have the potential for other moves or no moves. Whatever happens, we're going to build on our success so far in the second half, and any deals will be for this and future years."

The following day, one day before deadline, Koekkoek, more

impatient with every passing hour, charged into Oke's office after practice and demanded he do something, because he wasn't staying in Peterborough. When he returned to the dressing room, he bowed his head, telling teammates, "I want out, I want out, I've got to get out of here."

"We all realized," said one player, "that he didn't care about the team, us, or anything but getting out of here." The public speculation about Koekkoek being traded continued, but Oke said there had not been any offers that were attractive enough. The Petes knew he had another year of junior ahead of him—a valuable asset to OHL teams. Most teams had inquired about him, some about Quine, others about Mathers, who had told the team whatever happened was fine with him, rebuilding or not. Trades had to take place, but Hull worried about playing the next 28 games as a strictly defensive team if he lost too many good offensive players. He also worried about the dressing room if some of these moody players were not moved.

Word was spreading in the community that deals were tough to make because players didn't want to come to Peterborough.

"Imagine," said DiClemente, shaking his head. "Who would ever have thought the day would come that kids didn't want to come to the Petes?" Agents were worried about the lack of stability behind the bench and in the front office, with both key people in interim situations. But Czinder said players didn't mind coming to Peterborough at all. "The bottom line is you want to play hockey. I have no problems at all and don't believe any players would."

Kingston had drafted him, but he hadn't wanted to go there. "Windsor was closer to my home, so they traded for me." He wasn't surprised at his latest trade, because he wasn't happy with his ice time. "I had no hesitation whatsoever coming here. The coaches are smart, and like all teams, they treat you good. This is a great place to play."

Findlay, once unhappy with the Petes, agreed with that assessment and was pleased to escape the overage trade deadline. He was happier with Hull coaching.

And the Petes . . . well, they once again traded their captain, sending yet another message to those on the outside that the sailors were in control of the ship and if you asked for, or demanded, a trade, the team would give in.

The Petes got very little for Koekkoek from Windsor: Michael Clarke, Colorado's fifth-round pick the previous June, along with second-round picks in the priority drafts in 2014 and 2015. It was not the deal Ottawa got for Ceci, and not the deal the board had said it wanted for a star player. Hockey observers were surprised there wasn't another local uproar over the trade, but it never came.

Inside the Memorial Centre, the team massaged the trade as best it could, but the hockey world continued to ask what was happening to the Peterborough Petes. What was happening was that the team was afraid that if it didn't trade the disgruntled captain, the dressing room would worsen for the rest of the season. The Petes now painted the captain as a kid who didn't care and wasn't respected in the dressing room. Only four months after saying all those great things about Koekkoek when he was given the *C,* management now claimed the other players didn't respond to him and that he couldn't find the right balance between this team and his career.

It was an emotional time for Koeks. He was happy to be traded but in tears because he was leaving. He told fans he had set high expectations for this year, as had everyone, but those expectations bore no fruit and his frustration with losing caused him to want out. Strangely, for a kid who wanted to win so badly, he agreed to go to Windsor, a team that was in a situation similar to the Petes—they were in ninth place in the Western Conference and without much hope of making the playoffs. Koeks said goodbye to his teammates at the Memorial Centre, telling them he wasn't bailing on them, although many indeed thought he was.

Meanwhile, a surprised Clarke learned about the trade when the Windsor general manager called him late at night. "He said they didn't want to trade me, but they had a good offer, and the next day, here I was in Peterborough."

The adjustment took little time. "Having that first year under your belt, knowing what it was like to come to a new team, made it easier.

"Windsor had a different dynamic, with the coach being a part owner of the team, but both coaches here or there are intense. They were more vocal in Windsor, but that's only a coaching style; they are both very intense and know what they are doing." While his focus was on hockey, Clarke was one of the few players with a backup plan. He graduated from high school with a 75 average and was taking more courses to try to boost his grades so he could attend university if pro hockey didn't work out or he got injured.

The final trade deadline was January 9 at noon, and by then the Petes had another player requesting a trade. Koekkoek's good friend Quine wanted to be with a playoff team. The only surprise was that he had taken so long to submit his request. He had been talking about it with teammates for a month but had not told the team until now, although Oke and Hull were aware he would probably want to move. It was the second team he had requested a trade from, having demanded that Kingston move him to Peterborough. Plenty of teams had been asking about this creative centreman, and his agent even told Quine what other teams were offering the Petes.

The Soo offered the best deal, but Quine, who had a no-trade clause, made it known he would not report there. Talks continued on the morning of deadline day in Oke's office, the ever-present

President Devlin there with him. Quine paced, texted, left for drives or walks outside, or went into the dressing room, talking on his cell, waiting nervously in the hours before the noon cut-off point. Half an hour before the deadline, he sat in the Petes' assistant coaches' room only two offices down from Oke's, looking at a silent Verner. Out of the blue, he said, "You'd be doing the same as me. I just want to be in the playoffs. They're [the Petes] just messing around. I'm not going to the Soo, and I know they have at least four other options." The 18-year-old admitted he was shaking inside, his stomach churning. He fiddled with his phone and became silent with anxiety.

He also agreed with what Koekkoek had said: if the Petes had fired Pelino two months earlier and put Hull in charge then, they would not be in this predicament.

With only three minutes left to the deadline, Quine was called into Oke's office to approve a trade to first-place Belleville. It was his birthplace, it was just a two-hour drive from his family home near Ottawa, and its rink boasted the largest ice surface in the league, which was ideal for his skating style. The Petes got three second-round picks, giving them seven draft picks in three days. These were great assets to set aside for future drafts or trades, but they offered nothing to improve the team immediately.

Quine went to the dressing room, where Mathers, Seymour and Ritchie had drifted, and sat with the boys for one last time.

Petes director Pat Casey looked at the OHL trades and wondered where the league was going. Teens were moving all over Ontario—some of them four times just this season—changing cities, schools and homes, being uprooted in midseason. It didn't seem to fit the amateur image, but it did mirror the NHL.

The Petes did not even attempt to massage the trades in a press conference or media release. The team just sent out short announcements wishing Quine and Koekkoek all the best. There was no public relations machine, no staff meeting to rev up major announcements or explain why the deals were done. There was never any introduction of new players to the media. Coach Clark, teaching at school, got the news as everyone else did—on the radio or online.

Petes fans had just lost the team's top scorer in Menard; their top player, Koekkoek; and top centreman, Quine. The trades gave the Petes one extra pick this year, five more in 2014, four in 2015, two in 2016 and two more in 2017. They even had one pick in 2018—which, someone jokingly said, meant they could scout the 10-year-old atom players in an upcoming Peterborough tournament. The Petes' extra picks gave them good opportunities for the next few years of drafting and trading. To many of the fans, however, the season was over. The high hopes and expectations had slipped away earlier in the season, but today they had plunged into an abyss.

Hull had met with a confused Mathers the night before the trade deadline and told him Koeks would probably be getting traded and that he, Mathers, would be the new captain. Hull wanted Mathers to stay and was hoping the mood in the dressing room would improve. He hoped Mathers would provide the strong leadership a team of gritty, no-star players needed. The team had been moving in several directions at once. There had been an exclusive, not inclusive, leadership, which was not conducive to the team's efforts.

Mathers cherished the opportunity to be that leader.

Mathers (Diesel to his teammates) and Seymour (Seabiscuit) would both be good new captains in Hull's eyes. Diesel had opened his mouth last week about not wanting to be with the Petes in a rebuilding phase, and that bothered Hull a bit, but he knew the players looked up to Mathers. He thought Seabiscuit might return to the team next season, and he was well liked, but Diesel was his choice. Hull thought the hardest-working player, Pierog, could be an assistant, as could young Boland. He chose Boland, feeling that it might boost his confidence. Later, he added Findlay.

Oke had spent four days in purgatory leading up to the trade deadline. Now he could relax, leave his office and his shadow (Jim Devlin), and recharge his phone and himself. He was free, at least until tomorrow, when he and Hull had to go to the high school to discuss players' marks, which still were disappointing, although there were a few bright lights, like Cornel.

The trades and poor season made the fans angrier than at any time in the Petes history. On January 10, before the Kitchener game, Devlin, who had delayed a medical procedure until after the trade deadline, felt the brunt of the fans' displeasure when he was booed heavily while making some presentations at centre ice. It was believed to be the first time a team executive had received that treatment. He presented gifts to Petes assistant coach Wayne Clark and to Eric Cornel for their participation in the world under-17 tournament as well as to Peter Ceresnak and three Kitchener players for their play in the world junior championship. There was also a plaque for a Kitchener executive for the team's 50th year in the league. Unlike Devlin, Rangers coach Steve Spott, who had also coached Team Canada at the under-20 tournament, received a rousing ovation.

Puempel and Ritchie watched the game together. One longtime season ticket holder, spotting Puempel, called him a traitor and admonished him for "walking around like a celebrity." Pointing to the small Petes crowd, young Puempel threw a zinger back, to the effect that "we've got 7,000 in our place." Ritchie moved his friend along before a shouting match became something more.

That night, after several tense days, the team responded to the trades with energy. Ritchie watched this new team with glee, saying excitedly, "This team is good." Things were looser, Mathers's influence already having an effect.

"When they traded our top three players, we all kind of said, 'Oh shit, here we go. Now we'll go back to losing,'" said Mathers later, "but me and Seymour talked to the team and said, 'What do we have to lose? Nobody is expecting us to win—let's go give it a try.'

"There was no pressure now; every night, we could just go out and play hockey. It seemed to be working well. Our practices had more energy, more flow. Jody was a players' coach, the guy who would come in and have fun with the team, but now we didn't see him as often and he had to be the head coach. We had more push. He had caught our attention. He's been there, played the game, and he's all business, but he knew what it was all about. He had changed the atmosphere, and it was more fun."

Petes fans had seen this act before, most recently in Kitchener, when their team outplayed the opposition only to lose in a shootout. And again tonight, the Petes held the lead until the third period, when Kitchener forced overtime and then another shootout.

The first three shooters from each team failed, and then Tanus slipped one in. Spott, sensing the drama and irony of the moment, sent out Schoenmakers, the kid who wouldn't report to the Petes, who was Public Enemy #2 (behind Puempel) in Peterborough. Schoenmakers knew the significance, as did Dagger, and the 2,100 fans let loose the loudest boo heard in the centre since World Wrestling Entertainment came to town three years earlier. The roar resounded off the boards as Schoenmakers skated forward. Dagger stepped out, made the big save and gave a high fist pump as players buried him in hugs and the crowd's cheers boomed around the rink. The rejuvenated Dagger was the game's first star.

It was a happy team that Hull congratulated in the dressing room. His speech was a short one, telling the players to enjoy tonight but think about tomorrow. Hull believed that the fewer words he used, the more players would listen. Pelino, more of an academic, had studied his script and thought hard about what to say between periods. Hull, in contrast, went by gut instinct and kept it brief. "I don't want them thinking about 15 different things or worrying about remembering all that."

The Petes hadn't won the Memorial Cup yet, but the mood sure felt like it. Hull wanted to make sure the team knew it had won only one game, nothing more.

Following the game, young Cody Thompson, the strongest kid at training camp, who had worked his butt off in the pre-season only to have an injury keep him off the ice for two months, got his just reward. Oke invited him into his office and welcomed the happiest teen in the building to the team for the rest of the season.

CHAPTER 16

In the Basement, Looking Up

The Oshawa Generals promoted their home games against the Petes as the "greatest rivalry in junior hockey." This competitive intensity started in the NHL's "Original Six" period, when Montreal owned the Petes and Boston sponsored the Generals, and has been kept up over the years as Peterborough youth teams played Oshawa's. It was still a surprise, though, that the GM Centre was sold out on January 11, with a record 6,269 people officially in attendance—20 more than when Hall of Fame legend and former General Bobby Orr was honoured. Players love a big crowd to push and pull them, to become that seventh player cheering them on, but even visitors loved to have a lot of people jeering them—adding excitement and challenge rather than more pressure. It is what brings the magic to Showtime.

Outside, an Oshawa fan did what he said he has done for years before every Petes game: he urinated on a tire of the Petes' bus. Inside the beautiful arena, a game between eight- and nine-year-olds was being played. As the players gathered near their bench to tape sticks, they watched enviously. "God, I'd love to be out there," said Stephen Pierog, and Brandon Devlin finished his sentence: "To have the fun they're having."

"Look at that kid—he doesn't even know what wing he is on. Man, that was fun," said Giggy Giugovaz. And Diesel Mathers, ripping old tape from a stick with his knuckle-scarred hands, his tank top revealing his hilltop biceps, looked at the kids, smiled and said quietly, "Those were good times."

The season was more than half over, and yet, for all the time the team had been together, there had been hardly any team pranks or practical jokes. There had been some minor fooling around with butter, cream or salad dressing at team meals, but it hadn't amounted to much. Finally, with 27 games remaining, a team prankster struck. Perogi, jumping on the ice for the warmup, slipped, slid and scrambled back to the bench to discover that a piece of clear adhesive tape was stuck to the bottom of his skate blade.

"Bastards! Right in warmup," he muttered, laughing, while assistant trainer Larry Smith ripped it off. Perogi shook his head, wondering who did it and how he could get the prankster back. He would never learn it was Clark (Seabiscuit) Seymour.

Giggy, who hadn't played in three games after being pulled in his last one, started tonight, which everyone knew without being told because he sat alone in Giggy's world—ball cap, T-shirt and shorts on fidgeting, slurping, spitting his water, focusing his eyes straight ahead for about 10 minutes before heading to the dressing room to suit up. Dagger D'Agostini had been playing great, but coach Jody Hull knew Giggy needed to play and was giving him a chance against the powerful Gens.

The Windsor Spitfires, with a game the next night in nearby Belleville against Quine's Bulls, followed by one in this arena on the 13th, were spending the night in Oshawa, so Slater Koekkoek and Trevor Murphy were in the crowd. "This is so weird," said Koekkoek. "I really hope for the boys. They had a big win last night and I want them to win badly, but watching the maroon and white, while I'm up here, is definitely very weird." He hoped the fans understood that he just felt the move to another team was a decision he had to make. "It's different for sure, but it feels good and was the right thing." Murphy said he too was happy, living at home. He found that the greatest difference between the teams was "definitely coaching."

"We are all about systems, studying the game, setting up systems," he said. "I love it. I think if Jody had been hired months ago, things might have been different. They needed some players to turn themselves around, and I see some changes in their style, but Windsor is a different world." He said it was "first class all the way," using that familiar line, "They get us whatever we need."

The two former Petes were intense while they watched the game, murmuring when their old buddies made a familiar move or, as a play shaped up, remembering some of the old mistakes the players continued to make, but noticing a bit more energy and grit. They also saw their buddy Mathers, the heavyweight champion of the OHL, filling in on defence again.

The Generals fired six shots at Giggy in the first 2:10 and put one past him with their 11th shot—Peterborough had managed three on the Oshawa goalie. In the second period, the Petes were pounded, outshot 25–12, and Jenner got one to make it 2–0. Petes fans worried it would be a fiasco, but suddenly there was a shift in Mo.

Hull had said to them during the intermission, "Only one team showed up tonight, and our team better show up for the third."

The coach had been right to choose Boland as an assistant captain, although they had not sewn the *A* on his sweater yet, having forgotten to tell B-Man about the promotion. They hadn't told their fans, either, and never did. Their public relations machine needed some cylinders reground and some oil added, as well as someone to drive it.

When Eric Cornel got smucked by Tyler Biggs, who knocked the rookie on his can, his visor cutting his lip, Boland jumped in to look after Biggs. He got an extra two minutes and a 10-minute misconduct, earning Cornel's—and the rest of the team's—appreciation.

Perogi took the heart out of the nervous Generals fans when he tied it up in the third, and for the third consecutive game the Petes went into overtime, getting at least another point. They lost this game 4–3 in the shootout.

The Petes' home game against Sudbury on January 12 was their third in three nights. The players' bodies were aching, muscles bruised and burning, but the pain of a disallowed goal hurt more, making the team feel they had been robbed in their fourth consecutive overtime game—a fourth consecutive shootout that should never have been.

Hull was upset about having to discipline Hatcher for missing curfew—benching him meant that the team was left a player short. But he was even more upset about the disallowed goal. That one point could be very important for the Petes, and he knew it.

While the players were learning and developing in the league, so were the officials, but this was a strange night, made stranger when the puck, which seemed clearly to go into the net, wasn't counted. It had been a goal to all those in the biggest crowd (3,451) to attend a

Petes' game all season—there, finally, to make noise in a hockey rink the way it was meant to be.

Hull's night got worse. Five more veteran players missed curfew that night, on the very day he had suspended a player for the same offence. He was shocked, surprised, disappointed. The players claimed in a meeting with him that they had called for a cab that arrived late. Hull sarcastically wondered how the rest of the team managed to get home on time. He thought about sitting them for a few minutes to start the next game, but he didn't have enough play- ers, so he put them on a 9 P.M. curfew for a week instead of the team's usual 11 o'clock.

The Petes had played eight games under Hull, with five wins and three overtime ties for 13 of a possible 18 points. Five of their last six games had been shootouts. The season was not over until the mathematician told Hull it was. Still, they were 11 points behind their closest rival, which was now Kingston. As Sudbury rose in the standings, Kingston slid.

There was also a behind-the-scenes deal going on that only Mike Oke, Hull and eventually the other two coaches were aware of. A local defenceman, Nelson Armstrong, whom Wayne Clark had coached in minor midget and Hull had coached in Tier II, had gone the NCAA route, attending St. Lawrence College in Canton, New York. He was in his second year but was hinting he might come home. Oke, Hull and Clark liked him and moved quickly. For once this season, the team was able to keep its moves quiet. Notably, the staff didn't inform the board, the source of too many leaks, until they had to approve it.

Hull predicted this kid would be as valuable to the team as Koekkoek had been. (Koeks, in only his second game with Windsor, had wrecked his shoulder again and was done for the season. Hull,

Oke and Devlin saw the irony but felt sorry for the kid.) Their new recruit was six foot one, 205 pounds and a '93. He was big and fast, with quick feet. Hull was smiling when he introduced Armstrong to the team. And all he had cost them was an education package.

Oke had placed Armstrong on the Petes' protected list in 2010 after the Sarnia Sting, which drafted him in 2009 in the 10th round, had dropped him from theirs, but nobody had told the player. Oke had been in touch with his advisors regularly, so when they told Oke about two weeks before the signing that Armstrong might be interested in joining the Petes and taking some courses at Trent University, he wasn't surprised. Petes scouts hadn't been watching him, but they had old scouting reports, along with Clark's and Hull's memories.

At his first practice, Armstrong wore an old extra pair of Petes skates and some used equipment. His former school had not allowed him to keep a thing.

Just days earlier, on January 10, President Devlin and business development officer Reeves met with officials from the Canadian Broadcasting Corporation, including Greg Millen, the former Pete and current TV personality who had wanted to buy the team, to discuss some good news for the city and team. CBC's *Hockey Day in Canada,* a day-long live broadcast that had become a tradition in Canada, would be coming to Peterborough, giving national exposure to the city and the team, a great opportunity that wouldn't be announced until later.

This development affected Dagger one week later, on the day of their home game against Guelph. He was being followed all day by a CBC television crew preparing a feature on the Petes for the upcoming program. The crew spent hours with him, filming his story as player, student and humanitarian. Perhaps encouraged by the attention, he stopped eight scoring chances before Guelph got one by him. The team allowed two more to end the first period trailing 3–0.

Newcomer Nelson Armstrong was impressive in the team's 5–3 loss. He found the biggest difference was playing with and against players in his age group; in the NCAA, players were older and stronger, up to 24 years old. "You're 100 per cent fresh in the NCAA because you're not playing as often in college, which is more [of a] systems and defensive game with no fighting. Here it is dirtier, more hitting and more skills."

Assistant trainer Terry Bowser had a new nickname for any problem players, calling them "Larry's Kids," after fellow assistant Larry Smith. If a player missed school? One of Larry's Kids. Another chewed tobacco? One of Larry's Kids. Another missed curfew? One of Larry's Kids. Terry and Larry were like Mutt and Jeff and brought some much-needed jibing to the team.

All the kids played gritty, gutsy hockey on January 19 in St. Catharines, earning a 5–4 win and even fighting off a five-on-three power play in the dying minutes. The team completed its checks, and Mathers continued his six-game scoring streak. Dagger put in another solid game, his consistency the factor that was helping the Petes more than any other in their rising success. "I don't know what happened," said the goalie. "The coaching change, then the trades. Czinder and Clarke were character players, positive people. Negative thoughts were going away and the room became positive. Some of the younger guys were still goofing off and needed maturity, which was a concern all year, but the room became different. There were different influences and they were all positive."

Czinder, whose size and aggressive play added spark and courage to the lineup, went to the medical room to get a few stitches to his face from a Brett Ritchie fight. What the public wasn't told was the concern the team had over a possible concussion.

Public relations was not the team's strong suit. The board was set to announce the appointment of three new directors—big news for the team—on the same day they decided to hold a press conference at which they would also herald the return of Dick Todd, now as a consultant, and break the news that CBC's *Hockey Day in Canada* was coming to Peterborough. These were three momentous announcements, each of which deserved individual attention, but the team piled them into a single event.

The appointment of the new directors was among the worst kept secrets in town: the names of two had already been broadcast on radio and Twitter. Joining the board were high school principal Dave Lorentz, a former Petes captain who was now a high school principal and president of the team's alumni; Rod McGillis, a former NCAA player, teacher and part-time advance scout for the Windsor Spitfires and Ottawa 67's; and Dave Pogue, a truck company owner, Petes sponsor and fan. All were in their 40s, and Devlin said he hoped their appointments would silence critics who said the board was an old boys' club. The public never learned that the local member of Parliament, Dean Del Mastro, had also applied, been interviewed and been rejected as a candidate.

Inevitably, there was carping in the hockey community about the choices and they hadn't even started attending meetings.

For many in the hockey community, the naming of Todd as a consultant was bigger news than the addition of the new directors. Todd, who spent most of his winters in Florida, was not in attendance for the announcement, but his appointment was good for the team's image and good for morale. The Petes board said he would be a volunteer, although they would probably have to pay some of his expenses. His experience as a general manager and coach would be invaluable, adding yet another hockey voice in the offices of the GM and coach. His inclusion probably also signalled that Oke would remain as GM. It seemed unlikely that, if the board intended to bring in a more experienced Ontario Hockey League GM, such a manager would also want Todd's advice or welcome his presence.

Meanwhile, the part of the press conference at which the Petes had intended to release details of the *Hockey Day* banquet was cancelled when Devlin received legal documents pertaining to the event and foresaw problems.

The team's next game was another win against Belleville, but again, not in regulation play—oh no, the Petes wouldn't want to deny the fans value for their money. They went into their 10th overtime of the season. The five-minute extra period was unusual in that there wasn't a single whistle. The ovation when it was over, and the team's salute to their crowd, signalled that the fans were back on board. Peterborough had new directors, new players, a new coach, a new atmosphere and a new life.

"Good win, you earned it," said Hull to the players afterwards. "I told you after the second period, all we needed was two goals—don't worry about anything else, just get those two goals, don't worry about the rest. The resiliency and maturity of this team since the break is going to get us there. Like I said at practice yesterday, keep believing. Our goal is the playoffs, and it should be the goal of everyone in this room. We're eight points out and we're going to make it. We can control what we do and can't worry about the others. Great job, great job!"

Outside the dressing room, GM Oke stood with his cute, blond-haired four-year-old son, who was holding a paper airplane and waiting to see his hockey hero, Nick Ritchie. He looked at his dad and said what the hometown fans were thinking: "That was a good game, Dad."

Ritchie said, "The boys are playing great. It's not like we weren't playing hard before, but there's a different feel on the team." He had noticed when he returned that the mood and flow of the game had changed so much that it took him a few shifts to get used to it. It was a mood (upbeat) and flow (fast and no quit) that he liked.

Eric Cornel's wide smile made his surprise at being given the Burn the Boats Award obvious. He knew Dagger could have received it with 30 saves, none bigger than the two he made in the shootout, and many others deserved it too. The players were taking control of their own fate and that of the team, just as Hull had planned. Players were even taking the initiative after the game to get into the gym, to push themselves on the bikes and weights. When Hull heard this from Clark, he smiled. "Finally, it is their team."

In the last 11 games, Jonatan Tanus had 9 points and was a plus-6; Stephen Nosad had 6 points and was a plus-1; Steven Trojanovic had 8 points and a minus-1; Brandon Devlin had 8 points and a plus-9;

Derek Mathers had 5 points and a minus-1; while Stephen Pierog had 3 points and was minus-3. Dale Hawerchuk, the former NHL star who was coaching the Barrie Colts, warned his team before their January 26 game that the Petes had as many points as the Colts had in the last 10 games.

Dagger's goals against in his last eight games—of which he had won six—was 2.60, and his save percentage was .932, an incredible turnaround from the previous 40 games. The Petes were winning the close games they once had lost. Only two of their wins were in regulation time. Former coach Mike Pelino was glad for them but thought that, with the trades he had also planned to make, he could have turned it around. "Maybe that's just sour grapes," said Pelino, who, like Dave Reid, had never come back for a game or contacted Hull.

The Petes were nine points behind Kingston with a long, gruelling four-day road trip ahead, taking them to Windsor, Saginaw and Plymouth. Hull was on his 14th consecutive day of work: he had taken only two days off in the last 21 days, and his words echoed the obvious: "This isn't a job, it is a lifestyle."

On the Monday before leaving, the Petes participated in various charitable functions. On Tuesday night's schedule was a skate with season ticket holders, and even that would bring a dark cloud.

Nothing should be more innocuous than a community skate, but you couldn't miss anything with this team. Seymour was skating around, holding a fan's baby, when a youngster crossed in front of him, tripping him up. He fell face first, protecting the baby as he slammed into the ice, spraining his shoulder area. He wouldn't be able to play for two weeks. The baby obviously didn't know what was going on and wasn't injured.

Injuries were not strangers to Seabiscuit. He remembered his first game with the Petes two years ago, when his arm went cold after a hit. Training staff thought it was a pinched nerve, so he played through it for a few games, but it wouldn't stop, and finally a doctor discovered an artery was clogged that would need an operation. He was out for six weeks, but without the discovery it could have been much worse. Seymour was a happy-go-lucky, dedicated player from a hard-working family that had built the Kriska trucking group near Ottawa. His father, Mark, had played in the OHL. Seabiscuit could also have gone the NCAA route, but when he went to his first OHL camp, "the excitement of it all, the free sticks and equipment, the media attention was like a dream come true. I had talked with others who had accepted scholarships and found the NCAA was more about school and the OHL more about hockey, which was what I wanted."

Seymour's injury was bad news for Hull and Oke. So was their meeting that day with the players' high school teachers. Players' marks had not improved since the last meeting. When Hull played, the Petes' contracts stated you had to earn at least a 60 per cent average in high school or you didn't get your education package, but there were no such requirements or threats now. He didn't need these problems as the team prepared for the long weekend trip, but he swore to take action if players continued to ignore their schooling.

Mixing school and hockey at this level is difficult, as is making sure the players stay busy. As the players waited for Thursday's road trip, they were given their itinerary for the upcoming five days. Here's what they saw; it's an example of the regimented lifestyle the teams try to keep them under.

Windsor/Saginaw/Plymouth
Weekend Itinerary January 30th–February 2nd, 2013

Wednesday, January 30th, 2013

Depart P.M.C.	5:00 P.M. approx.
Meal @ Montana's PTBO	5:15 P.M.
Depart for Windsor	6:15 P.M.
Arrive @ Hotel in Windsor	11:15 P.M. approx.
Pizza @ Hotel	11:45 P.M.

Thursday, January 31st, 2013

Wake Up	9:45 A.M.
Breakfast @ Hotel	10:00 A.M.
Team Event	11:00 A.M.
Pre-game Meal @ Hotel	2:00 P.M.
Depart for Game vs. Spitfires	4:40 P.M.
Game vs. Spitfires	7:05 P.M.
Post-game Meal @ Hotel	10:00 P.M.

Friday, February 1st, 2013

Wake Up	9:45 A.M.
Breakfast @ Hotel	10:00 A.M.
Check Out of Hotel/Depart for Saginaw	11:00 A.M.
Arrive @ Hotel in Saginaw	1:30 P.M. approx.
Pre-game Meal	2:00 P.M.
Depart for Game vs. Spirit	4:45 P.M.
Game vs. Spirit	7:11 P.M.
Post-game Meal	10:00 P.M.

Saturday, February 2nd, 2013

Wake Up	9:45 A.M.
Breakfast @ Hotel	10:00 A.M.
Team Event	11:00 A.M.
Pre-game Meal	2:00 P.M.
Depart for Game vs. Whalers	3:00 P.M.
Game vs. Whalers	7:05 P.M.
Post-game Meal on Bus	

Recently acquired Mike Clarke woke up from his goal drought in Windsor, scoring two against his former team. He was named the first star. Brandon Devlin, another former Spitfire, went unnoticed by the media but played his best game, adding two assists. Ritchie, back from another injury, played a big game, using his body and strength as only this man-child could do.

Czinder, finally cleared for duty, hit a crossbar. Nelson Armstrong got his first goal as a Pete but had some teeth damaged, requiring the attention of a Windsor dentist. Former Pete Trevor Murphy played but did little against his old teammates, and the injured Koeks was there only to watch the game, meeting some of the players during warmup, going out with Seymour that afternoon for lunch and seeing others after the game.

That night, the *Examiner*'s Davies experienced some discomfort when his hotel room was pranked, his wake-up alarm reset, his bed turned around and some other minor alterations made. He initially blamed Coach Hull, but Hull had an alibi. Davies would never learn of the power of the B-Man.

Moving into February the next night in Saginaw, the Petes played a team that had been on a hot streak, winning nine of its last 10 games. "Muhammad Ali" Cornel got into his first fight, or at least dropped his gloves and wrestled for a while, earning five-minute majors for both himself and his opponent. He and the linesman both chuckled at his pugilistic weakness. The other rookie, Josh Maguire, got his first goal in a 4–2 win. The team had four points in two nights on the road, and with a Kingston loss in overtime, they were now only six behind. They could feel the team closeness and hear Hull's words: "We can do this."

The next night, they lost to Plymouth, but coming home with four of six points on the road was a good feeling. It was not so much that the Petes were winning, but how. Maybe it was the new dressing room leadership, with Mathers bringing the rookies into the fold, or Dagger's improved play or, more noticeably, Hull at the helm, but the team was changing.

"Definitely, it was the coaching change," said Cornel. "Jody came in, everyone respected him. He had played here, played in the NHL, knew where we were coming from. He brought everyone together. Before, the players were playing for each other; now they were playing for the team. He's a players' coach, holds us accountable . . . he treats us all the same. He made us all more comfortable. He was approachable; we enjoy playing. Even the bus rides were better. Plugger [Pelino] would get up and want music off, telling us we have a game to play."

Mathers agreed but added, "It was a little bit of both, firing the coach and trading the players, that turned it around."

A lot of players' families travelled to see their kids play three games in three nights, an incredible feat for bruised and battered teenagers.

When the bus arrived back on Roger Neilson Way at 4:30 A.M., after travelling 534 kilometres and four days away, Trojanovic, who hadn't played in Plymouth, limped down the steps. Nelson Armstrong, after his first goal, had a bent smile from his swollen lip and damaged teeth, which would have to be further examined Monday. Josh Maguire was still smiling from his first goal, the thrill of his young life. Mathers, stepping off the bus, showed Hull his blistered knuckles and asked, "Want to kiss it better, Coach?" Nick Czinder, using a hockey stick to scrape the early-morning frost from his truck windows, had returned from his concussion tests and appeared fine.

Jonatan Tanus, on a hot streak with 12 points in 13 games, had improved his English to such a degree that he could easily carry on a conversation that included swearing. He still came up with some classics, though: when he hit his head on the bus mirror, he explained, "I was watching down." Brett Findlay, finally dazzling crowds and teammates with his smooth style, now led the team in scoring; he hit the bus horn while disembarking.

Clark and Hull smiled as they watched the transformed players carrying their suit bags, stepping from the bus with goody packages families had brought them, and the players smiling back.

The training staff headed home an hour later, after getting the gear packed away. B-Man would return in the morning to do laundry. His assistants were seen but seldom heard, handling things so well they were barely noticed. The team had spent four days away with 23 players, two coaches, an assistant general manager, a trainer, four part-timers and three reporters and had not a single problem.

I reached inside my pocket upon arriving home and found a salt shaker. Now I knew why Seabiscuit had asked, after one of the restaurant stops, if I had any salt.

***

The Petes had a game in Ottawa on Wednesday, followed Thursday by their first home game in two weeks, against Windsor. Then Saturday was *Hockey Day in Canada* (finally announced only a few days earlier), a sold-out game in Peterborough on the Petes' special "Pink in the Rink Night," a salute to mothers and the season's biggest fundraiser, this time for breast cancer research.

The combination of the two special events in one night had been causing anxiety, tension and friction in the Petes' small office, where too few people were doing far too many things. Newcomer Kathleen Reeves was juggling too much. She quit later in the month for a job in Toronto where the company, unlike the Petes, had a job description, trained her for weeks and provided her with work manuals and appropriate resources. While she was no longer working in sports, it was a welcome change. Her duties reverted to Garfat.

The business side of hockey was of little importance to any of the players, even though it had a great effect on them. They cared about only one thing: they were four points out of the playoffs. As the team headed to Ottawa on February 6, the players seemed loose—too loose. Even Hull sensed it, but they won 10–6, the team's largest scoring output of the season. Dagger had a poor game, his first in more than a month, and angrily tossed his stick when the game ended. Even good kids get pissed off. Verner had mapped out the team's goalie statistics, showing the improvement since November 27. In 25 of the last 29 games, most of them Dagger's, they had had a save percentage of better than 90 per cent. Goalies have bad games; the trick was to not have many.

Hull told the team it was not a good game from a coach's perspective: they were getting away from their system. He acknowledged that a win was a win, but he'd rather win the coach's way, as a team. The bus, which had left Roger Neilson Way at 1 P.M., arrived home at 1 A.M. The high school kids had to be at school by 8, then ready for that night's game against the Windsor Spitfires, who had arrived last night to rest and prepare for battle.

The Petes had been 14 points out of a playoff spot and were now only four points behind Kingston, which just as remarkably had gone in the opposite direction, losing its 12th straight game. There were 16 games left in the regular season, two of them against the Frontenacs. There were bumps on the road ahead, though, and one of those bumps was the game against Windsor, when the Petes did not, as stick boy Iain once again predicted, win 5–0. Instead, they lost 9–4, before a small crowd, announced at just more than 2,000, but fewer were there. The Petes had been playing so well and getting close to making the playoffs, and yet the fan turnout was disappointing. It was disheartening to the team. To rub salt into the wound, the Spitfires had dressed only 15 players because of injuries and suspensions.

A winter storm dropped 40 centimetres of snow on Peterborough the next night. It brought with it a magical winter wonderland weekend for the city and for the Petes, followed by a wild, unimaginable and unforeseen fairy-tale-like journey.

CHAPTER 17

Showtime Magic

Every year, CBC Television picks a different locale from which to broadcast a day-long love-in with Canadian hockey. It's a tradition that was instituted more than a decade ago and has flourished happily ever since. *Hockey Night in Canada*'s regular Saturday night crew visits the city, interspersing the local sights and sounds with broadcasts of several NHL games. This year, the program's producers had no way of knowing the league's schedule until the lockout ended early in the new year, and they wanted to find someplace close to their Toronto headquarters so that their staff could organize and shoot the show with a minimum of logistical disturbance. They turned to Peterborough for help.

Community volunteers jumped at the chance, and the Petes were asked to play a major role. Devlin took over a so-called community committee that he set up to look after the Petes' part: putting on a big celebrity banquet the night before the Saturday game and making sure the CBC had the necessary access to the Memorial Centre the next day, when the Petes played the Soo. To the public, it looked like everything ran without a hitch. This wasn't quite the case.

The Petes would be the main thread running through *Hockey Day in Canada,* not only hosting their own game on February 9 but also basically turning over the facility to the national broadcaster. However, nothing seemed to come easily to the Petes, who apparently had told the CBC they had the use of the arena, though they were not in a position to speak on behalf of the city, which owned the arena and was less inclined to welcome the network than the Petes.

On January 17, there was to be a press conference announcing that *Hockey Day* was coming to Peterborough and that the Petes would host a banquet the night before, but Devlin was becoming aware of snags in the contractual relationship between the CBC, the city and the Petes. These issues became all-consuming: over the next few weeks, Devlin would spend close to seven hours a day dealing with them. The CBC and its major corporate partner, Scotiabank, wanted to take over the whole affair. The city and Petes worried about their other local commitments. Parks Canada worried about the size of *its* commitment and struggled with what it was allowing to take place on its property, which included the Trent Canal, where a huge outdoor hockey tournament was to take place, putting a lot of pressure on their local employees to make sure it all worked. There were also some personality clashes among local potentates. Small pictures were getting in the way of the big one. The CBC came close to saying, "To hell with the Petes and the Memorial Centre" and pulling out. Contracts weren't finally signed, and arrangements announced, until 10 days before the big weekend. It came that close to not happening.

And despite the best efforts of a variety of bureaucrats and officials to sabotage the event, the two-day hockey celebration was enchanting.

The biggest snowfall in a decade did not hinder the banquet on Friday night, which featured television celebrities including Don Cherry, Ron MacLean, Kevin Weekes, Elliotte Friedman and P.J. Stock, as well as NHL alumni such as Bob Gainey, Cory Stillman, Steve Larmer, Lanny McDonald, Steve Webb, Wendel Clark, Darcy Tucker, Mark Napier, Derian Hatcher, Dick Todd and many others. The National Hockey League Players' Association donated more than $50,000 worth of equipment to local teams. A CBC feature on Dagger and his contributions to cystic fibrosis and a special city boy stricken with the disease, to be shown coast to coast the following day, was played for the banquet crowd and all of his teammates, who could have teased him as some had expected, but instead gathered around and embraced their new leader.

The 40 centimetres of snow that fell that night cancelled two other OHL games, but as the mayor of Peterborough, Daryl Bennett, told the banquet attendees, the federal government was in charge of that weather; the municipality would clean it up and guarantee perfect weather for Saturday.

While those lucky enough to get tickets partied at the banquet, almost 300 volunteers shovelled snow on the Trent Canal late Friday night and early Saturday morning so the ice would be available for the tournament, which involved a thousand children. Participants woke up the morning after the snowstorm to see a cloud-free sky of robin's-egg blue and a corn-yellow sun. With a temperature of minus-4, it *was* perfect weather, and the CBC made the most of it.

Hockey Day in Canada host MacLean would be on the canal at the tournament for seven hours before heading to the Memorial Centre in the evening for another five hours of live broadcasting.

It was a phenomenal day for Peterborough, as its history, hockey and people were featured continuously over the airwaves. For the Petes, the weekend would be especially memorable, with the Saturday night game sold out and the Pink in the Rink fundraiser set to become a golden occasion.

Before that Saturday night game began, Perogi looked at the women wearing pink T-shirts, standing across the ice from board to board at the Petes' blue line, players' mothers and their landmothers all there in support of the annual Pink in the Rink breast cancer night. He thought of his own mother, who had died of a heart attack a few years earlier, before ever seeing him in the maroon and white of the Petes, and he imagined how much she would have enjoyed this moment. Perogi's mother had given him tenacity and what Pelino had so appropriately called the "junkyard dog" attitude. Tears welled up in his eyes. Coach Clark patted him on the back.

He was the only Pete to no longer have a mother, but adding to his emotional burden was the fact that his landmother, who stood with the group, as well as her mother, had both been battling the disease that won't leave any of us alone.

As the women stood on the ice, the "rock star" of *Hockey Night in Canada,* 79-year-old Don Cherry, emerged from a virtual mob scene in the lobby to step onto the red carpet and drop the puck. He was dressed in a green-and-black plaid suit, a leashed British bull terrier at his side. He had demanded the dog earlier in the afternoon; it was supplied just before game time. Fellow commentator Ron MacLean, who does more to provide information and support for hockey in Canada than many, accompanied him, waving to the Petes' largest and loudest crowd of the season. Peterborough native, former NHL star, and two-time Stanley Cup winner Cory Stillman, wearing a pink shirt under his suit jacket in support of his recently deceased mother, Sandra, waited at centre ice to drop the puck with them.

The Memorial Centre was abuzz, jammed from restaurant to rooftop. There had not been comparable community sports excitement here since the 1996 Memorial Cup. The week-long buildup to *Hockey Day in Canada* and the CBC broadcasting live from Peterborough all afternoon had been magical.

There were 3,907 people in attendance, the largest crowd for a Petes' game since 2006, when 3,996 witnessed an OHL finals game. The Memorial Centre was the venue for *Hockey Night in Canada* segments, including "Coach's Corner" and the "Hot Stove" panel, where MacLean was quietly cheering for a Dagger win after seeing the film demonstrating the teen's devotion to a young kid with cystic fibrosis.

The coaches didn't really have to encourage the players to get excited about the CBC's hockey weekend; they were primed and pumped for it. Their motivation was obvious: the full house, national television exposure, their mothers, their landmothers and the other women in their lives who would participate in the Pink in the Rink Night. Not to mention the continuing race for the playoffs.

The Petes, wearing one-time-only pink-and-black uniforms, played against the powerhouse Soo Greyhounds. The day-long entertainment package was wrapped in a ribbon of perfection when the Petes won, not disappointing the city, its people or the CBC. Dagger starred in the net on his perfect day, which ended when he gave a live interview in full gear with MacLean and Cherry.

There were so many wonderful tales that were never told. These included Cody Thompson (called Thumper by the boys) scoring after asking Hull to let him play in memory of his father, who died of a heart attack after prolonged cancer in 2010. The rejuvenated Findlay scored a goal and an assist and was named the game's first star against the team that had traded him away. Czinder scored the winner, and the team played a textbook game in a 3–2 nailbiter.

There had been several other loud ovations before the game for Pink in the Rink, the CBC, Cherry, MacLean and Stillman, but none came close to reaching the crowd's roar for their Petes when the final buzzer sounded. Few people had left the rink when the team saluted the crowd before accepting a special cup that Scotiabank gave to the winning team.

It was a fairy-tale day for the city and the Petes, for almost everyone.

Near ice level, watching the presentations and waiting for the team to leave the ice, were the mothers dressed in their pink shirts with their names on the back. I smiled thinking of Perogi, as well as Thumper's goal for his dad. But dressed in their street clothes, wearing their special team jerseys, standing at the bottom of the stairs below the mothers, unable to see the ice surface or be with their teammates, were healthy scratches Chase Hatcher, whose parents had driven from Philly for the big weekend, and Peter Ceresnak, whose parents were back home in Slovakia. Sitting the pair had been Hull's hardest decision of the day. For Hatcher, it was his turn to sit, while Hull hadn't been impressed by Ceresnak's play of late. Hatcher would have sat Thursday and played tonight instead of Thompson, if not for Thumper's special request. I told them to at least go up to the team's bench and stand with the coaches. They were nervous, though, and unwilling to push through the crowd of mothers. They stayed standing with their hands in their pockets. "This is really tough. Really tough. You don't know how hard this is," said Hatcher, as Ceresnak nodded his head in agreement. "It would have meant so much to be playing. This is difficult, especially tonight—this is such a special night."

You couldn't help but hurt with them. Nobody else was aware of their predicament. There was nobody involved with the team to at least urge them to ice level. It wouldn't have helped the hurt but might have comforted the pain if they had at least got there. I saw the HATCHER T-shirt his mom was wearing. She didn't know that her son was behind her, but she obviously wished he was before her on the ice. Hatcher and Ceresnak had not been forgotten, but in that moment, they had not been remembered, either. Hatcher shook it off quickly, turned around and said, "Big win for the boys, though; big two points, that's a good thing."

The other players finally left the ice, past the happy mothers, down four steps and along the corridor, 13 strides long, that led into the dressing room, Hatcher patting each of them on the back before he and Ceresnak joined them. Thompson walked by and said to me, "There's one for Dad." Stephen Pierog looked up as he passed me, and we both knew. We smiled. "A win for Mom," I said, so only he could hear. A huge open-mouthed smile came across his face. He didn't have to say a word; he just nodded vigorously.

Seabiscuit walked by, still glowing with the victory. "I can't wipe the smile off my face, and I don't want to."

Ritchie had been a horse among ponies tonight. He had played his best game despite recording only a single assist, which for some players might have been enough but for him was not even close. He laughed, soaked in the excitement. The officials, for once, had not taken away his hitting with penalty calls.

Inside the dressing room, behind closed doors, Tanus presented the Burn the Boats Award, saying, "There were a lot of big points tonight, like Zindy and Finner, but today is Dagger's day." The room erupted in cheers. Dagger, who had stopped 40 shots that night, broke into a smile. He and the rest of the team had been on a mission. It wasn't so much to win, but to make sure the team did not lose on this special night.

Dagger had written on the whiteboard before the game, "Every victory is won before you play under the lights." It was an echo of boxing great Muhammad Ali's line, "The fight is won or lost far away from the witnesses—behind the lines, in the gym and out there on the road, long before I dance under those lights." In other words, practice makes perfect.

"There were great individual efforts out there tonight," said Hull. "You all did your job, put in the effort that was needed. The entire defence played well. You can all look at the player beside you and know that he emptied his tank tonight. Remember this feeling, remember how tired the extra effort makes you feel, but remember that feeling is what we need. I think Ritch played a great game, showing that scoring points is not all that matters. It was just a great team effort." His pride in what they had accomplished was bursting from his breaking voice as he spoke. Some F-bombs lent them emphasis.

The Petes had played Hull hockey, textbook hockey, or as Dick Todd told the coaches, "There wasn't a player there that didn't buy into the team game tonight."

Inside their dressing room, after Hull's short talk, the players looked at each other knowing they had given it everything. Their tanks were empty. It was 9:50 P.M. Hull joked that curfew was 10. Stick boy Iain, who had again predicted a 5–0 win, quietly walked about the dressing room, then added more magic when he spoke up, saying more than his usual "Showstopper!" "Well done, guys, good game, play as a team. I mean it!" he yelled. The players, coaches and training staff cheered, clapped, laughed, bit into some pizza and cranked up their music, before hitting the ice again to auction off their jerseys.

A crowd of about 1,000 was waiting for the boys, now including Hatcher and Ceresnak, to auction their pink-and-black jerseys, which had arrived just this week but had been ordered by the methodical B-Man long ago. He had also, without recognition, sent requests to his NHL contacts for auction items such as signed sticks and jerseys for the night. In all, more than $80,000 was raised for cancer research. The jersey auction alone raised more than $14,000, led by Diesel's, at $1,300; Ritchie's, at $1,000; and Dagger's, at $850.

The players had heard the crowd chanting, no longer the familiar smattering of scattered applause and weak attempts at "Go Petes Go," but the sound of almost 4,000 voices, all wanting the players to hear them. They agreed that if they had this crowd to boost and urge them on every night, it would be a different team, a better team, a team assured that it had that seventh player with them during Showtime.

It was this night—not the firings, not the trades, not the past, but this night—that marked the turning point in the season. This night was when 23 players became a team. Assistant coach Clark wondered later if maybe this game would increase the crowds by even 300. The other coaches, although hopeful, were doubtful. It was special, and everyone knew it.

The restaurant/bar at the rink was still full of people after the game as the CBC continued to broadcast among them. Some people there didn't even know the score; they were so enthralled by *Hockey Day* and the alcohol they had been consuming that they hadn't watched the game in front of them. A surprise guest was Greg Millen, who had broadcast a CBC game that afternoon in Detroit and driven directly to Peterborough afterward. He hadn't received much credit or even thanks for helping to bring the event to town, but he was proud of the people who had only five weeks to put it all together. "The community came through, eh?" he said, smiling. It had.

Neither the Petes, the city, nor the Memorial Centre had anything on their websites about the banquet, *Hockey Day* game highlights or the jersey sales, maybe because they were understaffed or just unable to recognize an opportunity staring them in their faces. Millen and many others knew the people had come through, though. CBC executive producer Joel Darling, who put it together, as he had for most of the *Hockey Day* telecasts, knew about the struggles, arguments and frustrations, but he smiled at the result. He knew it had been worth it. When the night was over, his crew packed up and left behind another city brimming with pride at what CBC had revealed to the nation: that Peterborough was the best city in Canada.

Obviously, there would be arguments about that from people in almost every other part of the country, but for now, Peterborough, one of the best-kept secrets in Canada, was part of the public record from coast to coast. A national spotlight had been shone on the community, and it shone back. Every athlete knew, however, that sunshine could be quickly covered by a cloud. Would the team be able to continue basking in the glow of this weekend for the rest of the regular season?

CHAPTER 18

The Impossible Dream

The new Petes board met for the first time on February 11. As usual, the meeting, still without an agenda, went past midnight, and there were some interesting developments, the most significant being that coach Jody Hull and general manager Mike Oke were hired permanently and given two-year contracts. The board discussion wasn't about whether the "interim" qualifier should be removed from their titles but whether the length of their deals would be one or two years.

Hull, who had almost walked out in December when no changes were made, had done an excellent job of turning the team around, while Oke had made the deadline deals the board members felt were necessary for their present and future success. The team would also go back to having the GM and player personnel director roles combined: Oke assumed both jobs, just as all GMs before Reid had done.

By game time on February 14, the Petes were only two points behind the Kingston Frontenacs. Two points! Unbelievable.

It was the inspiring, incredible play of Dagger, making 46 saves, that saved the game in front of another surprisingly small hometown crowd, announced at 2,300—including Liberal Party leadership candidate Justin Trudeau. Dagger made saves he hadn't been making earlier in the year. His 22-year-old brother Matt, now a marketing intern for the Petes, was so happy for him. Last year, when the team was doing so poorly, he had watched his brother struggling and the fans turning against him, and he sympathized so keenly that he joined a Thursday night recreational hockey league in Scarborough to avoid having to attend the Petes games with his parents.

Most of the players now were playing like Perogi—they were junk-yard dogs. He continued to impress coaches and fans, making every shift count, while scoring another goal to tie the game against Menard's Brampton team. The final score was 3–1 in favour of the Petes.

They played in Ottawa Friday; Kingston was in Sudbury. The Petes could wake up Saturday morning tied for the last playoff spot. Brampton coach Stan Butler told the media he wouldn't be surprised to see Peterborough in the post-season.

The Petes' rise had caught the attention of the media and the rest of the league. Hull was getting a lot of the credit, but he deflected it, saying the players should get the praise. The players touted him, though. They respected what he had done and were willing to crash through walls for him. He hoped he was laying a good foundation for the Petes' future, knowing at least 17 of the players could return next season.

Kelly Hull remembered the nights when Jody came home so frustrated he couldn't sleep, when he was thinking of quitting because nobody seemed to be doing anything to turn the team around. Being out of the playoffs the last two years had made him miserable. Now he was losing sleep worrying about players missing curfews, their school marks and the team's playoff chances. He felt like the players' coach, father and mentor. Why continue to do it, given the grief? "It's hard to explain so people would understand. This isn't a job, it isn't work. It is the lifestyle. It's something you love to do, but you never consider it work," he said. It was a good attitude, because the hours were long, the days off during the season were few and the heartaches outnumbered the joys, although the joys were wonderful and lasting.

When he looked at the team statistics, even he was surprised at the improvement in the team and in individual players. His record was 11–6–0–3 since taking over, while Pelino's was 8–23–3–1. Ritchie had nine points in his last nine games since returning. Dagger was a new goalie, winning six of his last seven starts; he had won only one of 15 under Pelino. Findlay, who had almost left the team in October, said he was happy now that he hadn't left; only a visit from his sister, the Canadian figure skating champion, had stopped him. He had been oh so close, telling his parents he had had enough, wasn't getting the ice time he wanted or needed, and was the coach's whipping boy. He never disclosed this to the coaching staff or the media until much later in the season, when the Petes began to win. Findlay had 26 points in 20 games under Hull, but only 13 in 35 under Pelino.

Hull was not winning with smoke and mirrors, but with all of his players. Back in November, Hatcher and Cornel were getting five or fewer minutes per game; now they were averaging 11. Koekkoek had been eating up 27 to 30 minutes every game; now nobody was on the ice for more than 23.

Hull continued to tell the boys that they could worry only about what was in their control. He stopped one practice the next week to remind them that if they didn't want to concentrate and put the proper effort into the drills, they should get off the ice. They got the message, and practice got more intense.

Giggy continued to be a treat to watch, with his loose and carefree style. Before one practice began, he was lying on the ice as if asleep, then sweeping his stick at players' feet as they skated past. Former scout and teacher Don Barrie said it was something you'd see in "like, a peewee goalie." Nope, it was just Giggy being Giggy. As the kid said, "It's stopping the puck that will make me a better goalie," and there wasn't a player on the team that didn't have difficulty scoring on the kid in practice. He hated when they got one by him, and it didn't happen very often. "He's the toughest goalie we face," said Mathers, agreeing about his immaturity but confident in his talent.

Giggy had chosen this profession, saying, "It is a crazy thing we do," but as far as his mother was concerned, it was better than being a sulky driver, something her father, brother and uncle, all well-known at Ontario harness-racing tracks, had done to make a living. She was a secretary at a board of education; Giggy's father was a civil engineer and his sister had attended a university in Scotland on a scholarship. Pursuing dreams was acceptable and encouraged in their household.

Peterborough beat the 67's 5–1 in Ottawa, but Kingston won their road game as well. The two-point gap remained. The Frontenacs dropped a 10–7 decision the next night in the Soo, using up one of their games in hand on the Petes, but rebounded to win 7–4 on Monday the 18th in Mississauga while Peterborough suffered a 3–2 loss to Owen Sound in regulation time. The gap was back at four points.

There was nothing more pleasing for Petes fans than sending an Oshawa team back down the highway with a loss, but it hadn't happened since October 2010. Defeating the Generals on February

21 was like winning a lottery, tasting sweet juice from a tangerine, the Habs beating the Leafs—or vice versa.

The last time the Petes had played Oshawa, in GM City on January 11, they were down 3–0 and came back to tie it, only to lose in overtime; this time, the Generals came storming out in the first period and took a 2–0 lead. Hull was not happy. Oshawa had outhit his team, with 11 hits. "You look like you're scared of them," he said during the first intermission. "Start competing, quit moping around. If you're scared, take your gear off and stay here. Squeeze your nuts."

The team responded with an amazing comeback, not only tying the game but taking hold of it and ripping the Gens 6–3, with Mathers, who had 18 points in his last 21 games, popping two goals and two assists and earning the nickname Sid (as in Crosby) from his landparents' son. Oshawa's Justice Dundas tried to spear him following the game, and the two had a few words that ended in Mathers warning that he'd see Dundas on Sunday, when the teams next met. Dagger again made key saves to push Oshawa away from what could have been a 6–0 opening period.

The Petes were again only two points out of a playoff spot, but more importantly, the dressing room, office and rink were in a state of euphoria. Dagger, selected the hardest-working Pete for turning away 37 Generals shots, skated onto the ice with a radiant smile and did something he had not done this season. He turned to the crowd, pumping his arms three times in the air: thank you, thank you, thank you. The crowd—which included his critics, who had called him a bum earlier in the year—returned his salute with a wonderful ovation. As he left the ice, he gave his buddy Anthony, the boy with cystic fibrosis, a big high five.

Dagger was the key in helping this team win by getting rid of his early-season bout of rebounditis—his tendency to, as Slater Koekkoek had described it, allow that weak goal. He now had an incredible .914 save percentage, worked even harder with his training, and was stopping pucks that were once going past him. It was because of his work ethic—his no-nonsense approach—that in February he was leading the way, in the best shape an athlete could be, while other goalies in the league were fading. "Dagger has been the one we can count on," said young Cornel. "He works so hard, we count on him every night. We know we can make mistakes now."

As for Dagger, he gave credit to his coaches. "I always asked Andrew [Verner] if he knew who was playing goal the next game until finally he told me, 'You're playing until we tell you you aren't.' My confidence shot up to a different level. I clearly took it to a new level. I knew I had it in me. The coaches showed confidence in me. Everything went right. If you had told any of us at Christmas, after that first win, that we would accomplish so much, nobody would have believed you, but Jody thought we could."

Coaches, once shaking their heads in frustration, now kept pushing the troops, reminding them they could defeat and play against any team. Office staff, which once put on mourning faces when entering the building, now greeted people with smiles, hearty handshakes and even laughter. Fans, who once blistered the team with ignorant, shameful insults, were now full of praise and wonderment. The people who had predicted this team would not make the playoffs had conveniently forgotten their words and were saying, "Maybe they have a shot," as they cheered them on. Ticket sales, slow until recently, were up as well.

After the Oshawa game, Giggy gave the Burn Boats Award to the guy he jokingly called the team's "lightweight champion," Mathers. The captain had turned his game around since Christmas. The once-plodding winger now had some speed and had been working hard in the weight room and on the ice with his conditioning and leg strength. Since getting the captaincy, he had made sure all the players were included in team activities. Rookie Maguire noticed this when he and other rookies went out with the team to a Boston Pizza "for the best night of my life." Their inclusion was a first for the new kids. Mathers was leading off the ice and getting points on the ice.

Findlay, leading the team in points, went public, revealing to Davies his October contemplation of almost leaving. He now said what so many in the sports world preached: never quit or stop believing. He had been a minus player on a poor team; now he was a plus player on a good team. It was a remarkable turnaround. The fans couldn't believe his change, his creativity, his ability to find the open man or his effervescence when the team scored. Still, they wished he would shoot more. Fans are tough critics, always wanting more.

There was a loose hour-long practice on Friday, February 22. Near the end of it, Hull hid Giggy's catching glove, setting him off in a search-and-accusation episode. B-Man loaded a water bottle full of salt water to the surprise of Ceresnak and Betzold, the unfortunate ones who guzzled the drink during the on-ice cool-down. There was a short special-units practice with Wayne Clark scheduled for Saturday morning, and then the team was off to Belleville that night to face the red-hot Quine, who had 37 points in 17 games since leaving the Petes.

Saturday didn't start well.

Hull was at minor-hockey meetings in the morning while Clark had the special units practising, but Boland, a key man on the defence, had slept through his alarm. Hull had sat him for 10 minutes the last time he arrived late for a meeting; this time, he had no choice. The game's relevance didn't overrule the importance of team discipline. Boland was a scratch.

Belleville extended its seven-game winning streak to eight when the Petes, who had played shift for shift against the Bulls, took two penalties near the end of the second period and collapsed, giving up a 1–0 lead and allowing two goals during the penalties. They lost 5–2. Pierog's hot hand continued as he scored two goals. Quine, on a tear since moving to the Bulls, cooled down, with a single assist. Luckily, Kingston lost to Niagara so the Petes were still only two points out.

It was a tough loss, but after the game life was put into perspective once more. Josh Maguire's parents were waiting for him in the lobby. Josh's grandfather, Bryan Rose, one of his best friends and supporters, and a former junior player himself, had suffered a fatal heart attack without warning. Josh's parents didn't want him to find out by phone, so they were there to break the news. Hull had the family come into an empty dressing room and directed Josh there after he got dressed. A sobbing Josh went home with his heartbroken mother.

That weekend, the team came up short 4–1 to a much stronger and more talented Generals team before a crowd of close to 6,000. Mathers made good on his promise to Dundas. The right winger started the game on the left side instead and they dropped gloves immediately. Mathers won handily, but it was his 10th fight, which meant the OHL would suspend him for two games if he had another in the regular season.

There were more than a dozen NHL scouts watching Oshawa forward Cole Cassels and Giggy—outstanding in the nets, stopping 48 shots—as well as Betzold, who was still attracting attention.

The following week, Tyson Baker, the kick-boxing champion who had given up that sport for hockey, was welcomed to the team for the rest of the year. Hull talked with Maguire, Thompson and Hatcher, who had been rotating in and out of the lineup, to assure them that Baker, whose Junior B season was over, was only there in case there was an injury and to give him some experience around the team. He didn't want any apprehension or anxiety that yet another player was going to take up some of their ice time.

Giggy continued to live in Giggy's world, failing to get a high school paper in on time, so Hull sent him home before a practice to get it done. A high school goalie was brought in to replace him. An issue like this, as Mathers pointed out, shouldn't have been cropping up at this time in the season. Hull sent a clear message that this type of school effort was not acceptable and wouldn't be tolerated. He threatened to send Giggy home to Brampton for the remainder of the season if it continued. Two other players were late for school—one sleeping in, the other without an excuse—so they too had to be brought in with Oke and Hull for a talking-to before practice.

Giggy was back at practice the following day, February 27, when Hull told the team that the next eight games were their playoffs, a chance for veterans and rookies to get into the real post-season, and to give pro scouts even more time to watch them. Hull had addressed these playoff opportunities briefly before, especially after games when they were inching closer to Kingston during the last two weeks, but today he spent more time on the theme. It was nothing the players didn't already know, but he reinforced it as their main focus to build that playoff atmosphere for the upcoming games.

Not that everyone was always serious. Dagger had been waiting for his new mask for a month when it finally arrived. B-Man unwrapped it, but, rather than telling Dagger, he let Verner and Hull know. They then wrapped a plain white goalie mask and placed it back in the box. B-Man delivered it to Dagger in the dressing room, and he had a fit: this wasn't the mask he had ordered at all! He tore into Hull's office to tell them, and there was Verner, wearing the new mask, which was beautifully painted to show peaks and valleys—just like their season. Dagger had asked that several quotes be reproduced on the mask, one from Dr. Spencer Johnson—author of *Who Moved My Cheese?*—that said, "You change your valley into a peak when you find and use the good that is hidden in the bad time." There was also a quote from football player Ray Lewis, Dagger's favourite athlete: "If tomorrow wasn't promised, what would you give for today?"

Down the back of the maroon-and-white mask were words from the motivational speaker Eric Thomas that Dagger, an avid reader, thought summed up his season and philosophy: "Pain is temporary. It may last for a minute, or an hour, or a day, or even a year. But eventually it will subside, and something else will take its place. If I quit, however, it will last forever."

"You guys won't have to worry about me coaching here next year," Hull told them following the Ottawa game on February 28. "If you keep playing like this, I'm going to have a heart attack."

The team had just completed a 4–3 shootout win that had required two shorthanded goals (before this game, they had scored only two all year). Dagger stoned Ottawa in the shootout and Tanus got a nifty one to win it and put the Petes once again only two points behind Kingston.

Once again, a small crowd of 2,000 showed up to cheer the Petes on to a possible playoff spot. Later, when most of those fans were warmly tucked in their beds, one of the Petes' players still hadn't gone home. Unbeknownst to the team, he missed curfew by hours, causing a problem that wouldn't erupt for two days.

The team travelled five hours to Sudbury on Friday, March 1, lost to the Wolves and stayed in a rather beaten-up hotel on a broken street in the city. The next morning, they travelled another three and a half hours to the Soo on a two-lane highway that made the trip feel two hours longer.

It wasn't until later that Saturday that Hull learned Betzold had broken curfew in pursuit of *la femme* (curfew breaches are seldom because of alcohol or drugs; they usually involve a young woman). An upset Hull put him through a strenuous bag skate back and forth across the ice at the Saturday afternoon practice in the Soo and informed him he would be sitting out Sunday's game.

Betzold had put Hull in a terrible situation: now they'd be missing one of their top six forwards for an important game. Hull told the media upfront that the rookie was out for discipline, a curfew viola- tion. Agents complain about this degree of honesty from coaches, asking why the team just doesn't say they are out sick or a healthy scratch. In Hull's view, players should think of the consequences before they choose to hurt the team. He hadn't been an angel when he played for the Petes—he had also missed curfews—but he had picked his moments. Betzold was not the first, and wouldn't be the last, but hopefully he would be the last this season.

Betzold knew he was wrong and apologized. The normally talk- ative teenager was relatively quiet and more attentive for the rest of the season. It was obvious he had learned an important lesson.

If Betzold was quiet that night, Findlay was excited. He was coming home to where he had played minor hockey, where his mom had been power skating coach for the Greyhounds until the team traded her son. The Findlay family and friends treated the team to some nearby Echo Bay hospitality.

Echo Bay is a blink-of-an-eye hamlet of 600 people. When you looked across the water, you could see the United States; on the Canadian side, you saw lakes, streams and forests where the locals hunted, fished and rode snowmobiles. On Saturday nights, some of them went to the Elk Lodge, just down the street from a gas station that had a sign welcoming BRETT FINDLAY AND THE PETERBOROUGH PETES that night.

There were 33 on the Petes bus that pulled into the Elk Lodge, where Brett's dad, Bruce, along with relatives and friends, were cooking beef and pork on the spit. Inside the small hall, similar to many halls in countless Canadian communities, the Findlay women, including Brett's mother, grandmothers and aunts, were in the kitchen. Helping them were Findlay's Peterborough landparent as well as Petes office administrator Cathie Webster and the mothers of Dagger, Varga and Nosad, all of whom had driven from Toronto and Peterborough for a girls' weekend away. They prepared mashed potatoes, mixed vegetables, salads, perogies, buns and desserts, including Finner's grandmother's chocolate peanut butter balls, the room's favourite.

They not only fed everyone but also entertained them with a washers tournament (sort of a poor man's game of horseshoes that involved metal washers and a wooden box), billiard games, darts and shuffleboard. It was a good old country neighbours' night, with hands down the best meal of the season. As Davies, who had ridden the buses for close to 20 years, said, it was the best time the Petes had ever been shown. A close second was the Italian feast that Mike Martone's family, also from the Soo, had put on years ago in their home.

The players lit candles on a piece of banana cake and walked it over to an embarrassed Larry Smith as everyone chimed in with "Happy Birthday" for Peterborough's newest 60-year-old.

There were three hours of sheer fun, laughter and the filling up of bellies in Echo Bay that night, just what many had needed after a season of fast food, interrupted sleep and hurrying up to wait. It's too bad we couldn't have stayed.

Some of the players should have, because they might have got more sleep. Hours after returning to the hotel, a couple of the younger players were seen wandering the halls at 2:30 A.M., not a good signal that the entire team was focused. The coach didn't know, but some of the veterans did, and they were pissed off at their teammates. Nothing was said that weekend.

There were seven games in the OHL that Sunday, six of them played in the afternoon, but the Petes and Greyhounds did not play until 7:07 P.M. In a league that claimed to be about development and education, it was difficult to see this kind of scheduling as a glittering example of their philosophy in action. All the Petes players would miss school the next day after making their journey home through the night and early morning. The team had to wait out Sunday in a hotel, take walks, go shopping at the mall and check the results of the afternoon games on their cell phones and tablets. They made the short walk from the hotel to the rink at 5 P.M. for a game inside the Essar Centre, a clean, modern, four-year-old facility that welcomed close to 4,000 fans to that night's game. B-Man was there, stitching an old jockstrap, finding tape, sharpening skates, taping players. When asked if he needed help, his simple reply was, "Why, you a psychologist?"

Soo fans went home happy when their team defeated the visitors 4–0, but it cost the Petes more than two points. Mathers got into his 11th fight of the regular season, was ruled the instigator and was suspended for the next four of their final five games. He didn't know this until after the game, which he was allowed to finish after serving his five-minute major. It was a big blow to the team.

The loss made the journey home even more gruelling. Trying to sleep among 32 guys in a large steel box, where some were stretched out on the floor, others across seats, heads bowed, heads tipped, some with pillows, bodies wrapped in blankets or track pants, some watching movies, was not a joyous experience. The laughing, yelling, swearing and storytelling that preceded sleep were not appreciated. Worse were the grunts, snores and body odours that followed. The last three hours of the eight-hour trip that Monday morning, after silence had finally arrived and the blackness of the night descended, were not worth doing again, ever. In spite of the smelly and sonorous distractions, most of the passengers slept.

CHAPTER 19

Sprint to the Finish

There were 11 days and five games left in the regular season. Derek Mathers, Clark Seymour and Brett Findlay met with coach Jody Hull to assure him they were behind his philosophy, but they wanted to confirm that he would be playing only the guys who were "working their asses off." The veterans then held a players-only closed-door meeting.

"The older guys at breakfast club got together and thought things had to be addressed, especially after the last weekend, when the younger guys were out after curfew after Sudbury, and then the Saturday night," said Mathers. "Missing curfew on road trips, at the most important time of the year, and with some of the young guys out of their rooms, had to be addressed.

"We talked to the team about not having any distractions of this type and the importance of winning four of the next five games."

Standing before their teammates, Findlay, Seymour and Mathers said that Hull was going to be playing only those he felt were working their hardest. The meeting lasted only five minutes, but the players got the message. Mathers said the veterans had held similar meetings a couple of times earlier in the season, but the "players didn't listen. There was no respect for leadership at that time."

He also took curfew breaker Greg Betzold aside because "some of the guys were blaming Betzy for the Soo loss," and he assured him it wasn't his fault.

At practice, Hull reiterated what his veterans had said. There was only one focus: the next 11 days and five games. There couldn't be any disciplinary distractions, and only the players playing well, no matter how talented they were, would play.

The practice was lively, more tenacious, more deliberate and more attentive. You could feel the players' anxiety and attention. It felt and sounded different from every practice that had preceded it. This final stretch was their season in a nutshell: after 63 games, it came down to this. Few outside the team believed they could do it.

The following day, Hull gathered the players in the dressing room before practice to show them a video. He had taken hours to put it together. The three-minute film featured highlights of their past Kingston games: a Connor Boland fight, a Steven Trojanovic goal, a Betzold stickhandling display, a Jonatan Tanus goal, a Cody Thompson fight, a Nick Ritchie rush, a Findlay goal. Background music blasted from tape of a 300-instrument orchestra. The video finished with Sylvester Stallone as Rocky Balboa saying, "Life's not about how hard of a hit you can give. . . it's about how many you can take and still keep moving forward."

Hull looked around the room and simply said, "Let's get ready for practice."

In practice, pucks were going over Dagger's shoulder into the net. Giggy was stopping more pucks, more often. It didn't concern the coach. Hull was riding Dagger the rest of the way, riding the horse that had got them there for as long as he could.

Mathers, still pissed that he couldn't play, worked as hard as ever.

Hull yelled at the players to "never mind that tic-tac-toe; you won't be doing it in a game, so don't do it here."

It was a hard, fast practice. Near its end, Boland went over to the boards and slyly unscrewed some water bottles. Michael Clarke later grabbed one for a drink and instead tipped the water down his chin, neck and chest. He looked around for the guilty party. Long gone.

The players were not tense, but loose. Were they ready? They'd find out in 27 hours, when they played against Kingston at home in their most important game of the season . . . until the next one.

Just before game time on March 7, Tanus informed the coaches he had the flu and was out. Mathers, and now Tanus, would not be playing.

Inside the dressing room, Hull drew on words and phrases first uttered by past sports greats. "Tonight is about us being the best team we can be. Tonight isn't about the past or the future, it is about right now. You have to want these nights to last forever. You have to skate, pass, shoot and hit all night long. You've got to live in the moment, understand there will be adversity and there will be challenges: that is what has brought us close together as a team—the adversity and challenges. Live in the moment and go out and play as a team."

After the national anthem, there was a dedication to Stompin' Tom Connors, a legendary Canadian singer who had died a few days before. The crowd sang, a cappella style, the words to his "Hockey Song" while the players waited to do battle. The crowd had swelled to more than 3,400, but 43 seconds in, Kingston scored on its first shot—with an assist from former Pete Luke Hietkamp. Hull calmly told the team not to panic, to keep pushing; there was lots of game left.

Kingston got a penalty with two minutes left in the period and Ritchie, playing with new energy, skated in on a two-on-one. He fed Nelson Armstrong, who drilled one past former Pete Mike Morrison. Then, with 17 seconds left, the Petes paid the Frontenacs back for their early goal, and the scorer was none other than the notorious curfew breaker, Betzold, playing his best game of the season—and he had had some good ones. About his mistake, he said he intended to make it up to the team.

Mathers was in the crowd, pacing. "This is driving me nuts," said the captain, who wanted to be on the ice so badly. "You have no idea what this is doing to me."

A puck whizzed into the Petes' bench; Giggy ducked, and it deflected off B-Man, who reminded the goalie he was wearing $3,000 worth of equipment with which to stop the puck. Giggy just smiled and replied, "I have to protect my beautiful face."

The crowd was into the game. Their chants could be heard coming from every corner. In the third period, after the Petes had killed a five-on-three, the fans gave the players a loud blast of cheers and applause. The players soaked up that seventh-player feeling, one that hadn't been felt very often this season—maybe only twice before. It was a moment that pushed the team on, and Betzold scored for the second time.

Dagger proved Hull's decision right. He stopped three shots using his new mask and pocketed two beauties in his catching glove, keeping Kingston out of the game and allowing the Petes to salute to their approving crowd with a 4–1 win.

Betzold got the Burn the Boats Award and later said he owed his teammates after failing them last week. Hull told them, "That was a game of courage, the type of game which showed true character. That is far better than coming back from a 3–0 deficit. It was a game where you pushed for the entire game. Maguire and Thompson got only a total of about five minutes, but they didn't whine or complain. [Hull was dead on: they played 2:30 each.] Dagger was outstanding. It was a great game." The players slapped their sticks against the floor, then Iain came forward. "Great game," he said, pumping his arm and shouting, "Showstopper!" Troj cranked the team's victory tune, "Beauty and a Beat" by Justin Bieber and Nicki Minaj.

B-Man's tiny MASH unit was getting even more crowded before and after games. Ceresnak and Trojanovic were taped for wrist injuries. Clarke, Devlin, Seymour, Ritchie, Czinder, Nosad and Pierog were in for shoulder treatments. Most of them were also having trouble with their pre-game naps: they were nervous, anxious, restless but ready.

Mississauga lost to Nick's brother and his Niagara IceDogs in a shootout. The Petes were now three behind Mississauga, who had five games left, and two behind Kingston, who had six remaining. Those two teams were playing each other Saturday before the Petes took on Ottawa at home on Sunday afternoon. As Dagger said following the game, "They know we're coming now. We are a family now; we haven't seen that in a while, but everyone in that dressing room can look at each other and know they are part of our family. It feels good."

Before the afternoon game on Sunday, March 10, against Ottawa, Hull offered up a variation of a quote that may originally have come from U.S. basketball coach Dean Smith. "Somewhere behind the athlete you've become," he told them, "the hours of practice, the coaches who pushed you, the teammate who believes you and the fans that cheer you, there is a little boy who fell in love with this game and never looked back. Enjoy every opportunity and moment, because there are no second chances; there is only this moment and the next moment. Every one of these moments is a test that you get to take one time, and only one time. Seize the moment and take it."

It was Cystic Fibrosis Day at the Memorial Centre, and Dagger's little buddy, Anthony, was in full uniform to drop the puck. For perhaps the first time in Petes history, the two captains did not take the ceremonial faceoff, but Dagger, the Petes' heart and soul, and Ottawa goalie Jacob Blair. The Petes' goalies had raised more than $4,000 for the charity this season after a sponsor donated $2 for every save they made at home.

The visitors took an early 1–0 lead, but it was the only time the fans would worry. Everyone chipped in. Ceresnak scored his second of the season with his parents, visiting from Slovakia, in the crowd. Finner scored one, then skated into the corner, where *his* proud parents, visiting from Echo Bay, were sitting. He raised his arms and blew them a kiss as players surrounded him. Armstrong got four assists, won a fight and got the first star and the Burn the Boats Award. The final score was 7–2 in favour of the Petes.

Finner inaugurated a new award following the game: the Beer Goggles Award for the goofiest play. The first recipient was Seabiscuit, who, in the last minute of the game, while there was a scrum in front of the Petes' net, took the puck, skated the length of the ice, swept past one defender and then around two more—all three were watching the scrum—and scored on Blair with only one second left to play. The crowd's applause for his effort was mixed with laughter. "I gave it my best Bobby Orr," he said.

Many of the fans were equipped with smart phones and were tracking the Kingston–Mississauga game, which the Frontenacs won 3–1.

The Petes were two points behind both teams, though Kingston still had a game in hand. They would play the next night, against Quine's Belleville squad. The Petes would play the Steelheads Tuesday night at home and then in Kingston before traveling to Brampton Sunday for the final game. The math was simple: if the Petes beat Mississauga on Tuesday and Kingston lost Monday, all three would be tied. If Missy won only one of their remaining two games and the Petes two, the Petes were in.

The drama and winning ways had brought the curious back to the rink. "I can't believe this season," longtime board director Ken Jackman said." I haven't seen anything like it—it's like two seasons in one. Someone could write a book about it." Then he stopped, looked at me and laughed. He looked around at the packed crowd and said, "There are no better marketing tricks or gimmicks [for] getting fans out than there is in winning."

Hull woke up Tuesday knowing Belleville had defeated Kingston on a game-winning goal by none other than Quine, which led NHL scout J.J. Johnston to quip, "Good trade by Peterborough." Mississauga, Kingston and the Petes all had three games left.

For the game on March 12, both Missy and the Petes were pumped, nervous, afraid to make mistakes, wanting to make the big plays, looking forward to the meaningful game. Everyone, that was, except for Giggy. Astonishingly, he slept in and missed the 11 A.M. team skate. The team wasn't able to reach the 17-year-old until 11:55, when he finally opened his eyes and responded. Two players, Cornel and Baker, whom he was supposed to drive to the rink, had almost not made it, but they borrowed their landparents' second car. Luckily for Cornel, Baker had a licence.

These were distractions the team could do without, and Hull acted immediately, calling up Lindsay Muskies backup goalie Mathew

Robson. Giggy would sit in the stands. Mathers, still upset at not playing and unable to be around anyone without being miserable, sat elsewhere. He was disgusted by the goaltender's behaviour. "I would have sent him home two months ago," he said, adding, "That guy can stop pucks. He could be a great goalie. We can't get pucks by him in practice but he can't keep doing these things."

Even Giggy seemed to know it, although the coaching staff and Oke were not convinced he cared. He didn't telephone after the team finally reached him, nor did he head immediately to the rink. When he did arrive, he didn't apologize to Oke or Hull during an uncomfortable pre-game meeting. "It was a nice, upbeat day, going to be a good, easy skate," said Hull, "and then this."

Hull told his team before the game, "Don't ever let someone tell you you can't do something. If you don't believe in yourself and your teammates, it is over. Real simple: I demand your best. I am not perfect, no one is, but if you give us your best, then perfection is very close. One game, to be the best you can be. You have to fight and die for that guy beside you—that will be the difference between winning and losing. This is your time." And then, raising his voice only slightly but sharply, he looked at them and added, "If you want it, go get it!"

They did, and they did.

Mississauga had one of the best goalies in the league in Spencer Martin, who would probably be a top draft pick in the spring. The never-drafted Dagger, who had worked his way up to top-six stats in the league since December, outduelled Martin tonight. Both goalies were at their best, making early spectacular saves to keep their teams in the game. It was a tilt that fans, players and coaches expected: a tight, hard-fought, back-and-forth game, with the Petes taking the lead twice, only to have Missy tie it both times. Martin and Dagger continued with incredible saves in the third period, forcing the teams into overtime. Martin stopped several in the extra period, leading to a shootout in which Dagger stopped three of four, Martin only two.

Ritchie scored first, and then Betzold, who had turned 18 the day before, scored the winner, a birthday present to cherish. Even the shootout wasn't without controversy, as Tanus clearly scored on his shot—the video replay, viewed by OHL officials upstairs, verified the fact—but still it was not counted. The puck went in over the goal line and then slid out under the back of the net. The ref didn't see it. A win was a win, but that non-goal could've cost the team a playoff spot, the second time this season the team had lost a goal to the officiating.

Ritchie, steadily showing the fans why he could be the future of the Petes, had five hits and six shots to lead the team in all categories. His line with Czinder and Findlay had been unbelievable. Cornel showed why the Petes had made him their top pick, recording four hits and five shots.

Armstrong, who had received the last Burn the Boats Award, handed the plastic vessel (with past winners' names signed on it) over to "the obvious choice, Dagger." Laughter erupted when the Beer Goggles Award was handed to Nosad for falling forward to the ice earlier in the game with nobody near him. And the laughter continued when Iain toned down his usual "great game" description to "pretty good game" before yelling, "Showstopper!"

Lost in all of this was that, for some players, it may have been their last show on the Memorial Centre ice. Only a playoff series would bring them back.

An *Examiner* online poll asked, "Will the Petes make the play-offs?" Seventy-five per cent of the 138 respondents said no.

*** * ***

Hull wanted to change things up again, so 10 minutes before leaving for the two-hour trip to Kingston on March 15, he gathered the team into the dressing room. Below the video screen, he had written the words of football legend Vince Lombardi: "I've never known a man worth his salt who in the long run, deep down in his heart, didn't appreciate the grind, the discipline. I firmly believe that any man's finest hour . . . this greatest fulfillment to all he holds dear, is that moment when he has worked his heart out in a good cause and lies exhausted on the field of battle. VICTORIOUS."

Then Hull showed them the video he'd made. Anyone not affected by it would have been devoid of human emotion. There was a collage of Petes vignettes from their victories, their together times, their crowds, their saluting the crowd and their victory celebrations in which they locked each other in a circle of hugs, all set against actor Kurt Russell's voice from the movie *Miracle,* in which his character, Team USA coach Herb Brooks, told his team that this was their time, not the other team's, that the other team would lose, that this was their moment.

"Shit, I've got goosebumps," Perogi softly admitted, with the entire team's agreement. There was no loud cheer, just quiet confidence hanging around their anxiousness. Findlay, heading out of the dressing room, shouted, "Now let's make sure we get those two points."

It was a nervous, anxious team that got off the bus in Kingston. They knew they were going to be watched by some 5,200 people. A fan bus from Peterborough had sold out in two days, and another had been added. Altogether, Garfat expected 300 Petes fans, from Peterborough and elsewhere, would be waiting for them Friday night in Kingston. Many would be familiar faces, and some not as easily recognized.

Hull addressed the team. "In sports, you have guys that play smart, guys that play with their heads, but [if] you find a guy who plays with his heart, with every fibre in his body, that's what we have in this room. I want everyone to take a moment and look each other in the eyes [everyone scanned the room] and put each other in your hearts forever, because forever is about to happen. Let's go out and play with that heart and take it. Enjoy the opportunity."

A rallying shout from the players followed: "Let's fuckin' do it!"

It was indeed Showtime.

Dagger, as always when he started, led the team out the door, stopping briefly to pick up his water bottle in the hallway, where it waited for him before every game. Verner had compared Dagger's statistics to those of another goalie of similar age and OHL experience this season: top-rated Sudbury netminder Frank Palazzese, who had joined Sudbury from Kitchener in a trade on January 8. At the time, he had been, statistically, the league's best goalie, with a goals-against average of 2.10 and a .934 save percentage. Since then, he was 8–9–2–2, with a 3.16 goals-against average and a .910 save percentage. Dagger was ahead of Palazzese in every category since Christmas. Incredible.

Hull, Clark and Verner were a mass of nerves. For Verner, the wait before the game was the longest he had experienced all season, even though all of them had been the same two hours. Hull was not himself until the puck dropped. When players hit the ice, they heard the energetic cheers of hundreds of their fans seated above them, a thunderous roar.

A Kingston choir of more than 100 adults sang the national anthem (Perogi, as always, talked to his mother). They were singing not just to the fans in the arena but also to the national television audience, in a broadcast that featured the former Pete who had wanted to buy the team almost one year ago, Greg Millen.

The game was what everyone expected and was refereed the way it should have been, with only two minor penalties—a battle for the players only. It was a teeter-totter game, each team taking the lead in turns. Kingston tied the game in the last minute of the first, then took over in the second, but the Petes took back the lead in the last minute. Kingston tied it again in the third. Czinder played his best game. He not only had a goal and an assist but also was tenacious in his checking—displaying why he was known as the Big Hurt—his blond mane touching his shoulders, his black mouthguard constantly slipping from his mouth while in stride. His long reach and big hits made up for his awkward skating style; he was more a goose than a swan, an Esposito rather than an Orr.

Ritchie did what he was expected to do: be a power forward that the opposition had to chase down. Sixteen-year-old rookie Cornel, who was playing against four other 16-year-olds drafted this season against whom fans constantly compared him, set up two markers.

There was an "uh-oh" moment for Peterborough fans when Ritchie left the ice, followed a minute later by Findlay, but they returned in minutes, their skates resharpened by B-Man. Dagger, though he was not having his best game, made two great stops: a signature glove save from a shot in front of the net and a pad save in the second, the type usually reserved for the Roys, Brodeurs and Prices of the hockey world.

Kingston GM Doug Gilmour fidgeted in his team's suite, going for periodic walks whenever Peterborough scored, nervously rubbing his hands. Next door in another suite, Petes captain Mathers and others were doing the same.

The game went into overtime, as it should have. The Petes heard their boisterous fans as the extra period started. Kingston's fans were trying to drown them out, but even with their advantage in numbers, they couldn't do it. Mathers shuffled nervously on a stool beside me. "It's killing me, you have no idea. I couldn't be a coach or a GM—I'd have a heart attack."

And suddenly it was over.

Halfway through the overtime, with former Petes Morrison and Hietkamp trying to rub it into the faces of their ex-teammates, speedster Nosad raced in on a Kingston defenceman who suddenly lost his balance and fell. Nosad peeked at the streaking Pierog, the junkyard dog, and fed him a perfect pass that Perogi blasted in.

The Petes bench erupted and their fans rose, cheering, clapping, screaming, waving flags, giving them a rousing ovation. The players, after their family hug, recognized their fans with a salute as they left the ice for their own noisy celebration. Mathers jumped when Pierog scored, awkwardly trying to give someone a high five, his big paw striking a shoulder as a smaller hand hit his chest. "We'll have to practise that," he said, laughing as he headed quickly to the dressing room, where the team joined in what was a Memorial Cup-style victory celebration.

"I can't believe the resiliency of this team," Hull told them. "You just never give up, you all believe, you all keep coming. That was one helluva game. Just a great example of never quitting."

Dagger smiled and told his team, "This is so incredible, so exciting. I have to give the Boat to Pierog." There was no disagreement. They cheered and slapped each other.

Everyone in the room knew that the team, which had been 16 points out of a playoff spot, was now not only in a playoff position but also in seventh place, having leapfrogged over Mississauga, who had lost to the Bulls. Nobody could believe it.

More parents greeted their boys outside than at any time this season. They had driven from Brampton, Scarborough, Orangeville, Echo Bay and Ottawa to watch their boys. Now they were hooked, just like the fans, by the nightmare that turned into a dream.

Saturday, there was another quick practice, and Ceresnak became a prankster's victim. He walked onto the ice with his skate guards still on, taking the full fall in front of laughing teammates. Or maybe he had just forgotten to take them off.

The next day, Sunday March 17, was the last of the Petes' regular season. Hull wrote words on the dressing room whiteboard: "Choose your direction, and then act with all your heart. Tomorrow belongs to those who take action today."

The mood during the two-hour bus trip to Brampton that morning was loose. The sun shone, although not enough to warm the minus-6-degree outside air as the bus was unloaded and the players made their way into the arena. The players were anxious, the coaches quiet, as they got ready to clash with their old friend Francis Menard and the Battalion, who were starting their backup goalie. The Petes assumed that Kingston would win today, as Missy had yesterday. The Petes had to win to survive and cap off the most incredible playoff drive in team history. They had not won a game in Brampton since 2005, and they were ending their regular season on the road once again.

At the 12:30 meeting, Hull gave his last pre-game talk of the regular season. "Some people listen to themselves, rather than listen to what others say. These people don't come along very often, but when they do, they remind us that once you set out on a path, even though critics may doubt you, it is okay to believe that there is no *can't, won't* or *impossible.* They remind us that it is okay to believe 'impossible' is nothing. Go out and enjoy this great opportunity."

The players were pumped. Their big captain, Diesel, was back. Changing a winning lineup, one that had won four straight for the first time this season, was not done very often, but there was never a question that Mathers would dress.

"Did you see all the vandalism out front?" asked B-Man as we looked at the nearly empty rink. "They soldered the doors shut. That's why there are no fans." But the crowd grew, and by game time there were a couple of thousand—including, once again, several hundred who had made the trip from Peterborough. This time, though, they were spread throughout the rink with no chance of creating a seventh-player push.

By the time the game began, Kingston was already into the third minute of play and leading its game, 1–0. By the 3:46 mark of the first period in Brampton, Peterborough was winning by the same score on a deflection by Clarke off Diesel's slapshot. The period ended that way.

Hull had little to offer in the intermission other than instructions on how to keep playing Brampton and telling the team to keep moving forward. They hadn't played poorly, but Dagger did have to stop a couple of excellent scoring opportunities.

Just a few minutes into the second period, Menard, the former Pete who had not wanted to be traded and the only one disappointed that he was, tied the game, and then, with 3:15 remaining in the second, Brampton took a 2–1 lead. There was not much Dagger could have done on either goal. It looked like the team that had played in Kingston Friday had stayed there. Some old habits were showing up: players slamming doors on the bench, hitting their sticks against the boards, criticizing teammates. Perhaps, after all, they were unable to handle the do-or-die pressure.

Meanwhile, Kingston was still leading their game.

Brampton had a 3–1 lead in the third period but took a penalty, giving the Petes hope and a power play. But the Petes gave up a short-handed goal. Hull was dejected, quiet on the bench, while Ritchie was yelling, "We can still do it! Let me out, we can still do it!" Findlay scored one later from Ritchie, but Hull had to pull Dagger for the extra attacker. Menard, alone in front of the empty net, could have scored but unselfishly passed the puck to an oncoming teammate to end the game 5–2.

The Petes' season was finished.

They had gone 4–1 in the last five games. The two teams they were chasing had won only one of their last five, but they each won the only game they needed.

Neither Barrie nor Belleville, waiting to see who they would meet in the first playoff round, wanted to play this doggedly determined Peterborough team. Their coaches knew how dangerous they had become. Surprisingly, Brampton coach Stan Butler told the media following the game that he felt sad for the Petes. He said they deserved to make the playoffs, but it was also his team's last regular-season game in that rink (they were moving to North Bay for the 2013–14 season) and they wanted to win it for the team and fans. "I felt for their team," he told Davies. "It was a bittersweet win. That may sound corny. I was happy we won, but I felt bad for them, because what a comeback they made."

As the Petes left the ice, Findlay, who had just played his last OHL game, cried while heading to the dressing room. The others had not yet succumbed to such emotions, but Finner, the team's emotional leader, couldn't hold back. Tears flooded from his eyes.

None of the coaches immediately entered the dressing room. Hull went into a corner of the arena near the Zambonis, wanting to be alone, thinking of the season, the disappointment and what to say to his team. Clark leaned against a wall with his eyes closed. Verner stood silently, head down, in another corner. They were alone in their disappointments, shocked to realize that the season was over.

When Hull finally entered the room, he allowed the boys to continue their moments together, telling them to take their time.

They did. Each player sat in full gear, none daring to be the first to begin undressing. More than half of them were sobbing uncontrollably. Big Diesel, Seabiscuit, Clarke, Dagger, Troj, Perogi, Hatcher, Boland, Thompson, Cornel, the Big Hurt, Tanus, Nosad and Ritchie, proving standardbreds have tears, all wept. The others, maybe still not realizing what had just happened, or feeling too brave to weep openly, sat in silence as Findlay spoke through his gushing emotions. "I'm proud of you guys—so proud. I will always remember you. I'd go to war with any of you. I know that I pissed you off sometimes. I know, and I'm sorry, but I know what we have done, what we have been through. I'm so proud of you."

"If anyone had ever told me at Christmas we would be here tonight, fighting for a playoff spot, I would have doubted them," said Hull, finally standing before his team, Oke and four members of the board of directors who had joined them. "There is not a player in this room that can't look up and say they didn't give it everything they could. I'm proud of you all.

"There are things I could say about each one of you, but this is not the time. It was one helluva ride."

After circling the room, hugging his players and shaking hands, he added, "I only have one more thing to say. When you guys leave this dressing room, when you get back to Peterborough and spend the next few days in the community, hold your heads up high. You believed in yourselves, and what you have accomplished since Christmas is incredible. Hold your heads up high."

It was the longest the team had stayed in the dressing room all season, as parents, agents and friends waited outside in the evening air.

After 73 games (including exhibition), 164 times on the ice and 37 days off (nine of them at Christmas) in 201 days, with only nine days off in the 76 days since January 1, it was over. After more than

14,000 kilometres and more than 165 hours on a bus, with few complaints from players or coaches other than "Is that all there is to eat?" after thousands of pounds of victuals had been devoured in 54 restaurants and 30 bus meals together, it was finished.

After eight nights in a hotel and more than $100,000 spent on the road, the regular season—actually, two different seasons—had ended as it had begun.

Stephen Pierog could finally rest his aching body after never taking a shift off during the entire season. He had made his mother in heaven proud. Dagger, who apologized to Petes fans for not getting them to the playoffs, had no reason to be sorry. He had done his job, as had his teammates. They had arrived last year as boys and would leave as growing adults.

In the last months, they had burned the boats, taken no days off.

As director Ken Jackman said that last day, "You have to lose to learn." They had lost and learned that they never wanted to lose again.

In the end, another victory was probably too much to ask of these young people. At times throughout the season, many had forgotten they were not professional hockey people, not even men yet. They were boys, just teenagers learning their trade in the OHL apprenticeship program. They were children like yours and mine—children who had a special talent, but still the minds and hearts of young people.

The Petes' next season would again bring many peaks and valleys in another journey of dream-chasing, but every single person connected to this 2012–13 team, friend or foe, past or present, knew there would never be another season like this one on Roger Neilson Way. Never.

Findlay was the last to leave the dressing room that night, his eyes still damp. I had waited for him. We were alone when we glanced at each other and hugged. "Thanks for the journey, young man," I said. "Thanks for the journey." And he replied, wiping away his tears before going outside: "Sorry we couldn't get you that good ending, Eddie."

But they did.

CHAPTER 20

Overtime

After the game, Beamer pulled the bus out of the Brampton arena parking lot for the last time. We ate our last bus meal together—cheeseburgers and fries—and got our last candy from Larry. There was silence while we ate. Jody Hull, Wayne Clark and Andrew Verner sat perplexed, burnt, beaten up by the emotional roller coaster the season had been. Dave Reid sent Hull a text congratulating him on the season, as he had done on Friday. Mike Pelino also sent a text of congratulations, their first contact since the firing. They understood. There was nothing personal.

The quietness ended 45 minutes into the ride, almost as if the funeral service was over. There was jabbering among coaches and players, although not from the disappointed Andrew D'Agostini, who had spent four years trying to get into the playoffs. Younger players were laughing as Greg Betzold told another of his stories that many doubted, Nick Ritchie's big laugh erupting from the centre of the bus as it had on almost every trip this season. Hull had already talked with his wife, Kelly, "the General" of the Hull home, who told him what many others were saying: "If you had made the playoffs, you would have done some real damage." His son texted him with the big news that he had been accepted at the University of Toronto if he wanted to go there. Hull's mood brightened.

We finally arrived and unloaded for the last time—for most until next season, for others forever. The players would disperse, leave Peterborough within the next few days, most going back to their homes, where they would be lost without their new family, the hockey team. Players in the Neilson era used to stay in Peterborough for the entire school year, even when the Petes didn't go deep into the playoffs. But now junior teams allowed them to go home because parents preferred it. It also saved teams money and freed them of their responsibilities.

Kingston lost to Barrie in four straight in the first round. Mississauga lost to Belleville in the first round. London won the OHL championship in the final game of a series against Barrie, scoring the winner with one second remaining in the game.

In sports, only half the teams win the game, and only one team wins the championship. London got to the Memorial Cup, but the Halifax Mooseheads won it all.

The Petes' players had learned about living away from home. They had matured, added life skills, learned valuable lessons while figuring out what worked within a team. Most importantly, they had learned that nothing in this world could be achieved without commitment and that you should never quit. They had also learned that today was yesterday's tomorrow. Live for today.

There are critics who question chasing these dreams, who can't imagine parents doing what some do, and would do, for their children, but they miss the point. These players are not chasing dreams, but doing what so many others would love to be doing . . . they are *living* them.

Team president Jim Devlin had said at the end of 2011–12: "I'd be very disappointed if we don't go deep into the playoffs next year. If we're sitting here next year with the same thing, yeah, we have a problem." A year later, he was content with the results and thought the team was finally on its way to success.

The new board, together with general manager Mike Oke, worked to develop a business plan and hold regular staff meetings. They advertised for a communications director who also would have to do game-night staging and hired a young Burton Lee, who had worked with the Sarnia Sting. They also hired a community events coordinator and marketing assistant: Dagger's brother, Matt D'Agostini. The board dropped any plans to sell shares and joined a consortium to try to get a new sports complex built in the city.

Aaron Garfat's role was finally defined and his title changed to director of sales, marketing and advertising. He no longer travelled with the team.

The Petes lost money again in 2012–13. And while fans were embracing the club, their landlord certainly wasn't. The City of Peterborough, which had donated the rink and parking for a Stompin' Tom memorial, sent the Petes a bill for an extra three hours of arena time following the *Hockey Day in Canada* game because the CBC crew was still on the restaurant stage after the game was over. Nobody was using the ice, but the Petes got charged for it. The directors also got a letter telling the team the city was approving ice time for the Petes' annual May rookie camp in 2014 but could not promise it in future years. Veteran and rookie board members were perplexed and dumbfounded.

The board met near the end of the season and decided the Peterborough economy wouldn't allow it to raise ticket prices for next season.

Board member Dr. Bob Neville was appointed the president of the OHL and chairman of its board, a first for the Petes team. Former long-time Petes GM Jeff Twohey left the Oshawa Generals at the end of the 2013–14 season after leading his team to the Eastern Conference finals. During his two seasons with the Generals Twohey led his team to the playoffs both years. He has since gone back to scouting for Phoenix in the NHL.

A disheartened, shocked, surprised and disappointed Wayne Clark was told in April by Hull and Oke that his services would no longer be required. Longtime professional hockey player Bryan Helmer was hired as an assistant coach. Hull also brought former Lindsay Muskies coach and GM Paul Mattucci aboard as an assistant coach and kept Andrew Verner as goalie coach.

Dave Reid joined TSN, back in television broadcasting, where he was happy and informative.

Mike Pelino was inducted into Welland's Walk of Fame in May 2013. He joined another former Petes coach, Mike Keenan, in Russia to coach Metallurg Magnitogorsk in the Kontinental Hockey League. They won the KHL championship in Russia. Keenan became the first person to coach both a Stanley Cup– and Gagarin Cup–winning team. He and Pelino became the first Canadian coaches to win the European title.

Captain Derek Mathers was called up to the Adirondack Phantoms of the American Hockey League immediately following the OHL season. He scored his first professional goal and won several fights. He spent the summer getting in even better shape for the Philadelphia Flyers' NHL camp and again made their AHL team.

Peter Ceresnak went home to his beloved Slovakia, where the Petes' coaches suspected his heart had been for months. They did not invite him to camp in 2013. He played for his hometown team, Dukla Trencin, in the fall.

Brett Findlay was presented with four awards at the Petes' team banquet: leading scorer, most assists, most goals and most gentlemanly player. He cried during his goodbye speech. His captain, Derek Mathers, stood alone to applaud, and then the rest of the crowd joined him. The next season, Findlay and Nick Czinder caught on with the San Francisco Bulls of the ECHL and made it into the playoffs. They signed contracts with the team for the fall, but the team went bankrupt. Finner moved to Anchorage, Alaska, to play, while Zimmer went to the University of Prince Edward Island. Findlay's Alaska Aces won the ECHL Kelly Cup championship in 2014. Their head coach was former Pete Rob Murray.

Brandon Devlin got top defenceman—even though he had spent only half the season with the team, he had proved himself worthy.

Stephen Pierog shared the award for most goals with Findlay. He also received the award for most improved player. He was invited to the Carolina Hurricanes' 2013 training camp and in January 2014 was traded to his hometown Guelph Storm, one of the OHL's top teams.

Greg Betzold and Jonatan Tanus shared rookie-of-the-year honours, while Eric Cornel got the scholastic award for academic and on-ice performance. Tanus played for Finland, which won the bronze medal at the world under-18 tournament in Sochi, Russia, and returned to the Petes in the fall. Betzold went home to Maryland

and waited for the June NHL draft, but for the first time since 1968, not one member of the Petes was drafted. The St. Louis Blues invited Betzold to their fall training camp, and he returned to the Petes, where he had a rather dismal season recovering from a persistent injury received at that camp.

Frankie Menard, still searching for his birth parents, attended St. Mary's University in Halifax in the fall of 2013.

On October 4, Steven Trojanovic was traded to the Guelph Storm for a third-round draft pick. He became a plus-40 player on a first-place team, an incredible OHL accomplishment and turnaround. In their first OHL playoffs, former Petes Pierog and Trojanavic, now of Guelph, won the OHL championship against North Bay for the first time since 2002. Guelph made it to the final against Edmonton, and although they lost, they proved once again that small-market teams with good facilities, proper management, strong players and enthusiastic fans can still make it.

Luke Hietkamp attended Wilfred Laurier University in 2013.

Andrew Rieder, who played only five games after being brought in from the Western Hockey League, played for Dalhousie University in 2013–14.

Chase Hatcher, who had been recognized the night before in a home game as the Petes' hardest-working player, was released by the team on January 11, 2014. He immediately went to Muskegon of the United States Hockey League, a Tier II junior league.

Clark "Seabiscuit" Seymour joined Pittsburgh's AHL farm team, the Wilkes-Barre/Scranton Penguins, for the rest of their season and, after a lengthy fall tryout, returned to the Petes for his final OHL season.

Slater Koekkoek finally signed his three-year entry-level deal with the NHL's Tampa Bay Lightning. His shoulder healed well. He was invited to Team Canada's junior summer camp but didn't make the final cut. In 2013–14, he had one of the best plus-minus statistics in the league—plus-44, good for fifth in the league—was named Windsor captain and was third in scoring among OHL defencemen with 15 goals and 53 points in 62 games. Near the end of the season, he was injured once again, his other shoulder requiring surgery. The Western Conference coaches named Slater the best offensive defence-man and third best defensive defenceman in 2014. His coach called him a great leader. He was named to the First All-Star team selected by league general managers.

Trevor Murphy continued to play for Windsor but broke his leg.

Alan Quine did not sign with Detroit and was drafted again, this time by the New York Islanders, in the sixth round in June 2013. He played in the American Hockey League for the Bridgeport Sound Tigers the following season.

Connor Boland was invited to the Buffalo Sabres' fall camp, returned to the Petes and was named captain.

For two weeks in the summer of 2013, Brian "B-Man" Miller was the trainer and equipment manager for Canada's gold-medal repre-sentatives at the Israel Maccabiah Games.

Mike Davies won the 2012 Ontario Newspaper Award for sports-writing, including the story he did on his own blindness and the exclusives he had garnered while covering the Petes the year before. Probably more exciting to him was that he also played hockey again, at the invitation of a visually impaired hockey team that had a tour-nament in Toronto. He hadn't played in 12 years. His equipment was so old he had to ask B-Man for some help.

On April 6, 2013, the Petes made another controversial draft-day decision, deciding not to take 15-year-old Sean Day, a big defenceman and an excellent skater who had been granted exceptional-player status, as the third-overall pick. Instead, they took defenceman Matthew Spencer of the Oakville Rangers. Day was taken fourth, by the Mississauga Steelheads. Only time will tell whether either or both teams made the right choices.

The OHL quietly changed player compensation after union threats the year before. Instead of $50 weekly stipends, players get up to $470 monthly and $1,000 for summer training. Overagers get up to $900 instead of $500 monthly. A player leaving the OHL at age 19 has 30 months to start his education package and can still sign an AHL deal while retaining his education package.

The Petes began the 2013–14 season once again with seven newcomers to the OHL and still with no playmaker to help Ritchie. The season opener was a disastrous 11–4 loss before only 2,271 fans, the team's worst opening-night thrashing since 1957, but then they went on a three-game winning streak led by Ritchie's five goals in four games and Eric Cornel's seven points.

The breakfast club continued, with 14 members no longer attending high school, but more than half were enrolled in online higher-education courses at community college and university.

In February 2014, the Petes, in what they called a major announcement, invited the community to the Memorial Centre and told them that next season, for the first time since 1967, the Petes wouldn't be wearing maroon and white. Instead the uniforms would be cream, maroon and black. More than 200 people had come to the press conference at centre ice expecting a bigger announcement, many of them hoping the team was offering shares. They left disappointed, wondering why the team couldn't have revealed the future look at the next home game.

Andrew "Dagger" D'Agostini, who had been named the team's 2012–13 MVP (voted on by the players), was named most dedicated player and was the player with the most three-star selections. He realized his dream of one day playing pro hockey, anywhere, when he signed an amateur tryout contract with the ECHL's Cincinnati Cyclones and played a period for them as well as getting called up to the Milwaukee Admirals of the AHL for a game. He went to Australia in the summer of 2013 for hockey instructional camps.

The next season, he again got the majority of work after Christmas and improved his game. Halfway through the season, he got a new maroon and white face mask dedicated as a thank you to the community. It featured the team logo, the city's old slogan—"I'd Rather Be in Peterborough"—a canoe, the lift lock and the town clock. He again won the title of team MVP.

Michael "Giggy" Giugovaz went home to Brampton after the 2012–13 season. The OHL's general managers selected him to the league's second all-rookie team. He graduated from high school and returned to training camp with his hair cut and his face clean-shaven, determined to do better. Coach Jody Hull said he had a different attitude. But not all had changed. At a photo session where pictures were to be taken of the players in shirt and tie, Giggy forgot and was on the ice in full uniform. He took off the sweater and shoulder pads but put his shirt and tie on while still wearing his hockey pants and goalie pads. He also continued to be late for team functions. The Petes had had enough, and midway through the 2013–14 season, he was traded to Belleville. Giggy is Giggy, still a growing, developing teenager and another reminder these hockey players were still kids.

Eric Cornel was invited to the Team Canada under-18 camp but was cut. Connor McDavid and Roland McKeown, drafted before him, made the team, as did Jared McCann, Michael Dal Colle, Spencer Watson, Robby Fabbri and Sam Bennett, all drafted after him. That summer, Cornel gained 20 pounds and became a leading point getter for the Petes in 2013–14. He was third in points, scoring 25 goals and 37 assists, after registering only 4 goals and 12 assists. He began getting interest from several NHL teams. He was a perfect example of what hard work, experience and growth can do for these young players. Cornel was drafted in the second round, 44th overall, by the Buffalo Sabres in the 2014 NHL draft.

Nick Ritchie came to fall camp weighing 235 pounds. He was in his NHL draft year and was expected to be selected in the top round. He led the team in scoring with 39 goals and 35 assists, 39 more points than last season. In February, Ritchie scored five goals in one game. The last OHL player to do that was his brother Brett, the previous season against the Petes. Nick more than doubled his previous year's totals while improving to a plus player. He was on a mission and was one of the last guys off the ice at practices. In 2014, he was named the best body checker in the Eastern Conference by league coaches and was rated third for best shot and shootout shooter. Yet, strangely, he was not named to the popular Subway Series game versus Russia. He was a great example of a player arriving at 15 and who, by 18, was maturing physically and mentally. Ritchie was drafted 10th overall in the first round of the NHL's 2014 draft, to the Anaheim Ducks.

Petes office administrator Cathie "the Big Boss" Webster, three days after the final 2012–13 game, said: "Mark my words, I can feel it, next year is our year."

Jody Hull was selected by Hockey Canada to be Don Hay's assistant coach for Canada's under-18 team in Russia in April 2013. He was away from home for 25 days with another Pete, Ritchie. They brought home gold medals after defeating the United States, which hadn't lost this tournament in four years.

Hull took the Petes into the playoffs in 2014 after a four-year drought. They were 20 points behind the first-place division winners, Oshawa. The team had its first winning season in eight years without one member in the top 20 scoring. And they became part of team history in the first round against Kingston. The Frontenacs took a 3–0 lead in the best-of-seven series, but the Petes didn't quit, coming back to win the seventh game in overtime in Kingston on a Ritchie goal. It was the first time in team history the Petes had come back from a three-game deficit. D'Agostini was incredible in the nets. They lost the next round four straight to the Oshawa Generals, but a crowd of close to 4,000, the largest since the rink renovations in 2003 and Hockey Day in Canada, gave the team—and last-year players D'Agostini, Seymour and Armstrong, who were also named the three stars in the home loss—a rousing standing ovation. Jody Hull was named Team Canada under 18 coach in 2014, heading the team playing in Slovakia. He and Oke were given new three-year contracts.

The Petes' fans, missing during many regular-season games, finally gave the team the spark they needed in the playoff home games. Every player loved the atmosphere and admitted that, had these fans been present all year, it would have helped. Players love big crowds. Sadly, Peterborough, mythically known as a hockey town, usually only supports "their" team this way if they make the playoffs.

Before the playoffs, the team was selling T-shirts boldly proclaiming WE'RE BACK.

Time will tell if the team is back to its historic winning ways, but one thing remained consistent at Showtime for every home game: stickboy Iain Norrie was back, still encouraging and cheering on the boys in the dressing room with his shout of "Showstopper!"

ACKNOWLEDGMENTS

I'd like to acknowledge everyone mentioned in this book—they all helped in their own ways—but without the cooperation of former Petes GM Dave Reid, who believed in the book from the beginning, it would never have happened. He knew the risk he was taking, even warned me there might be new faces as the season progressed, but he opened the doors and let me in. It was all approved by the board of directors—Jim Devlin, Dr. Bob Neville, Pat Casey, Ken Jackman, Wilf Hughes and John Oke, who, while not allowing me into all of their meetings, did open the doors a crack at some of them.

The coaching staff of Mike Pelino, Jody Hull, Wayne Clark and Andrew Verner were wide open. They knew as professional coaches they would be under the microscope, but also knew there was a story that should be told. They allowed me to help load and unload the equipment and to sit in on dressing room conversations and pre- and post-game talk.

Player personnel director—and later GM—Mike Oke was more than cooperative with information and opening the doors not only for scouting trips and meetings but to his scouts as well, who were especially helpful, notably Steve Ritchey, Chris McNamara and Ron Ringler.

The Petes' office staff of Aaron Garfat and Cathie Webster, Don Sharp and Kathleen Reeves were always helpful. Jim Devlin was at all times transparent, and as anyone knows, with books of this sort, that can lead to good and bad things.

The arena staff, especially the ushers, were always helpful as I toured not only the Petes' home rink but also all the others of the OHL.

The training staff of Brian Miller, Larry Smith and Terry Bowser (and his two sons, Clayton and Avery) and statistician Adam Murray were a joy to be around. I hope I didn't get in the way too often.

The most difficult part of the journey was staying in the middle, knowing what I knew and never being able to share it with parents, players, staff, management or fans, for fear of losing their trust. There were times I bit my tongue, wanting to tell someone what was happening with their team, but at no time did I compromise. I was the fly on the wall, and the view from there is in these pages. It was only 13 months in the life of a single OHL team, a year that will probably never happen again—or, as board member Ken Jackman said, a "year that should be a book."

There were others not employed by the team who should be acknowledged, including the landparents, Walter DiClemente, Greg Millen, Mike O'Connor, *Examiner* sports director Mike Davies, radio play-by-play man Rob Snoek, Cogeco television staffers Pete Dalliday, Brian Drumm, Dan Pollard and Dave Gilbert, CHEX-TV sports director Tyler Calver and *Peterborough This Week* writer Todd Vandonk, Don Barrie, Kevin Varrin, Gary Baldwin, Gary Dalliday, Ian Laperriere, David Branch and J.J. Johnston.

The pages of the *Peterborough Examiner* proved invaluable, and I thank publisher Darren Murphy for his support and the liberal latitude he granted me to quote from its pages.

The most important people in the book were the players, whom I thank for their frankness, openness and dedication to their dreams. They, more than anyone else, wanted the book to be real; they opened up more than anyone; and they, more than anyone connected with the team, wanted the book to have a winning ending. They worked harder than anyone else to make it happen, but many now know they will have to work even harder to make dreams come true.

Readers should realize these players are depicted in this book as they were: teenagers growing up. All of them were learning, growing and trying.

Finally, this book wouldn't even have happened without support of the people at HarperCollins, especially Jim Gifford, who took a chance on a project without knowing what direction it might take, and Brad Wilson, Erin Parker, Noelle Zitzer and Lloyd Davis, who helped it along, making a good story a better book. The other people around me who gave invaluable insights included Jonathan Webb, who made so many great suggestions and helped pull together a manuscript that had once flowed with more than 300,000 words— thank you for your patience.

Family and friends always showed support, and I thank them for indulging me, especially my wife, Lorna, who had to listen to a subject she really couldn't care less about and patiently accepted all those days and nights I was away with the team (although maybe she craved those moments). There was also my Stoney Lake friend, who listened and cared, but I'm sure by the end of the journey he was tired of his friend's obsession.

What really pushed me onward were the hockey fans who, all through the year, would stop and wonder how the book was going, reminding me after each new controversy that "you sure picked a good year for a book."

Yes, it was a bad year for the hockey team, but a good one for a book.